Learner-centredness as Language Education

CAMBRIDGE LANGUAGE TEACHING LIBRARY

A series covering central issues in language teaching and learning, by authors who have expert knowledge in their field.

In this series:

Learner-centredness as Language Education

Ian Tudor

CAMBRIDGE
UNIVERSITY PRESS

PUBLISHED BY THE PRESS SYNDICATE OF THE UNIVERSITY OF CAMBRIDGE
The Pitt Building, Trumpington Street, Cambridge CB2 1RP, United Kingdom

CAMBRIDGE UNIVERSITY PRESS
The Edinburgh Building, Cambridge CB2 2RU, United Kingdom
40 West 20th Street, New York, NY 10011–4211, USA
10 Stamford Road, Oakleigh, Melbourne 3166, Australia

First published 1996
First printed 1996

Printed in Great Britain at the University Press, Cambridge.

A catalogue record for this book is available from the British Library

Library of Congress cataloguing in publication data applied for

ISBN 0 521 48097 3 Hardback
ISBN 0 521 48560 6 Paperback

CE

Contents

Contents

Acknowledgements

The author would like to express his appreciation for the comments made by two anonymous reviewers, which were of great assistance in helping him clarify a number of ideas expressed in this book. Many thanks also to Alison Sharpe of Cambridge University Press for her encouragement and support throughout the process of writing, and to Gill Lucy for many stimulating discussions and much good advice. The shortcomings which remain are, of course, the responsibility of the author himself. The author also wishes to thank Joelle Herzet, who typed the manuscript.

The author and publishers would like to thank the following for permission to reproduce copyright material:

Z. Dörnyei for figure 2 on p. 47 from 'Conceptualising motivation in foreign language learning' in *Language Learning* 40: 45–78; National Centre for English Language Teaching and Research, Macquarie University, Sydney for figures 3 and 4 on pp. 49 and 50 from the Adult Migrant Education Program (AMEP), *Teaching How to Learn* (Teacher's Guide); G. Ellis and B. Sinclair for figures 5 and 6 on pp. 55 and 63 from *Learning to Learn English* Teacher's Book, Cambridge University Press; J. C. Richards and T. S. Rodgers for figure 10 on p. 119 from *Approaches and Methods in Language Teaching*, Cambridge University Press; C. Kennedy for figure 11 on p. 135 from 'Evaluation of the Management of Change in ELT Projects' *Applied Linguistics* 9, Oxford University Press; T. Lynch for figure 20 on p. 187 from Peer Evaluation in Practice in A. Brookes and P. Grundy eds. (1988) *Individualisation and Autonomy in Language Learning* Modern English Publications and by permission of Prentice Hall; R. Oxford for figure 21 on p. 203 from *Language Learning Strategies: What every teacher should know*, Heinle and Heinle; J. M. O'Malley and A. U. Chamot for figure 22 on p. 206 from *Learning Strategies in Second Language Acquisition*, Cambridge University Press.

Figures 8 and 9 on pp. 111–112 and 116 are taken from K. Willing (1988) *Learning Styles in Adult Migrant Education*. Adelaide: National Curriculum Resource Centre; Figures 13, 14, 15 and 16 on pp. 176, 177 and 178 are taken from M. Oskarsson (1980). *Approaches to Self-Assessment in Foreign Language Learning*, Pergamon Press, for the Council of Europe. We have been unable to trace the copyright owners of these materials and would welcome information.

Preface

During the 1980s and 1990s the term 'learner-centredness' has come to occur with increasing frequency in books and articles on language teaching. Two main trends, however, are discernible in the way in which the term is used. For some members of our profession, 'learner-centredness' is viewed in positive terms, as representing the direction in which language teaching should be moving. Indeed, one sometimes has the impression that the term 'learner-centred' represents, for certain writers at least, a cachet of respectability as was the case with the term 'communicative' in the 1970s. In very general terms, this perspective is perfectly understandable: if our teaching is not centred on our students – their goals, aspirations, learning preferences and so on – one might legitimately question what it should be centred on.

On the other hand, a number of writers, as well as a not inconsiderable number of teachers, have expressed reservations about what the concept of learner-centredness actually refers to, and what it has to contribute to the practical, everyday concerns of language learners and teachers. Hutchinson and Waters (1987), for example, express unease with the term 'learner-centred' because they feel it is understood in too individualistic a manner, and thereby fails to take account of the social constraints which shape learners' communicative needs and, thereby, their learning goals. They prefer to use the term 'learning-centred' to emphasise the goal of teaching as that of 'maximising learning'. O'Neill (1991) is rather scathing about the superficiality with which 'learner-centred' teaching is sometimes interpreted and quite sensibly argues for 'the importance of doing ordinary things well'. Holliday (1994a) develops further the point made by Hutchinson and Waters about language learning as a socially constrained activity, and takes exception with the culture-centredness of many of the teaching procedures which are typically linked with learner-centred teaching.

Should these comments be taken to indicate that the writers in question are unconcerned about language learners, or that they are *un*learner-centred? Presumably not. They do, however, indicate at least two things. The first is that there is a considerable degree of confusion in the literature as to what the term 'learner-centredness' should be taken to mean. The second is that our profession still needs to do some serious thinking about what 'centring teaching on the learner' actually involves and how this goal (to which most teachers would, in general terms at least, subscribe) can best be achieved. In the light of this somewhat confused state of affairs, it would seem only reasonable to clarify the way in which the term learner-centredness will be understood in this book and the specific perspective on learner-centredness, and thereby on language teaching, which will be developed in the coming chapters.

To begin with, the term learner-centredness will not be used in a restrictive sense, to refer to any one set of teaching procedures, which is one of the aspects of certain views of learner-centredness criticised by Holliday (op. cit.), and which is also implicit in O'Neill's (op. cit.) remarks. In this book learner-centredness will be seen rather as a broadly-based endeavour designed to gear language teaching, in terms of both the content and the form of instruction, around the needs and characteristics of learners. In this sense, learner-centredness may be seen as a concept which encompasses a set of concerns which have underpinned many of the main developments in language teaching since the 1960s.

One of these concerns is with the authenticity of learning content which is found in both communicative and humanistic language teaching. These two movements conceive of authenticity in different terms: communicative language teaching focuses principally on the functional needs of learners, while the humanistic school of language teaching emphasises personal relevance and the affective content of communication. In both cases, however, there is a clear recognition of the importance of basing the content of language study on the communicative agendas which learners bring with them to their language study. Another recurrent concern over the last three decades relates to the role which learners are expected to assume in their language study and, specifically, to how they may be helped to assume a more active and self-directive role in the learning process. Research conducted in the 1970s drew attention to the types of learning strategies employed by language learners and, thereby, to the importance of studying learner behaviours in parallel with teaching procedures. Learning strategy research provided impetus and working tools for subsequent developments in terms of learner training and learner autonomy, both of which seek to foster the informed and active involvement of learners in their language study. This perspective on the role of learners has found further expression in the concept of the learner-centred curriculum, with its emphasis on the active involvement of learners in the shaping of their study programme. This line of thought, which has had a profound influence on language teaching in recent years, may be seen as being learner-centred by virtue of its concern with the quality of learners' involvement in their language study, and is thus complementary to interest in the authenticity of learning content.

These and a number of other trends which have had a formative influence on language teaching since the 1960s may all be seen as learner-centred in that they explore how language teaching can be made more responsive to the needs of language learners, with respect either to the selection of learning content or to the way in which the learning process is structured – or to both. In this sense, learner-centredness may be seen as a deeply rooted agenda which our profession has been pursuing, albeit in a varied and exploratory manner, over the last few decades. Chapter 1 will provide a survey of a number of trends which have emerged in language teaching during this period and will assess their contributions to our profession's current understanding of what 'centring teaching on the learner' can entail. The global perspective on learner-centredness that will underpin the approach to language teaching in this book is that of the learner-centred curriculum developed by Nunan and other researchers in Australia. This rests on two main principles. The first is that language learners should be the main reference point for decision-making with respect to both the content and the form of teaching. The second is that this should be realised by a process of consultation and negotiation between teacher and learners. This perspective on language teaching will be discussed further in Chapter 1 but has two implications which need to be brought out at this stage.

One implication is that language teaching needs to acknowledge and work constructively with the diversity and richness of human experience that learners bring with them to their language study – which leaves little scope for neat, pre-packaged solutions to language teaching problems. The reason for this is, in a very real sense, inherent in the concept of learner-centredness itself. Language learners differ from one another on a number of counts and, if a learner-centred approach is to be coherent with itself, it must inevitably acknowledge these differences and their implications with respect to both course design and the more detailed level of classroom pedagogy. One pole of diversity relates to the terms in which *learning goals* are defined, which can vary from the functionally-oriented type of learning generally associated with specific purpose language teaching, to contexts in which language learning goals are defined in far more general terms as part of students' general education alongside a variety of other subjects. Another pole of variance relates to the area of *subjective needs,* or the way in which learners' psychological and cognitive characteristics interact with their language learning. Research in the areas of individual differences and of learning style preferences has revealed how varied learners' reactions to teaching procedures can be, and how strong an influence these reactions can exert on the quality of learning. It has thus seriously weakened the plausibility of the concept of 'method' in the sense of a discrete set of teaching procedures which are presented as the optimal way of teaching language with virtually any kind of learners in virtually any context. A third pole of variance which has begun to receive more attention in recent years relates to the role played by *culturally-based traditions of teaching and learning* and the expectations and interactional norms to which these traditions give rise among both teachers and learners. Language learners are undeniably individuals who differ from one another on a number of psychological and cognitive parameters: they are also, however, members of a given sociocultural community and are therefore likely to be influenced by the social norms, role expectations and learning traditions proper to the sociocultural group to which they belong. To be coherent with itself, then, a learner-centred approach to teaching must work with the sociocultural aspects of learners' identity as much as with the more individual aspects of their identity. As a result of these many sources of diversity, learner-centred teaching will be seen in this book as an inescapably open-ended endeavour which cannot be made synony-mous with any one pre-determined set of teaching procedures.

The second implication of a learner-centred approach to teaching arises out of the participatory or negotiative approach to decision-making which it recommends. Learner participation in decision-making has the goal of enriching the knowledge base upon which decisions are made in the light of the knowledge and insights which learners as well as teachers bring with them. This, however, implies that learners are called upon to play a more active role in decision-making than is the case in traditional, teacher-driven approaches. Some learners will be relatively well-equipped in strategic and attitudinal terms for this role; many more, however, will not. The successful realisation of a participative approach to course development is thus heavily dependent upon learners' ability to interact with the process of language learning in an informed and self-directive manner. In this sense, language education is an enabling condition for the active participation of learners in their language study. Above and beyond this facilitative or enabling function of language education, however, the view of language teaching upon which this book rests involves the belief that education, in whatever field, should seek to provide students not only with discrete knowledge and skills, but also with the capacity to operate in an informed and self-directive manner in the skill area in question, within the wider context of their chosen life goals. In this perspective, education is seen as a means of empowerment. This argument clearly has a social dimension, since it recognises that language learners are members of a social group, and views language education as a means of enabling them to fulfil their language-related life goals within this group in a constructive and socially responsible manner.

To sum up, then, there are two main components to the perspective on learner-centredness, and thus on language teaching, that will be adopted in this book. The first is that language teaching needs to acknowledge and work with language learners as complex and varied human beings, not just in individual but also in social and cultural terms. The second is that language teaching is an educational endeavour which should seek to empower learners by enabling them to assume an informed and self-directive role in the pursuance of their language-related life goals.

These principles will underpin the book as a whole. Chapter 1 will survey a number of trends which have emerged in language teaching since the 1960s and evaluate their contribution to our profession's current understanding of what 'centring teaching on the learner' can mean. On this basis, the view of learner-centredness which will underpin the rest of the book will be discussed in more detail and related to the content of the subsequent chapters. Chapter 1 may thus be seen as an overview both of learner-centredness and of the book as a whole. Chapter 2 deals with learner training and provides an introduction to the educational perspective on language teaching which underpins the rest of the book; it also suggests a number of activities designed to initiate the exploration of learners' learning goals and beliefs about language learning which will be considered in more detail in Chapters 3–5. Chapter 3 examines objective needs analysis and argues for a learner-based approach to the establishment of learning goals involving the exploration of the communicative agendas which learners bring with them to their language study. Chapter 4 looks into the complex area of subjective needs, i.e. those needs which relate to the process of learning itself: this will be examined with respect to individual differences and learning style. Chapter 5 considers the contextual dimension to language teaching, which relates in part to the pragmatic and organisational conditions under which teaching takes place, but also to the cultural expectations of the learners concerned. Chapters 3–5 are thus intended to provide insights into the main learner (and learning-context) variables which the teacher needs to keep in mind in order to be able to centre teaching on the learner. Chapters 6 and 7 discuss a number of teaching-learning activities designed to foster the active involvement of learners in their language study. Chapter 6 focuses on self-assessment, which is presented as having a pivotal role between the establishment of learning goals and the strategic selection of the learning activities by which these goals may most effectively be attained. Chapter 7 argues for the creation of a strategy-rich learning environment in day-to-day teaching activities so that learners can deepen their understanding of language learning and, at the same time, play an active role in the shaping of their study programme. Chapter 8 shifts the focus of attention to the role and responsibilities of the teacher within a learner-centred approach to teaching. Without pre-empting what will be said in Chapter 8, a few basic points need to be made at this stage about the implications of a learner-centred approach for the teacher in order to provide readers with an indication of how they might most appropriately make use of the book as a guide to their own reflection and teaching practice.

As indicated above, a key aspect of the view of learner-centredness that will underpin this book is a constructive acknowledgement of learner diversity as a component of decision-making in language teaching. Learner diversity may be seen on the individual level in terms of a variety of psychological, cognitive, and experiential factors; it also arises out of the sociocultural context within which language teaching will be conducted. While few teachers would question the *desirability* of such an approach to language teaching, it would be unhelpful not to recognise the complexities which it entails. An honest and coherent attempt to work with learners as they are, with all their diversity and complexity in both individual and sociocultural terms, not to mention the differences that exist between different learning contexts in pragmatic and organisational terms, implies that teaching programmes cannot be constructed via the more or less automatic implementation of any one set of teaching procedures. Teaching decisions, both at the strictly pedagogical level and in terms of course structures, need therefore to be made *locally*. This aspect of learner-centred teaching has a number of significant implications for the role and responsibilities of the teacher. One is that the teacher has to learn to 'read' both her students and the context within which they are working in order to identify those variables which need to be incorporated in decision-making. Another is that the teacher has to master a sufficiently broad range of pedagogical and course planning options to be able to respond to diversity of needs in a flexible and appropriate manner.

In addition to this, the view of learner-centred teaching as an undertaking whose ultimate goal is the empowerment of learners by means of language education is not without implications for the teacher. This educational perspective on language teaching, which entails the linked processes of learner training and learner involvement in decision-making, makes the teacher's task more complex than in an approach to language teaching based on a pre-established content syllabus realised by means of a set of approved teaching procedures. Furthermore, the idea of learner involvement in decision-making, which will be discussed in subsequent chapters, has implications for role relationships both between teacher and learners and between the teacher and other participants in the educational hierarchy.

In a number of ways, then, the adoption of a learner-centred approach to teaching can represent a significant challenge to teachers, in both professional and personal terms. For this reason, readers should use this book to explore what learner-centredness means not only for their students but also for themselves as teachers. In certain branches of oriental medicine it is usual for the doctor to take her pulse and assess her own physiological condition prior to examining her patient, the idea being that without an understanding of her own condition the doctor will be unable to make an accurate diagnosis of her patient's. A similar situation prevails within a learner-centred approach to teaching, which has implications for the way in which teachers should approach their reading of this book.

If it is understood coherently, there is something inherently novel and exploratory about a learner-centred approach to teaching, if only for the reason that no one learner or group of learners will ever be quite like another. The book will therefore not seek to offer neat, easily applicable solutions to teaching problems. Ways of analysing situations will, of course, be offered within the general framework of goals outlined briefly above, and strategies for action will be suggested. It is, however, up to individual teachers to assess for themselves the way in which the suggestions made can most appropriately be realised within their own teaching contexts in the light of the human, attitudinal and pragmatic characteristics of these contexts. In other words, the practical realisation of the suggestions made in this book needs to be decided upon *locally* in terms of what is practically feasible and appropriate within each context. This brings us to the role of the tasks which appear throughout the book.

The *tasks* constitute an integral part of each chapter, and are designed to help readers think through the various topics dealt with. Many tasks are based on readers' own experiences of learning or of teaching languages, and their subjective reactions to these processes. This is meant to involve readers in a personalised form of reflection on the pedagogical issues in question, so that they can come to feel the subjective implications of these issues 'from the inside' and thus be better able to understand their students' reactions. Wenden rightly observes that:

> ... teacher education is an essential ingredient in the management of educational change. In the promotion of new methods and materials, the teacher is the main change agent – not the

materials or techniques in which innovations are packaged. Their acceptance and success will depend on the teacher. ... The implementation of new methods and the use of new materials will depend on the creativity of a committed and informed teacher. (Wenden 1991: 7)

The personalisation of the content by means of active reflection and exploration by the reader is thus an essential part of the book, and the tasks are meant to provide guidelines for this process. There is rarely a 'right answer' to any of the tasks: they are exploration- rather than solution-oriented activities. The desired outcome of the tasks, on the other hand, is clear, namely the ability to better understand one's students, one's teaching context, and one's own subjective interaction with the processes of language teaching and learning.

Some of the tasks call for more or less substantial action research, and readers may not wish to undertake this systematically throughout the book. Such tasks are best approached in two stages. They should, to begin with, be thought through in order to get a feel for the topic under consideration. Subsequently, as and when the reader wishes or needs to explore the topic in more depth, the task can be carried out in full, either individually or with colleagues. For example, if a group of teachers decided to experiment with a more learner-centred approach to needs analysis and goal-setting, the tasks contained in the relevant chapter (Chapter 3 in this case) could be used as a basis for a series of seminars designed to analyse current practice and come up with practical avenues for change. The tasks therefore have two purposes. The first is to help readers to personalise their understanding of the topics dealt with by means of individual reflection and exploration. The second is to provide a framework for action research, which may be conducted individually or with colleagues. In either case, though in the second in particular, readers should feel free to modify the format of the task or (depending on the task in question) to provide parallel input data from their own experience or teaching context.

On a more detailed level, the tasks may be divided into three main types – personal reflection (REF), data study (DAT), and pedagogical action (PED). Each task is preceded by the relevant code. *Personal reflection* tasks ask readers to reflect on their understanding of the literature they have encountered (including their reactions to what is said in this book), their experience of learning (language learning or, in certain cases, other learning activities) or of teaching. *Data study* tasks involve readers in analysing data which is provided in the text or which they are asked to gather for themselves. *Pedagogical action* tasks ask readers to consider the practical implications of the relevant topic with reference to a teaching situation with which they are familiar. The three task types frequently merge, and where there is a strong element of two task types, this is indicated: REF/PED, for example, indicates a task whose primary focus is personal reflection but which leads into the assessment of the pedagogical implications of the topic in question.

'He' and 'she'

In what follows the personal pronoun 'he' will be used to refer to the language learner and 'she' to refer to the teacher.

1 Learner-centredness: an overview of trends

1.1 Did you say 'learner-centredness'?

The desire to find means of making language teaching more responsive to learners' needs, and thus more 'learner-centred', has been a consistent feature of both writing and practical experimentation in language teaching since the 1960s. In part, this grew out of dissatisfaction with 'traditional' language teaching practice. In more positive terms, however, it reflects a widespread desire in the language teaching community to develop means of allowing learners to play a fuller, more active and participatory role in their language study. Few teachers will have been unaware of this trend, and most will have their own opinions about learner-centredness, some positive or enthusiastic, others reserved or even sceptical. One relatively widespread reaction to learner-centredness which the author has encountered, however, is uncertainty as to what the term means, what a learner-centred approach to teaching actually involves, and how it might be realised. This uncertainty, or even confusion, is all too understandable. In consequence, this chapter will have two main goals: the first is to help readers gain an overview of the trends of thought which have led to our profession's current understanding of what a 'learner-centred' approach to teaching might mean; the second is to help them to find their way through the sometimes confusing thicket of terms and concepts they are likely to encounter in the literature.

A first point to be made in this respect is that 'learner-centredness' should not be taken as a label that is attached to a single, clearly delimited school of thought with unambiguous definitions and a clear programme of action. Our profession's interest in learner-centredness should rather be seen in terms of a broad church or community of believers who share two main sets of concerns. The first of these arises out of the belief that language teaching will be more effective if teaching structures are made more responsive to the needs, characteristics and expectations of learners, and if learners are encouraged to play an active role in the shaping of their study programme. The second involves the desire to explore the practical means by which such a qualitatively enhanced involvement of learners in their language study may be realised in day-to-day teaching practice.

A second point that has to be borne in mind when perusing the last three decades of research and experimentation around the general concept of learner-centredness is that one is dealing with an *emergent trend* within the language teaching profession, one that reflects differing perspectives and lines of thought, each with its own emphases and specificities. It is therefore unhelpful to look for the presence of a *deus ex machina*, calmly guiding our profession in a pre-ordained direction. Rather, one is faced with a complex and evolving social and educational system within which students, teachers and researchers have somehow felt that 'things could be different' and have, on this basis, explored ways of realising this 'difference'. This explains why the terminology used is sometimes confusing, and also why the way in which terms such as 'autonomy' are understood has evolved over time. This is not to say that writers in applied linguistics are sloppy or careless. It is rather that the terms which are used represent in themselves an attempt to encapsulate aspects of a complex reality which we have not, as yet, fully come to grips with. This is the case in many areas of applied linguistics, but it is particularly marked with respect to learner-centredness – as we will see at a number of points in the chapters that follow.

The goal of the present chapter is to present an overview of the main trends of thought in the general area of learner-centredness and then to introduce the perspective on learner-centredness which will be developed here. 1.2 will provide an historical survey of the main trends of thought which have served to shape our current understanding of the place and role of learners in the language teaching process, while 1.3 will examine those perspectives on learner-centredness which are currently the most influential. The distinction between 1.2 and 1.3 is not clear-cut: the 1960s and 1970s are hardly ancient history, and many of the ideas looked at in 1.2 are still very much part of current language teaching practice. The distinction between formative exploration (1.2) and current understanding (1.3) is nonetheless a useful one. In 1.4 a number of terminological and conceptual distinctions central to the view of learner-centredness put forward in this book will be considered, and 1.5 will present an overview of the rest of the book and will relate the content of subsequent chapters to the perspective on learner-centredness put forward in this chapter.

REF. In the light of the comments made above about the confusions surrounding the term 'learner-centredness' in the literature, it may be useful before reading further to take stock of your current attitudes to the concept of learner-centredness, even if it may seem somewhat vague or imprecise to you. If this is the case, do not worry. You are not alone!

- How would you describe your own spontaneous reaction to the concept of learner-centredness – enthusiastic, convinced, reserved, sceptical ... or whatever?
- List what *you* feel to be the main advantages of a learner-centred approach to teaching and also the main difficulties you feel could arise in the implementation of such an approach. You may do this in general terms, with a given teaching situation in mind, or on the basis of your own experience – either as a teacher or as a learner.

1.2 Formative trends

As was pointed out above, the trend towards a more learner-responsive, or learner-centred approach to language teaching should not be seen as the product of a single, coherently structured school of thought but rather as the confluence of a number of sometimes overlapping, sometimes differing perspectives on language teaching. These perspectives need therefore to be examined firstly in their historical context, and then in terms of their contribution to our current understanding of what learner-centred teaching can mean.

1.2.1 Humanistic language teaching

The humanistic movement in language teaching represents an eclectic grouping of ideas developed, in the first instance, in the fields of general education and psychology. Influential authors in the development of the ideational basis of humanistic education in general include Maslow (1970) and Rogers (1961). Underhill identifies seven main themes in humanistic psychology:

1 High-level health and well-being
2 The whole person
3 The human motivation towards self-realisation
4 Change and development
5 Education as a life-long process
6 Respect for an individual's subjective experience
7 Self-empowerment (1989: 25)

Stevick, in a well-balanced and insightful evaluation of the humanistic movement in language teaching, recognises five main strands or 'overlapping components' in humanistic thinking, which he labels H1–H5. These are:

(H1) *Feelings*, including both personal emotions and esthetic appreciation. This aspect of humanism tends to reject whatever makes people feel bad, or whatever destroys or forbids esthetic enjoyment.

(H2) *Social relations*. This side of humanism encourages friendship and cooperation, and opposes whatever tends to reduce them.

(H3) *Responsibility*. This aspect accepts the need for public scrutiny, criticism and correction, and disapproves of whoever or whatever denies their importance.

(H4) *Intellect*, including knowledge, reason, and understanding. This aspect fights against whatever interferes with the free exercise of the mind, and is suspicious of anything that cannot be tested intellectually.

(H5) *Self-actualisation*, the quest for full realisation of one's own deepest true qualities. This aspect believes that since conformity leads to enslavement, the pursuit of uniqueness brings about liberation. (1990: 23–24)

The ways in which these psychological and educational principles can be implemented in second language (L2) teaching have been explored by authors such as Moskowitz (1978) and Stevick (1976, 1980). However, it is probably methods such as Asher's Total Physical Response, Curran's Community Language Learning, Gattegno's Silent Way, and Lozanov's Suggestopedia, that have most forcibly struck popular imagination as embodying the 'humanistic approach' to language teaching. A brief look at two of these methods may help to bring out the ways in which the basic principles of humanism can be realised at classroom level, and also the differing emphases within the movement (readers are referred to the relevant chapters of Richards and Rodgers [1986] and Stevick [1990] for fuller accounts).

Caleb Gattegno's Silent Way (1972, 1976) is best known for its use of coloured *cuisinière* rods and the orchestrative but non-interventive role of the teacher. The external form of a Silent Way class may seem rather strange to an outsider: the teacher orchestrates learners' oral production via a carefully planned use of coloured rods and pronunciation or vocabulary charts, but keeps her own spoken intervention to a minimum and avoids explicit judgment or correction of learners' production. The Silent Way's rather unconventional teaching procedures are, however, designed with the explicit goal of generating a problem-solving approach to learning: by limiting her intervention, the teacher places the responsibility for generating language and identifying mean-ingful patterns on the learners themselves, a process which Gattegno describes as 'subordinating teaching to learning'. In this way, learners are meant to develop independence, autonomy and a sense of personal responsibility for their learning. Stevick sets out this goal in the following terms:

> . . . our proposals have been designed to free students deliber-ately from dependence and aim at autonomous and responsible learners. By using what each student brings to the task and by being acquainted with how one learns what is implicit in skills and capacities, we can help others become free of inhibitions, of anxiety, of all the hampering moves and at the same time make them experience an expansion of their self in the new universe open to them. (1990: 12, citing Gattegno 1988)

Although expressed in terms typical of humanistic psychology, what Gattegno is describing here are the processes of 'learning to learn' and of learner empowerment, concepts which will recur throughout this book. Not surprisingly, therefore, Stevick sees Gattegno as adhering in parti-cular to the fourth and fifth humanistic tenets listed above, viz. human intellectual development and the shaping of the unique self.

Charles Curran, the originator of Community Language Learning (CLL) (1972, 1976), was a Catholic priest who taught psychology and counselling, and CLL bears the mark of both of these aspects of Curran's experience. Curran conceptualises the language learning process in strongly theological terms (cf. his use of the terms 'incarnation' and 'redemption') and his approach to teaching is heavily influenced by the methods of counselling therapy. In a CLL class, learners typically sit in a circle and talk naturally about a subject of personal relevance. The learners formulate what they wish to say either in their first language (L1) or in the L2. The teacher stands beside the learner who is speaking and either gives the L2 form of what the learner has said in his L1, or gently reformulates his L2 utterance in an appropriate manner: each learner then repeats his contribution to the conversation, and so it moves on. The resultant conversation is recorded and replayed at the end of the class, various tasks being performed on the language it contains in order to aid retention. CLL thus has no pre-set syllabus, the language content being derived directly from the interests and concerns of the learners themselves. In CLL, the teacher (or, to use Curran's term, the counsellor) plays two main roles: the first is that of resource person who helps learners to formulate in the L2 the messages they wish to convey; the second is to create a supportive and non-judgmental atmosphere and to foster open and trusting relations among class members.

Stevick (1990: 98) finds that CLL embodies four of his five humanistic principles. Most conspicuous, he feels, is a concern for personal feelings and for the establishment of social relations (principles 1 and 2), though he also identifies a concern with responsibility and with self-actualisation (principles 3 and 5). Two aspects of CLL which will recur in subsequent chapters are the priority given to the generation of learning content by the learners themselves, in terms of both the topic and the precise form of expression desired, and the role of the teacher as learning counsellor.

The humanistic movement in language teaching has contributed to the development of our profession's understanding of learner-centredness in two main ways. The first is by allocating a central place in language teaching to the subjective and personal concerns of learners, and thereby moving away from a view of language teaching in which centre stage is held by the language code rather than the messages learners wish to convey. This has led to the incorporation into mainstream language teaching of a variety of affectively-oriented or personal-expression based activities whose origins lie in the humanistic movement. The second contribution of humanistic language teaching is its concern with the learning process itself, in particular with respect to learners' affective involvement in their language study.

This having been said, the degree to which humanistic ideas have been taken on board by the language teaching community as a whole has been limited by certain factors (cf. Atkinson, 1989, for one writer's reservations about humanistic language teaching). One is the heavy emphasis placed on affective input by some humanistic writers. True, every individual's affective concerns are very important to that indivi-dual, but this does not mean that these concerns need necessarily constitute the central focus of the person's language learning experience. Humanistic language teaching thus tends to pay insufficient attention to the situationally-constrained or real-world language needs of learners, needs which may be of considerable importance to the life goals of the learners concerned. Much the same applies to the closeness of the relationship that some humanistic writers wish to see established within the learning group. It *may* be desirable for learners to establish close or caring relationships with their fellow students or with their teacher, but this should never be imposed, nor should it be pursued as a goal in itself without due consideration of the cultural background and expectations of those concerned (both students and teachers). A second cause of the unease some teachers experience with humanistic methods is the feeling that the methods have been developed with insufficient regard to the practical constraints under which much language teaching takes place. Stevick acknowledges this problem and explains it in the following terms:

> Many of the devisers of unconventional methods have been
> people from outside the language teaching profession ... Their
> positions as outsiders have allowed them to come up with
> 'brilliant insights' ... that had never before been systematically
> exploited within the language teaching profession, and for this
> we must be grateful to them. But as outsiders they also designed
> methods that do not take into account the full range of social
> and curricular realities within which most language teaching is
> done. (1990: 142)

To sum up, the humanistic movement has made a considerable contribution to the language teaching community's understanding of what learner-centred teaching can entail, and it has expanded the range of insights and pedagogical resources available to teachers. At the same time, a genuinely learner-centred approach to teaching is more complex, and raises a far wider range of questions, than many humanistic writers have been willing to acknowledge, a point made by Brumfit (1982). The essential problem is that most humanistic writers seem to be involved in the search for 'the' way of teaching language. In itself, this is of course a laudable endeavour. Language learners, however, differ on a number of counts, which include the purposes for which the language is being learned, their subjective needs arising out of a variety of psychological and cognitive factors, as well as the expectations generated by the social norms and traditions of learning proper to the learners' home culture. These sources of variance, which will be considered in Chapters 3–5, are accorded insufficient attention by humanistic writers, and this seriously limits the transferability of these writers' frequently exciting insights into different language learning contexts. In terms of learner-centredness, then, most humanistic methods fail to take sufficient account of learner variability and of the ways in which this influences the processes of teaching and learning.

1.2.2 *Communicative Language Teaching*

The trend which has come to be known as Communicative Language Teaching (CLT) originated in the mid-1960s as a result of two related concerns. One was discontent with the essentially code-based view of language teaching found in the approaches most widely practised at that time (audio-lingualism and the grammar-translation method); the other was the desire to develop course design structures which were more flexible and more responsive to students' real world communicative needs.

An important role was played in the early development of CLT by the

Council of Europe's Modern Languages Project (MLP), which was set up in 1963. The MLP was an ambitious and wide-ranging initiative designed to promote language teaching and learning in Europe, both at school and in the context of adult permanent education. It aimed at promoting a 'learner-centred, motivation-based' approach to teaching which, according to Trim, was:

> ... anti-authoritarian [and which encouraged] individual initiative and responsibility in the exercise of choice of objectives and methods, and self-assessment in the monitoring of progress and performance. (1980: 47)

Inevitably, this called for a re-thinking of the terms in which the goals of language teaching were formulated. In this respect, Trim says that the MLP rejected:

> ... a systematic taxonomic division of language as subject matter in favour of an analysis of learning situations [since it] makes little sense to subscribe to a 'learner-centred, motivation-based' approach unless the needs of learners find direct expression in the context of courses and associated tests and examinations (Op. cit.: 53)

The resulting approach to the identification of learning goals (cf. Richterich 1973) involved an analysis of learners' target uses of the language in terms of language *situations* (defined by *agents*, the persons involved, together with the categories of *time* and *place*) and *operations* (*functions* to be fulfilled by the relevant communicative act, the *objects* to which it relates, and the *means* by which it is produced). In other words, the approach to goal-setting developed within the MLP was based on an analysis of the functional and communicative demands of the situations in which learners would be required to use the language.

The MLP was not, of course, the only attempt in the late 60s and early 70s to make language teaching more responsive to learners' functional language needs. The expansion of language teaching worldwide and, in particular, the growing need for specific purpose language teaching (LSP) which arose out of the economic expansion experienced by many newly independent countries during this period, starkly demonstrated the inadequacies of the traditional code-based approach to teaching. The pressing need for a variety of language skills within a rapidly evolving social and economic context made it essential for the language teaching profession to develop appropriate tools for identifying learners' communicative needs and for translating them into coherent course structures. This needs analysis–based approach to course design found its most coherent expression in Munby's *Communicative Syllabus Design* (1978), which will be discussed further in 3.1 and 3.2.

In parallel with this pragmatically-driven attempt to make course design procedures more responsive to learners' real-world communicative requirements, the same period witnessed a reformulation of the theoretical framework within which language, and hence language teaching, should be viewed. Hymes' (1972) concept of 'communicative competence', for example, included considerations of communicative effectiveness and awareness of the TL (target language) culture, and thus represented a more integrated view of the goals of language instruction than that implicit in the narrowly linguistic view of language competence defended by Chomsky during the same period. Halliday (1970: 145) developed a functional view of language based on the description of speech acts or texts since, for him, 'only through the study of *language in use* are all the functions of language, and therefore all components of meaning, brought into focus' (emphasis added). In the field of applied linguistics, Widdowson (cf. his significantly entitled *Teaching Language as Communication*, 1978) advocated an approach to language teaching based on the analysis of the communicative acts involved in both spoken interaction and the production of written texts.

These trends shifted the focus of language teaching away from the linguistic code viewed in a restrictive sense to language as a system for expressing messages and achieving functional and communicative goals in real-world interactive situations. Richards and Rodgers sum up the main characteristics of 'this communicative view of language' as follows:

1 Language is a system for the expression of meaning.
2 The primary function of language is for interaction and communication.
3 The structure of language reflects its functional and communicative uses.
4 The primary units of language are not merely its grammatical and structural features, but categories of functional and communicative meaning as exemplified in discourse. (1986: 71)

This change in emphasis regarding the content focus of language teaching went hand-in-hand with a re-thinking of the process side of language study. The communicative movement sought to develop a mode of teaching and learning which was experientially-based, involving the use of communicative tasks whose content mirrored the learners' target uses of the language. This led to a concern with 'authenticity' in terms of the language and materials introduced into the classroom, as well as the tasks that learners were asked to perform.

The communicative movement effected a profound change in the way in which language teaching was conceived, and gave rise to what remains the dominant paradigm in language teaching. Its contribution to the development of learner-centredness may be seen on two main levels. Firstly, and most importantly, the communicative movement accorded a central place in course design to the communicative goals of the learners concerned, i.e. to the messages they needed to receive or convey in real-world interactive situations. Secondly, on the methodological level, CLT fostered an experiential form of language study in which learners' real-world experience and concerns were given a central role in learning activities. This having been said, mainstream CLT has suffered from a number of weaknesses (cf. Hutchinson and Waters 1984). These relate to a somewhat mechanical approach to needs analysis and inadequate attention to the process side of learning, points which will be looked at in Chapters 3 and 4 respectively. Nonetheless, it is difficult to over-estimate the contribution of CLT to our current understanding of the place of the learner's communicative needs and goals within the language learning process.

1.2.3   Learning strategy research

Research conducted from the early 1970s (cf. Rubin 1987 for an overview) into the attitudinal and behavioural characteristics of L2 learners served to introduce the concept of 'learning strategy' firmly into the terminology of L2 teaching. Learning strategies, in general terms, are purposeful activities undertaken by learners with the goal of promoting their knowledge of and ability to use the TL. These activities may relate to very detailed aspects of learning, such as the organisation of vocabulary lists, or may be much broader in focus, such as deciding whether to follow a language course or to seek out social contacts with TL speakers. The learning strategy research of the 70s will be discussed further in 2.2 within the framework of learner training, and two categorisations of learning strategies will be discussed in 7.2 with respect to the active involvement of learners in their language study.

The learning strategy research conducted in the 1970s (e.g. Rubin 1975; Naiman *et al.* 1978) studied the attitudes and behaviours which characterised more and less successful language learners. The methodology used was explorative, employing questionnaires and interviews, so as to allow the researchers to gain insight into learners' subjective perceptions of language learning. One motivation behind these studies was to identify the behavioural and attitudinal characteristics of 'good' (or successful) language learners, with the idea that such a profile might provide an agenda for strategy training with less successful learners. One such list of 'good learner' strategies will be given in 2.2. With hindsight, it is clear that the idea of pedagogising a list of successful behaviours and 'teaching' them to less successful learners was perhaps somewhat simplistic. Nonetheless, the learning strategy research of the 1970s has provided an invaluable impetus to the development of a more learner-centred perspective on language teaching. To begin with, learning strategy research represented a coherent attempt to 'listen' to learners and to use learners' own insights and preferences to shape language teaching practice. In other words, it acknowledged the role of learners' subjective involvement in their language study, and thus prepared the path for subsequent research into subjective needs, individual differences and, in general terms, the process side of learning. On a more concrete level, the learning strategy research of the 1970s provided our profession with the methodological and conceptual parameters which have guided subsequent research into learner training and learner autonomy. This movement from learning strategy research to learner training and learner autonomy, which will be discussed in the next section, emerges very clearly in Wenden and Rubin (1987) and Wenden (1991).

1.2.4   Individualisation

Any account, however brief, of the development of learner-centred thinking in language teaching would be amiss if it failed to mention the work on individualisation which took place during the 1960s and 1970s (cf. Altman 1972, 1977; Altman and James 1980; ETIC 1978; Gougher 1972). Altman defines individualised instruction in the following terms:

> An individualized foreign language program is one in which the structure of the program – i.e. presentation and composition of content, role definition of teacher and learner, system of evalua-tion – is allowed to be flexible in an effort to accommodate, to the extent possible, the interests, needs and abilities of individual learners. (1977: 76–77)

The impetus towards work on individualised instruction arose out of a concern with 'breaking the *lock-step* [of traditional classroom instruc-tion], and allowing learners to progress at varying rates suitable to each individual' (Dickinson 1978: 9. Original emphasis). It was thus an attempt to make instructional procedures more flexible and more responsive to individual learning pace and needs. Interest in individuali-sation may be seen as a recognition of the importance of individual variability and of learners' subjective needs. In this way, it represents an attempt to get to grips with the process side of learning.

The practical results of work on individualisation, however, were often rather disappointing, which explains why far less attention has been paid to individualisation since the end of the 1970s. A major reason for this dissatisfaction is that, in practice, individualised instruction tended to be very materials- and teacher-centred. Holec (1979: 7) expresses this reservation by observing that 'in the minds of most of its advocates individualisation [remained] a "method" of teaching and [gave] rise to the elaboration of teaching procedures and not learning procedures.' More fundamentally, perhaps, the concerns underlying the initial interest in individualised instruction came to find expression in the more powerful concepts of learner autonomy and self-directed learning. In fact, in an article discussing these three approaches to language teaching Dickinson (1978) says that individualisation 'misses the point' because, despite its acknowledgement of the importance of individual differences in learning, it fails to cater for two factors crucial to the successful accommodation of these differences. The first of these is flexibility in teacher-student role relationships to allow for direct learner consultation with regard to teaching content and form. The second is the systematic development of learners' understanding of the learning process as a basis for meaningful learner involvement in programme development.

> *REF.* How far does the perspective on the formative trends in learner-centredness (humanistic language teaching, communicative language teaching, learning strategy research, individualisation) provided above coincide with the impressions you have formed from your own reading?
>
> - Do you feel that this perspective casts a helpful light on the reading you have done in the past?
> - If not, try to identify why and specify the way(s) in which your understanding of the literature differs from that presented above.

1.3   Current practice

This section will focus on the three perspectives on learner-centredness which have received the most attention in recent years: these are learner-centredness as a principle for activity organisation, learner autonomy, and the course design perspective on learner-centredness (best known in terms of Nunan's concept of the learner-centred curriculum). There is, of course, no neat historical divide between these perspectives and the trends dealt with in the last section: many teachers, for example, still subscribe enthusiastically to one or another school of humanistic language teaching and CLT continues to provide the dominant paradigm in mainstream language teaching. Nonetheless, certain developmental relationships are relatively clear. Work on learner involvement in activity organisation, for instance, owes a considerable debt to the importance accorded by both the humanistic movement and by CLT to relevance of learning content (even if the two schools conceived of relevance in different terms). Recent explorations of autonomous learning have built on the pioneering research into the nature and role of individual learning strategies conducted in the 1970s, and Nunan's work on the learner-centred curriculum operates within the general parameters established by CLT, even if it adds to them in a number of significant ways, particularly with respect to learner participation in decision-making.

1.3.1 Learner-centredness as a principle for activity organisation

Campbell and Kryszewska (1992) and Deller (1990) provide an interesting survey of the range of learner-centred activities which have made their way into mainstream language teaching practice. This sub-section will therefore be based on the activities described in these two books. The authors' accounts of the ways in which they developed their interest in a learner-centred approach to activity organisation relate to certain aspects of the theoretical background outlined in the last section as well as to a number of very down-to-earth pedagogical considerations. One influence on Deller (op. cit.: 2) was Curran, and she suggests that the activities in Curran's book represent an alternative way of generating the personally relevant learner input favoured by CLL. Another formative influence for Deller was her work as a teacher of ESP (English for Specific Purposes) and Business English with students whose content knowledge in the relevant specialist fields was greater than her own, which thus made the learners themselves the most fruitful source of learning material. Campbell and Kryszewska mention this point, too:

> In certain areas [our students'] knowledge was often considerably greater than ours. This taught us to respect them as learners, and see them as individuals rather than as 'a class of foreign students', and to call upon their specialist knowledge in the lessons. (Op. cit.: 5–6)

On a very practical level, Deller says that she found learner-centred activities to be a means of countering the difficulties caused by large classes, low-tech materials or inadequate coursebooks. The last point is echoed by Campbell and Kryszewska, who found that a learner-based mode of teaching offered a way of overcoming the dissatisfaction generated by coursebooks which 'did not meet the real needs and interests' of learners (op. cit.: 5).

Before looking at the activity types suggested in these two books, it is well worth considering the advantages which Campbell and Kryszewska see in adopting a learner-based approach to activity organisation:

1 **The potential of the learner**
   Students bring a lot with them. They all have their own ideas, opinions, experiences, and areas of expertise. All of this is important to them. What they need from the language classroom is the language to express all this, and thereby themselves in the TL.
   Encouraging learners to express their own ideas freely is a more direct route to fluency than one where the teacher imposes irrelevant topics in the hope that with time learners will be able to say what they really want to.

2 **Constant needs analysis**
   If activities are chosen in the light of the current needs of the learners concerned, teachers can monitor for gaps in the learners' language competence and introduce suitable practice activities in subsequent lessons. In learner-based teaching, then, needs analysis is an ongoing process.

3 **Topicality**
   Learner-based teaching makes it possible to introduce local or international issues and ideas which are of current interest to particular groups. Learner input may be especially important where there is no up-to-date coverage of such topics in published language teaching materials.

4 **Previous learning experience**
   A learner-based approach caters for an open-ended learning experience. A framework is given, but the learners bear the responsibility for filling in the details, so that the same framework can evolve in completely different ways with different groups. This can be a refreshing change for learners who have already worked through a number of published coursebooks.

5 **Learners as authors**
   Language practice is doubled in learner-based teaching because learners are involved in preparing as well as using the practice materials.

6 **Pace**
   It may seem much easier to hand out texts at the beginning of a lesson, rather than asking the learners to prepare their own. However, as the activity progresses, the pace increases. Also, the involvement of the learners is total throughout.

7 **The element of surprise**
   As materials are not available in advance, there is a strong

element of surprise. Not only do the learners not know what is coming before the lesson starts, but they are often unable to predict how the lesson will develop.

8 **Peer teaching and correction**
Learner-based teaching encourages students to work together and learn from each other. Activities are structured so that learners *have* to pay attention to what their colleagues are saying. They can teach and correct each other. Working together, the class can pool whatever individual resources they have, and work towards creating 'group grammars' and 'group lexicons'.

9 **Group solidarity**
Learner-based activities help to foster a spirit of group solidarity in which everyone has a valid contribution to make, regardless of overall linguistic ability. Learners are working with one another, not in competition with one another. (1992: 7–9. Adapted)

The books by Deller and by Campbell and Kryszewska present a wide range of activities (54 and 70 respectively), many with a number of suggested variations. In both books, however, the activities are presented under relatively conventional headings such as *vocabulary, writing, icebreakers, grammar exercises and drills*, or *games*. Within the present context, it may be helpful to look at these activity types under more general headings which bring out more clearly the specifically learner-centred nature of the learning processes they are designed to foster. Thus, four main categories of activity may be identified. Table 1 provides an overview of these activity categories with an illustrative example or two taken either from Deller or from Campbell and Kryszewska.

The first activity type, involving the use of learner knowledge as an input resource, is based on the idea that an activity is likely to produce more relevant language and be more motivating if learners are allowed to invest it with a content which is 'their own'. This can be seen in 'My country/district', where learners are asked to draw up a list of the advantages and attractions of their home country or area. In a similar way, 'Beat the expert' allows learners to assume the role of 'expert' with regard to their fellow students on the basis of one of their hobbies or personal interests. The same principle applies in terms of learners' professional knowledge, as in 'Listen to our meeting', where learners prepare a role play based on their knowledge of the company they work in.

The second activity type involves the use of learners' L1: this, however, should not be confused with traditional translation exercises, which generally involve narrowly language-based work on a text with little or no link to learners' real-world communicative concerns. The L1-based activities suggested by Campbell and Kryszewska, on the contrary, acknowledge that for many learners their L1 is the medium in which they formulate the greater part of the messages they wish to convey, and the activities suggested build on this to bring learners' own 'communicative agendas' into the L2 classroom. In 'Telephone call', for example, learners recall in detail the last call they made in their L1 and then try to transcribe it in the TL.

The third activity type, direct learner involvement in activity development and organisation, serves two learning goals. To begin with, it requires learners to survey a much wider range of TL materials than would be the case if the teacher were to select materials. In 'Newspaper search', for example, learners select and skim through a whole newspaper to prepare a set of comprehension questions for their fellow students. Secondly, such activities draw learners into the teaching-learning process in an active and reflective manner: 'My grammar problem' and 'We test you, you test us', for example, involve learners in aspects of diagnosis and evaluation which are generally considered to be the teacher's prerogative (cf. Chapter 6). In this way, these activities provide learners with insights into the nature of their learning goals and thus constitute a form of learner-training (cf. Chapter 2).

Finally, the affectively-based activity category has clear links with aspects of humanistic language teaching in its recourse to personal expression and imagination/creativity. 'Interest pies', for example, centres around learners pooling their personal interests with fellow students, and activities such as 'Dr Jekyll and Mr Hyde' or 'Invent your own country' allow learners scope to use their imaginative skills, creativity and sense of fun as means of generating language.

The two books by Deller and by Campbell and Kryszewska contain a rich and varied collection of activities which make active use of learners':

- personal interests and concerns;
- professional and/or specialised knowledge;
- willingness to work with fellow students to achieve shared goals;
- prior learning experiences and perspectives on the process of language study.

In this way, they provide teachers with a variety of valuable guidelines as to how they can make their teaching more learner-centred. It is difficult, however, to avoid a feeling of unease with respect to the wider framework of reference within which the two books are operating. Is learner-centredness seen as one option or resource alongside others at the level of activity development, or is it seen as a guiding principle for course design? As both books appeared in the category of 'resource book', it is difficult to judge which perspective the authors themselves actually prescribed to: the question, however, is important with respect to the use and evaluation of the activity types in question. Useful as they are, one cannot help wondering how profound a change the activities suggested by Deller and by Campbell and Kryszewska would effect in teaching practice unless they are integrated into a coherent framework of goals at course design level.

Table 1: *Categories of learner-based activity*

1 *Use of learner knowledge as an input resource*	
a General knowledge and personal interests	
e.g. 'My country/district'	C. and K*: 21–22
'Beat the expert'	C. and K.: 32–34
b Professional and/or specialised knowledge	
e.g. 'Listen to our meeting'	Del. +: 42–43
'Ask me my questions'	Del.: 45–46
2 *Use of learners' L1 as an input medium*	
e.g. 'The telephone call'	C. and K.: 76–77
'What is your text about?'	C. and K.: 80–81
3 *Direct learner involvement in activity development and organisation*	
a Student provision of language study materials	
e.g. 'Newspaper search'	Del.: 30–31
b Self- or peer diagnosis of language	
e.g. 'My grammar problem'	C. and K.: 26–28
c Examination preparation	
e.g. 'We test you, you test us'	C. and K.: 107–108
4 *Affectively-based activities*	
a Personal expression orientation	
e.g. 'What I like about you is . . .'	Del.: 26
'Interest pies'	Del.: 26–27
b Imaginative/Creative orientation	
e.g. 'Dr Jekyll and Mr Hyde'	C. and K.: 29–32
'Invent your own country'	C. and K.: 50–51
'Neighbours'	Del.: 44

(From *Campbell and Kryszewska [1992], + Deller [1990])

1.3.2 Learner autonomy

Learner autonomy has been one of the dominant topics in language teaching over the last 15 to 20 years (cf. Brookes and Grundy 1988; Holec 1979; Wenden 1991; Wenden and Dickinson 1995; Wenden and Rubin 1987, as just a few instances of a large and growing body of research on the topic). Inevitably, however, the nature and the implications of the concept of learner autonomy have evolved and become clearer over time: in this respect it may be instructive to recall that in

1979 Holec (op. cit.: 3) described the use of the term 'learner autonomy' as 'semi-anarchical'! The main ambiguity surrounding the use of the term that readers are likely to encounter is whether it is used to refer to a certain *mode of study* or to a *qualitative involvement* of learners in their language study. In the former sense, autonomy refers to various forms of independent or self-directed learning involving limited teacher intervention, generally outside a traditional classroom setting. In the latter, qualitative sense, autonomy relates to notions of awareness of learning goals, participation in decision-making, and personal assumption of responsibility. Over time, it is the second view of learner autonomy that has become the central object of concern, and it is in this sense that the term tends to be used in more recent writing: readers should, however, remain attentive to the way in which a given writer is actually using the term.

The reasons for this shift in emphasis are relatively clear: learners may or may not wish to study in an independent manner, but their ability to make this decision and to implement it effectively is dependent upon their strategic and attitudinal preparedness, in other words, on qualitative factors. It is in this perspective that Holec defines autonomy as:

> ... an <u>ability</u>, a 'power or capacity to do something' ... and not a type of conduct, 'behaviour'. 'Autonomy' is thus a term describing a potential capacity to act in a given situation – in our case learning – and not the actual behaviour of an individual in that situation. (Op. cit.: Original emphasis)

Wenden views autonomy in similar terms, describing the autonomous learner as one who:

> ... has acquired the strategies and knowledge to take some (if not yet all) responsibility for her language learning and is willing and self-confident enough to do so. (1991: 163)

Crabbe identifies three main reasons for fostering learner autonomy. The first, the *ideological* argument is that:

> ... the individual has the right to be free to exercise his or her own choices, in learning as in other areas, and not become a victim (even an unwitting one) of choices made by social institutions. (1993: 443)

Crabbe relates this argument back to the work of educationalists such as Freire (e.g. 1972), though it clearly shares a lot of ground with the humanistic movement's concern with responsibility, intellectual development and self-actualistion (cf. 1.2.1 above). Crabbe's second argument is *psychological* and:

> ...is simply that we learn better when we are in charge of our
> own learning [and that the resultant learning] is more mean-
> ingful, more permanent, more focused on the processes and
> schemata of the individual when the individual is in charge.
> (Op. cit.: 443)

This argument recalls certain tenets of humanistic thinking, as well as
the importance given to learners' personal strategic involvement in their
language study by learning strategy research. The third argument in
favour of autonomy advanced by Crabbe is *economic* and is based on
the recognition that:

> ... society does not have the resources to provide the level of
> personal instruction needed by all its members in every area of
> learning [so that] individuals must be able to provide for their
> own learning needs .... (Op. cit.: 443)

This economic argument has come, in Western Europe at least, to be
linked with an ideological argument different from that put forward by
Crabbe. This maintains that individuals *should* assume responsibility for
their learning in an active and self-directive manner and should not
expect 'the other', whether it be the State or an educational institution,
to pre-digest or organise their learning for them. Ironically perhaps, this
line of reasoning, based on liberal or free-market principles, places
teachers and students before a very similar set of challenges as those set
by a writer such as Freire, albeit for rather different reasons.

There are thus many good reasons for pursuing the goal of learner
autonomy, i.e. for helping learners to interact with their language study
in an informed and self-directive manner. Indeed, Brumfit's (1982: 11)
comment that 'no sensible person should want to be anti-humanistic'
applies equally well to the development of learner autonomy: no
sensible teacher should want to maintain or foster dependency in her
students. Addressing the issue in programmatic terms, however, raises
at least two important questions. The first relates to what autonomy
actually entails, and the second to the means by which it can be
developed. These two questions have been at the heart of a large part
of the work that has been conducted on learner autonomy over the last
two decades.

Huttenen (1986: 232) succinctly but pertinently defines autonomy as
'the willingness and ability of the learner to take responsibility for his
own learning'. This is fine, but a more detailed breakdown of the
component parts of autonomy is useful in assessing how it might be
developed. Dickinson identifies five characteristics of autonomous learners:

1 they understand what is being taught, i.e. they have sufficient understanding of language learning to understand the purpose of pedagogical choices;
2 they are able to formulate their own learning objectives;
3 they are able to select and make use of appropriate learning strategies;
4 they are able to monitor their use of these strategies;
5 they are able to self-assess, or monitor their own learning.
(1993: 330–31)

This is quite an impressive array of learning skills, and not all students will spontaneously master them at the outset of their learning career. Consequently, concern with the development of learner autonomy has given rise to research into the means by which learners can be helped to acquire the insights into language learning, the relevant attitudinal traits and, crucially, the learning strategies they need in order to operate in an informed and self-directive manner. This process is generally referred to as learner training (cf. Chapter 2), and will play a key role in the perspective on learner-centredness which will be adopted in this book.

Interest in learner autonomy, and in the closely related area of learner training, has moved language teaching in a learner-centred direction in three main ways. The first, and arguably the most important, is that it explicitly recognises the central role which learners can and should play in the management of their language study. The second is that it has focused the attention of the language teaching profession on the development of pedagogical procedures whereby learners can be helped to become full and active participants in rather than more or less passive recipients of language teaching. This has led to a number of imaginative initiatives both in adult education, of which the work of Holec and his colleagues at CRAPEL is perhaps the best known, and within the context of school-based language study (cf. Huttenen, op. cit.). The increasingly widespread establishment of self-access facilities is one of the more tangible manifestations of this trend, as it enshrines (in the form of a self-access centre) the importance of learner choice and self-direction in language study. The third is that by focusing the attention of the language teaching community on learning processes in addition to learning products, it has generated interest in those learner-specific factors which influence learners' interaction with various aspects of language study. This has given rise to research in the field of learners' subjective needs (individual differences and learning style preferences), which will be discussed in Chapter 4. It has also led to reflection on the interaction between learners' cultural background and expectations, and their perceptions of concepts such as autonomy, as evidenced by Riley's

'The ethnography of autonomy' (1988), which will be examined in 5.3 with reference to the cultural implications of a learner-centred approach to teaching.

These trends have played a significant role in promoting reflection on aspects of learner-centredness within the language teaching profession. Nonetheless, learner autonomy is something which is frequently grafted onto or runs in parallel with more or less traditional types of learning programmes. In other words, there are still a number of ambiguities about how the concept of learner autonomy can be integrated into course design in a systematic manner, a problem which was mentioned in 1.3.1 with respect to learner-centredness as a principle for activity organisation. This difficulty is expressed by Crabbe in the following terms:

> The important point ... is that autonomy as a goal needs to pervade the whole curricular system and not simply be an occasional part of it. ... Autonomous learning needs to become a reference point for *all* classroom procedure. (Op. cit.: 444. Original emphasis)

1.3.3 The curriculum design perspective

Probably the most coherent large-scale attempt to realise the principles of learner-centredness at course design level was made in Australia as part of the Adult Migration Education Program (AMEP) by researchers such as Brindley, Nunan and Willing, and which gave rise to Nunan's (1988) concept of the learner-centred curriculum. The main idea underlying this approach to course design is that learners should be taken as the reference point for decision-making as regards both the content and the form of teaching, and that this should be achieved via a process of consultation and negotiation between teacher and learners. The work of AMEP was situated within the conceptual paradigm generated by CLT, namely that the real-world communicative needs of learners should take centre stage in goal-setting. The curriculum design perspective on learner-centredness developed by Nunan and his fellow workers, however, adds to the basic CLT paradigm in three main ways. The first relates to the procedures used to identify learners' objective needs, the second to the criteria used in selecting methodology, and the third to the nature of decision-making.

Nunan (1988: 24) suggests that the needs analysis procedures developed within CLT are 'only superficially learner-centred' because they favour 'data about the learner, rather than incorporating data from the learner'. Logically, then, Nunan proposes that needs analysis procedures be expanded to accommodate more direct input from learners, and that needs analysis should be a developmental process, allowing goal-setting to emerge gradually, as learners come to understand and acquire the ability to formulate their insights into their communicative needs. In terms of the selection of methodology, Nunan and his fellow researchers accorded a crucial role to the subjective, or process-oriented needs of learners, in other words, to the way in which various cognitive, affective and attitudinal factors influence learners' reactions to teaching procedures. This led them to suggest that methodological choices be made in the light of learners' subjective needs rather than on the basis of what might, in theoretical terms, be considered to be 'good' teaching practice. The third main tenet, an insistence (mentioned above) on the active participation of learners in decision-making via ongoing consultation and negotiation, constitutes the channel by which the first two innovations are realised. Learners explore both their objective and their subjective learning needs in collaboration with their teacher as part of a shared process of discovery, and this is one of the main contributions of Nunan's work to our understanding of what learner-centred teaching can mean.

Viewed from a certain distance, the conceptual bases of Nunan's approach to course design (e.g. 1988: 22–24) are not terribly novel with respect to the other perspectives on learner-centredness which have been surveyed in this and the last section. The key distinction is that the concept of the learner-centred curriculum has integrated within a coherent planning framework the various insights which have been explored over the last two to three decades – relevance of learning content, flexibility of learning from and the strategic involvement of learners. In this way, it has provided the language teaching profession with an intellectual framework within which it can explore the many challenges and complexities of learner-centred language teaching in a more systematic manner than has been possible in the past.

REF/PED.

- On the basis of a language teaching programme you have been involved in recently, either as teacher or as learner, analyse the degree to which the three perspectives on learner-centredness dealt with in this section (i.e. learner-centredness as a principle for activity organisation, learner autonomy, and the learner-centred curriculum) were present. This may have been explicitly stated in programme goals and structure, or may have been realised more or less implicitly in terms of certain types of teacher-learner interaction or of activity organisation.
- Then, list the changes which, in your opinion, could have been made in this programme to move it in a more learner-centred direction, and give the rationale for your suggestions.

Thinking on learner-centredness, and indeed on language teaching in general, has moved on since Nunan published *The Learner-centred Curriculum* in 1988, and the perspective on learner-centredness that will be put forward in the following chapters will seek to reflect these developments. Nonetheless, the approach to learner-centredness that will be developed in this book is largely similar to that put forward by Nunan, namely that it is the learners themselves who should be taken as the central reference point for decision-making regarding both the content and the form of language teaching, and that this goal should be realised interactively by a process of consultation and negotiation between the participants in the learning situation. Learner education thus constitutes a key enabling factor in Nunan's view of language teaching, learner participation in goal-setting and in the selection of methodology depending crucially on the development of learners' understanding of language and of language learning. Nunan's work has thus introduced into mainstream language teaching a profoundly educational set of concerns, and these same concerns will underpin the approach to language teaching which will be developed in this book. This educational perspective on learner-centredness will be discussed in 1.4.2 and 1.5 will contain an outline of the content of the following chapters together with the rationale for the structuring of the book as a whole.

1.4   A few key distinctions

If nothing else has emerged from the last three sections, it should be clear that the concept of 'learner-centredness' is a broad one that has been, and still is understood in a number of different ways. The perspective on learner-centredness that will be adopted in this book should not, therefore, be viewed as being definitive. In the time that elapses between the writing and the reading of these pages, changes will have occurred and thinking will have moved on, and readers should actively seek to evaluate what is written here in the light of these new developments. Nor should the suggestions which will be made in this book be viewed in a restrictive sense, as an attempt to limit or box in the analysis of the complex network of relationships that exist between teachers, students and the wider social context of learning. This would, in fact, be in contradiction with the very idea of learner-centredness. With these general points in mind, this section will look at the concept of 'method' and its relationship with learner-centredness, and will then look more closely at the educational perspective on learner-centredness which will underpin this book.

1.4.1 Learner-centredness and the concept of 'method'

One reason why learner-centredness has received a rather bad press among certain teachers and writers is that it is sometimes made synonymous with a limited set of teaching procedures. Learner-centredness has thus been seen as a 'method' in the restrictive sense of the term. It is therefore helpful to look at the relationship between the view of learner-centredness, and thus of language teaching, which will underpin this book and the concept of method. Allwright (1991: 7–8) defines the 'historical concept' of method as 'a unitary/unified set of principled answers to all the main questions of how language is to be taught' and considers this concept to be 'highly problematic' for six reasons:

> 1 It is built on seeing differences where similarities may be more important, since methods that are different in abstract principle seem to be far less so in classroom practice.
> 2 It simplifies unhelpfully a highly complex set of issues, for example seeing similarities among learners when differences may be more important, since methods making universal claims to validity are simultaneously making the claim that all learners are essentially similar in all relevant respects.
> 3 It diverts energies from potentially more productive concerns, since time spent learning how to implement a particular method is time not available for such alternative activities as classroom task design.
> 4 It breeds a brand loyalty which is unlikely to be helpful to the profession, since it fosters pointless rivalries on essentially irrelevant issues.
> 5 It breeds complacency, if, as it surely must, it conveys the impression that answers have indeed been found to all the major methodological questions in our profession.
> 6 It offers a 'cheap' externally-derived sense of coherence for language teachers, which may inhibit the development of a personally 'expensive', but ultimately far more valuable, internally-derived sense of coherence .... (1991: 7–8)

In Allwright's use of the term, 'method' refers to a restrictive, there-is-only-one-right-way view of language teaching, one which most language teachers will have encountered at some point in their careers. Such a view of teaching is diametrically opposed to a learner-centred approach to teaching, which, virtually by definition, must reject neat, pre-set recipes or generally applicable formulae. Indeed, reformulating Allwright's criticisms of the concept of method in positive terms can provide a number of valuable insights into the nature of learner-centred teaching:

1 A learner-centred approach accepts and seeks to learn from the perspectives on language teaching contained in any method or approach, as well as from the insights teachers derive from their everyday teaching experience; it does this in the belief that openness to a variety of experiences and insights makes the language teacher better able to respond to local needs.

2 A learner-centred approach positively accepts diversity between learners, learning contexts and learning goals; it rejects the contention that there is one universally 'right' way either to teach or to learn.

3 A learner-centred approach is concerned in the first instance with the learners involved and with the quality of their learning; the means by which this is achieved are secondary, and are to be chosen in response to the characteristics of the learners themselves and of the learning context.

4 A learner-centred approach is open to insights from any source, within or outside language teaching, providing better understanding of the needs of learners is achieved and more effective teaching and learning procedures are identified; it does not set up ideological barriers.

5 A learner-centred approach generates a healthy dissatisfaction with current practice, as it maintains that there is no once-and-for-all right answer, but only appropriate, local responses to local needs; learner-centred teaching is always novel, since each new group of learners is always different from the last.

6 A learner-centred approach seeks coherence in terms of the adequacy of its response to the needs of each new group of learners; its coherence is to be sought locally, in terms of the human and educational development of each new group of students.

In brief, then, a learner-centred approach to teaching seeks to work with human complexity and diversity, and cannot therefore expect to find neat, pre-packed solutions. Rather, it seeks to find *local* solutions to *local* problems in the light of the human and pragmatic characteristics of each learning context.

1.4.2   Education as a means of empowerment

The various trends surveyed in 1.2 and 1.3 arose out of one or both of two complementary but nonetheless distinct sets of imperatives. One is social in origin and involves the endeavour to create learning structures which are responsive to the needs of the clients of language teaching – the students themselves in the first instance, but also the wider social group to which the students belong. This social imperative inspired CLT's attempt to create structures for gearing teaching content more closely to the real-world functional needs of learners at a time of rapid change in both the social and the economic fields of life in many parts of the world. More recently, our profession has been called upon, often for reasons of a budgetary or organisational nature, to create learning structures other than the traditional teacher-plus-class-group formula. Cost-effectiveness and flexibility are thus terms which have come to assume a significant place in the vocabulary of the language teaching profession, and have led to various innovations, particularly in terms of the development of different forms of (semi-)independent study. The other imperative is educational in nature, and is concerned with enhancing the quality of learners' involvement in their language study. These two imperatives should, of course, go together, the educational perspective providing the pedagogical insights which are necessary to ensure the successful realisation of alternative modes of study. Some-times, however, the confluence of these two sets of imperatives gives rise to ambiguities as to what the main point at issue really is, the development of alternative (generally independent or semi-independent) modes of study or the qualitative involvement of learners in their language study.

The focus of this book will be first and foremost on the educational side of the debate. This means that it will focus on the pedagogical considerations which underpin the effective realisation of a learner-centred approach to teaching. In doing this, the formula of a teacher working on a more or less regular basis with a stable group of students will be taken as the main reference point. There are two reasons for this. One is that despite increasing interest in (semi-)independent modes of study, the teacher-plus-class-group mode of teaching is still the most widely practised. The other and more fundamental reason is that the processes of language education can be illustrated more easily with respect to the teacher-plus-class-group formula. The same pro-cesses do, of course, need to be catered for in independent modes of study via consultation and the preparation of guidance materials: indeed, the less access learners have to the advice of a teacher and the moral support of fellow students, the greater is their need for prepara-tion in both strategic and attitudinal terms. In what follows no distinction will be made *in principle* between a teacher-plus-class-group and (semi-)independent modes of study, although real differences clearly do exist in terms of organisation and learner support. In the light of these remarks, a few terminological distinctions need to be made. The terms *self-directive* and *self-direction* will henceforth be used to refer to the strategic and attitudinal traits of a learner who is able, or who is in the process of developing the ability to make informed decisions relative to his language learning, and who accepts this assumption of responsibility in a free and willing manner. In other words, 'self-direction' will be used in much the same sense as 'autonomy' is used by writers such as Holec and Wenden (cf. 1.3.2, above). The term 'autonomy' will be avoided because of the ambiguities which surround its use in the literature. The teacher-plus-class-group mode of study will be taken as the unmarked form, and will not be explicitly signalled. The term *independent* (or *semi-independent*) *study* will be used to refer to study modes in which learners have limited direct contact with a teacher or learning counsellor, and therefore undertake much or most of their language study alone.

As indicated in 1.3.3, this book will operate within the curriculum design perspective on learner-centredness, namely that learners be taken as the central reference point for decision-making, and that this be realised interactively via a process of consultation and negotiation between teacher and learners. There are two justifications for this approach to language teaching. The first is that, in purely language teaching terms, the quality of learning will be better if learners are actively involved in shaping both the content goals and the methodological form of their study programme. The second is broader in nature and relates to the belief enunciated in the Preface that any educational programme should seek to do more than simply impart a discrete body of knowledge or skills. The latter approach is essentially closed in the sense that it sets goals which, once attained, do not necessarily set an agenda for further learning; it also fosters dependency, because learners remain dependent upon 'another' for the establishment of learning goals and the planning of how these goals can best be attained. An educational approach to language teaching cannot, of course, exempt itself from satisfying specific short-term learning objectives, whether these be defined in terms of mastery of a given body of structures or the ability to perform a certain number of functional tasks in the TL. It should, however, look beyond this to help learners develop the understanding and insights which will allow them to pursue their language study in an informed and self-directive manner – whether they decide to do this within a formal learning context or by means of some form of independent study. Within this perspective, the ultimate goal of a learner-centred approach to teaching is learner empowerment, which is realised by means of language education. This is represented schematically in Figure 1. *Language education* involves the acquisition by learners of an understanding of language, language use and language learning, and of their own subjective interaction with the process of language study. This need not be an academic understanding, but something that is living and personalised which learners can use to direct their language-related behaviour in an informed manner.

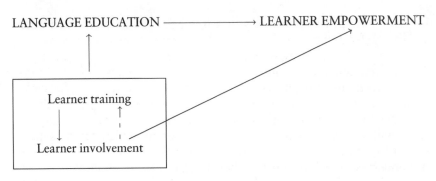

Figure 1 Components of a learner-centred approach

Learner empowerment is the result and practical realisation of language education. It relates to learners' ability to assume an active and informed role in their language study and, ultimately, to pursue those of their life goals which pertain to language use and learning in a self-directive manner.

Two sub-processes exist within language education: learner training and learner involvement. *Learner training* involves the initiation of learners into the process of language study, and *learner involvement* refers to the direct participation of learners in the shaping of their study programme at any level from the provision of materials for a specific learning task to negotiation of assessment procedures or study mode. Learner training will logically precede learner involvement, as it entails learners acquiring the knowledge and insights they will require to make reasoned choices about different aspects of their language study – hence the solid arrow from learner training to learner involvement. Nonetheless, in the course of their involvement in programme development, learners are likely to encounter situations in which they will need to acquire new skills, which may call for a new cycle of learner training – hence the broken line from learner involvement to learner training. Any involvement in programme development, however, whatever its scope and at whichever level of the course hierarchy it takes place, is empowering – hence the solid arrow from learner involvement to learner empowerment. The distinction between learner training and learner involvement will be discussed further in 2.7.

1.5 Chapter overview

As has already been mentioned, this book will operate within the general framework of goals established by Nunan's concept of the learner-

---

REF. How far does the perspective on learner-centredness outlined in 1.4 correspond with the views that you have worked with so far?

- List any differences between the two and identify the aspects of teaching they relate to.
- Now, look closely at the perspective on language teaching put forward in this section and list your reactions to it in terms of:
  – Positive approval: what you like or agree with.
  – Reservations: what you do not like or are unaware of.
  – Questions that you feel need to be answered, either on the theoretical level or in terms of teaching practice.

---

centred curriculum. This approach to language teaching has two main components. One is that language learners should be the main reference point in decision-making with respect to both the content and the form of teaching. This component clearly implies a constructive acceptance of learner diversity. Learners differ on a number of counts – their learning goals and perceptions of the learning process, their subjective learning needs, and their culturally-based expectations of the learning process: centring teaching on learners must therefore involve the willingness to interact constructively with these poles of variance, which leaves little scope for the belief in easy, pre-packageable solutions. The other main component involves the desire to make decision-making a shared process between teacher and learners which is realised by means of consultation and negotiation. For this to be feasible, however, teaching needs to involve the systematic development of learners' understanding of language and of language learning, so that they can assume an informed and self-directive role in their language study. This relates to the role of language education as a means of attaining the goal of learner empowerment. These two elements, viz. *the constructive acceptance of learner diversity* and *the pursuit of learner empowerment by means of language education*, underlie the approach to language teaching that will be developed in this book. With these two principles in mind, it may therefore be appropriate to look at the topics dealt with in the subsequent chapters.

Chapter 2 looks at learner training which, as the first stage in the reflective involvement of learners in their language study, plays a fundamental role in a learner-centred approach to teaching and needs therefore to be understood before any other topics are approached. Learner training will be presented as having two main purposes. The first, and most obvious, is to provide learners with the basic insights into language and language learning that they require in order to initiate an informed and reflective approach to their language study. The second is to create a forum within which the teacher and her students, by the sharing of their respective knowledge and insights, can begin to establish the educational relationship upon which the effective realisation of a learner-centred approach to teaching depends so heavily. Chapter 2 will therefore examine the rationale for learner training from both the learners' and the teacher's point of view; it will then survey certain basic learner training activities and discuss a number of points to do with the practical organisation of learner training activities. Finally, it will discuss further the distinction between learner training and learner involvement. The rationale and procedures of learner training will thus underpin the exploration of learners' knowledge, insights and attitudes to learning covered by Chapters 3–5, as well the pedagogical means by which learner involvement can be realised, which are the focal point of Chapters 6 and 7.

Chapter 3 examines the means by which the objective learning content of a course can be established. Subsequent to a survey of recent trends in needs analysis and of the data collection procedures which are available to teachers and researchers, an analysis will be made of the knowledge structures which learners bring with them to their language study and which can be exploited to inform the establishment of objective learning goals. It will be suggested that an expert-based approach to needs analysis can only go so far in identifying learners' real communicative needs and should be complemented by a learner-based form of needs analysis involving the exploration of learners' existing communicative agendas. In this way, it will be suggested, it is possible to personalise learning content and thus make it reflect more closely the communicative needs and intentions of the learners concerned. The chapter concludes with a few practical suggestions for a learner-based form of needs analysis.

Chapter 4 examines the area of subjective needs, i.e. those needs which arise not from learners' intended functional uses of the language, but from the process of learning itself. This will, in the first place, involve consideration of the areas of individual differences and of learning style preference, and of the influence which such factors exert on learners' interaction with language study. It will then be suggested that virtually no pedagogical option is neutral in learning style terms, the goal here being to bring to teachers' attention the ways in which their pedagogical decisions may interact with their learners' subjective needs. In conclusion, recommendations are made regarding the accommodation of subjective needs in the development of a learning programme.

Chapter 5 considers the contextual dimension to teaching. In part, this will involve a discussion of the influence exerted on pedagogical decision-making by the pragmatic and organisational conditions under which teaching is conducted. It will also involve consideration of the concept of classroom culture, or the grouping of beliefs and expectations which go to form the sociocultural identity of learners in the classroom. The classroom culture of a given group of learners arises in part out of their general cultural background as defined in national or regional terms. This view of culture, however, is too general to serve as a useful guide on a detailed level of pedagogical decision-making, and needs to be complemented by a more local analysis of the sociocultural realities of the peer group to which learners belong and of the institution in which teaching is being conducted. In the light of the profound differences which can exist among learners and among learning contexts, a distinction will be made between the *underlying goals* of learner-centred teaching and the *manner in which these goals may most appropriately be achieved.* While the former will remain stable, the latter have to be selected in response to the pragmatic features of the teaching context and the attitudinal dispositions of each group of learners, and may therefore need to vary to a more or less significant degree from one situation to another. For this reason, openness of mind and flexibility are essential qualities in the realisation of a learner-centred approach.

Chapter 6 examines self-assessment, which plays a key role in the active involvement of learners in their language study. Self-assessment is presented as an activity which is located centrally between the establishment of objective learning goals and the exploration of the means by which these goals may best be attained by means of the choice of appropriate learning activities. This will involve a discussion of the role and rationale for self-assessment together with a survey of studies into the validity of language learners' self-assessments; it will also be suggested that learners' assessment of their language abilities should be coupled with an evaluation of their strategic awareness of the learning options that are available to them. A number of self-assessment activities will then be described and evaluated, and the chapter will conclude with some practical suggestions for developing learners' strategic awareness.

Chapter 7 takes the last point further and suggests that a learner-centred approach should incorporate a systematic attempt to develop learners' strategic skills as part of the goal of learner empowerment. This, it is suggested, involves the creation of a strategy-rich learning environment within which learners have the opportunity to explore and develop their understanding of language learning as part of day-to-day teaching-learning activities (i.e. and not as 'something separate'). The chapter contains a discussion of two categorisations of learning strategies and an illustration of the strategies that can be activated by a number of teaching-learning activities. In conclusion, suggestions are made with respect to innovation in methodology.

Chapter 8 considers learner-centredness from the point of view of the teacher, and suggests that learner-centred teaching represents a challenge to the teacher in both human and professional terms. This arises out of the inherently novel nature of learner-centred teaching, resulting from the fact that no two groups of learners and no two teaching situations will ever be quite the same. In addition, by virtue of the linked goals of language education and learner empowerment, a learner-centred approach calls for a variety of educational skills above and beyond those which are required in a content-based approach to teaching. The chapter contains an annotated list of recommended reading materials for the teacher wishing to explore the literature on learner-centredness further on her own. In conclusion, some practical advice is offered to the teacher wishing to adopt a more learner-centred approach to her teaching.

Readers are of course free to use this book in the manner they find most appropriate to their own needs and interests. It may, however, be helpful in the first instance to read through the book as a whole relatively quickly in order to gain an overview of the approach to teaching it presents. This may make it easier for readers either to re-read the book in more detail or to focus on the specific topic(s) that are most relevant to their own concerns. Throughout, however, it should be borne in mind that my goal has been to offer lines of reflection and to stimulate exploration, and not to provide neat solutions. Readers are thus actively encouraged to interact with the suggestions made in this book in the light of their own personality, needs and experience of teaching. The tasks play an important role in this process and readers may therefore find it helpful to refer back to the rationale for their use provided in the Preface.

1.6 Summary

The following points are addressed in this chapter:

a) The endeavour to create teaching structures which are more responsive to learners' needs, and thus more learner-centred, has inspired many of the main developments in language teaching since the 1960s. This endeavour, however, is not the result of a single school of thought, and reflects a variety of different perspectives.

b) These perspectives reflect one or both of two sets of concerns. One relates to the relevance of learning content and has the goal of making the content of instruction reflect the communicative needs and intentions of the learners concerned; the other relates to the form of instruction and seeks to create learning structures which are responsive to the subjective or process-oriented needs of learners.

c) Four formative trends (the humanistic school of language teaching, communicative language teaching, learning strategy research, and individualisation) and three current perspectives on learner-centredness (learner-centredness as a principle for activity organisation, learner autonomy, and the learner-centred curriculum) were reviewed and their contribution to our profession's understanding of learner-centredness discussed.

d) This book operates within the general framework of reference established by the learner-centred curriculum, which is based on two main principles: one is that learners are the main reference point for decision-making regarding both the content and the form of teaching, and the other is that this may be achieved by means of consultation and negotiation between teacher and learners.

e) The specific perspective on learner-centredness adopted in this book has two main components – language education and learner empowerment. Learner empowerment relates to learners' ability to pursue their language-related life goals in an informed and self-directive manner, and is the ultimate goal of teaching. This is achieved by means of language education, which involves the interplay of learner training and learner involvement.

2　Learner training

2.1　Rationale

A learner-centred approach differs from traditional approaches to teaching in that it is based on an active involvement of learners in the development of their study programme in terms of goal-setting and choice of methodology. This has a number of advantages, not the least of which is that course design decisions are made on a broader knowledge base than is the case in a traditional teacher- or expert-based approach. Participation in programme development, however, calls for a great deal of reflection and personal investment, something for which not all learners will be prepared. As Holec (1979: 27) points out, 'few adults are capable of assuming responsibility for their learning . . . for the simple reason that they have never had occasion to use this ability'. The knowledge and personal qualities that learner involvement requires cannot be taken for granted, and need to be developed over time. A learner-centred approach needs therefore to contain an element of awareness development, which is designed to help learners deepen their understanding of language learning and develop their ability to play an active and self-directive role in their language study.

Holec (op. cit.) suggests that two separate processes are needed to help learners assume this self-directive role. These are:

- a gradual *'deconditioning' process* which will cause the learner to break away, if only by putting them into words, from *a priori* judgements and prejudices of all kinds that encumber his ideas about learning languages and the role he can play in it . . .
- a gradual *process of acquiring* the knowledge and know-how [the learner] needs in order to assume responsibility for his learning . . . (Op. cit.: Original emphasis)

In other words, learners need to *grow into* their self-directive role by means of a critical assessment of their current beliefs and attitudes, accompanied by the acquisition of a body of knowledge and study techniques which will allow them to manage their learning in an insightful and self-directive manner.

This process of awareness development and preparation is generally referred to as *learner training*. Ellis and Sinclair describe the goals of learner training as being:

> ... to help learners consider the factors that affect their learning and discover the learning strategies that suit them best so that they may:
> – become more effective learners;
> – take on more responsibility for their own learning. (1989a: 2)

These are certainly desirable goals. The question arises, however, as to how they can be realised in practice. In other words, what should learner training include, and which specific objectives should it set itself? Given the complexity of language learning as an undertaking, it would be less than helpful to opt for quick and easy answers. Furthermore, the term learner training is used in the literature to refer to training in a variety of different learning-related skills. For example, the term has been used to refer to training in all of the following areas:

1 Clarification/Verification: the learner asks for examples of how to use a word or expression, asks for the correct form to use, etc.
2 Making judgements about how to learn a language, about what language learning is like.
3 Using gestures when you cannot think of how to say something.
4 Self-management: understanding the conditions that help one learn and arranging for the presence of these conditions.
5 Memorising words through grouping them according to the similarity of their endings.
6 Learning how to organise self- and peer assessment of written composition.
7 Learning that language has several different functions – e.g. for description, for negotiation and for self-expression.
(Cited in Dickinson 1988: 47)

Given the range of processes contained in this list, Dickinson (op. cit.) comments that 'the term "learner training" is so broad that one might query whether we aren't really talking about the whole of language learning'. In a sense, of course, we are. If learners are to assume a genuinely responsible and self-directive role in their language study, the wider their knowledge of language learning, the better it is. So broad a view of learner training is not, however, very helpful to a teacher wishing to set up a learner training programme. With this in mind,

Dickinson suggests that learner training should incorporate the following components:

- training in processes, strategies and activities which can be used for language learning;
- instruction designed to heighten awareness of the nature of the target language, and instruction in descriptive metalanguage;
- instruction in aspects of the theory of language learning and language acquisition. (Op. cit.: 48)

While not identical, Dickinson's suggestions share common ground with the topics that Ellis and Sinclair see as requiring attention in learner training, namely:

- the language itself;
- language learning techniques and processes;
- the learners themselves as language learners. (Op. cit.)

Combining the suggestions made by Dickinson and by Ellis and Sinclair, three main target areas would seem to emerge for learner training instruction:

1 *Language learning and language learning processes*
The first, and probably most obvious objective of learner training is to help learners develop their understanding of language learning and of the learning options that are available to them. In the first instance, this can allow them to understand and participate more fully in the learning activities proposed to them by their teacher; it can also help them to select those learning activities which correspond best to their personal preferences and which seem most likely to help them attain their learning goals.

2 *Language structure and language use*
Learners also need to develop their insights into the nature of language and of language use. There are two reasons for this. Firstly, it can enable them to perceive the TL as something other than a confusing and alien blur, so that they can understand the intended outcomes of learning activities, set realistic and attainable goals, and monitor their progress. Secondly, on a more general level, it can allow them to understand how language is structured and used to achieve communicative goals, and thereby to analyse their own communicative needs.

3 *The learners themselves as language learners*
It is also very important that learner training should help learners to look at themselves honestly and realistically in their role as language learners, and to take stock of their motivation, their attitudes to learning, and their willingness to invest time and effort in their

language study. This third element relates to learners' psychological and affective involvement in the learning process, and is essential in a learner-centred approach to teaching, one that is so dependent on the active and willing involvement of learners.

Learner training could therefore be defined as the process by which learners are helped to deepen their understanding of the nature of language learning, and to acquire the knowledge and skills they need in order to pursue their learning goals in an informed and self-directive manner. Learner training therefore constitutes the starting point and an enabling condition for the reflective involvement of learners in their language study. It also plays an important role from the teacher's point of view (cf. 2.3) by allowing her to make an evaluation on the one hand, of her students' learning goals, their perceptions of these goals and their overall motivation; and on the other, of their beliefs and expectations about language learning. These factors will be examined in 2.4 and 2.5 respectively. Learner training does not, therefore, simply involve a one-way flow of information, in which the teacher provides learners with knowledge and skills they might not possess – even if it will certainly entail this. It also caters for the creation of a forum within which teacher and learners exchange insights and perceptions of the learning process and thereby initiate the shared exploration of language learning which lies at the heart of a learner-centred approach.

REF. A fine balance exists in learner training as in other aspects of education between, on the one hand, helping students to develop their own insights and self-directive potential and, on the other, 'training' them in a restrictive sense to use a pre-established set of techniques: the latter may well be effective in the short term, but has less educational value and transferability.

With this distinction in mind, analyse your own teaching practice and the advice you give to your students under the following headings:

– the areas in which you provide the most advice;
– the form this advice usually takes;
– whether you generally suggest specific activities, or rather encourage students to work out their own solutions to their learning problems. How significant a part does this type of activity assume in your teaching as a whole?

2.2 Strategy training in context

A number of questions need to be addressed with respect to both the content and the organisation of learner training activities. Before doing this, however, it seems appropriate to look briefly at the concept of 'learning strategy' (cf. 1.2.3) which occurs frequently in the literature on learner-centredness, and to consider the role which this concept plays within learner training and, thereby, within learner-centredness in general. A learning strategy may be defined as any purposeful activity that learners engage in to promote their learning and knowledge of the TL. A number of studies were conducted in the mid-70s and early 80s (cf. Rubin 1987, for an overview) to investigate the learning strategy usage of more and less successful learners with the goal of identifying the behavioural characteristics of 'good' language learners. One of the motivations for this line of research was the belief that an identification of the behavioural traits of individuals who have attained a good level of success in language learning could provide an agenda for strategy training with less successful learners.

Rubin identifies seven main strategies which characterise the learning behaviour of successful learners:

1 The good language learner is a willing and accurate guesser. The good language learner is comfortable with uncertainty and is willing to try out his guesses. A good guesser gathers and stores information efficiently, and uses all the clues situations offer.

2 The good language learner has a strong drive to communicate or to learn from communication. He is willing to try out a range of options to get his message across.

3 The good language learner is often not inhibited. He is willing to appear foolish or to make mistakes in order to promote communication or to learn. He is willing to live with a degree of imprecision.

4 In addition to focusing on communication, the good language learner is prepared to attend to form. The good language learner is constantly looking for patterns in the language.

5 The good language learner practises. He may practise by pronouncing words or making up sentences; he will seek out opportunities to use the language with native speakers, or by going to the cinema or to cultural events. He will initiate conversations with his teacher or fellow students.

6 The good language learner monitors his own speech and the speech of others. He is constantly monitoring how well his speech is being received and whether his performance meets his goals.

7 The good language learner attends to meaning. He attends not

only to grammar and surface forms, but also to the context of the speech act, the relationship of the participants, interactive conventions and the mood of the speech act. (1975)

Useful as this analysis of the behaviour of successful language learners is, it would be misleading to assume that these strategies can be neatly pedagogised and 'taught' to learners in a straightforward manner. They grow out of a general approach to language learning which is active, inquiring and attentive, and can only be acquired integratively – as expressions of such an approach. Some learners may well enter a course of study with this approach reasonably well embedded in their personality and will therefore need little more than encouragement and a few guidelines to develop a very effective array of learning strategies. Other learners may have a very different set of attitudes, and may need a lot of 'deconditioning' and awareness development work. Furthermore, what constitutes an effective set of learning strategies depends on a number of factors relating to the learners themselves and to the wider context of learning. Rubin lists six such factors:

1 *The task.* Learning goals influence what is a more or less useful activity or strategy.
2 *The learning stage.* Different strategies may need to be used at different stages in the learning process: what may be effective at intermediate or advanced levels may be inappropriate at beginner level, and vice versa.
3 *The age of the learner.* Adults may feel at ease with strategies that younger learners would find difficult to handle, or for which they would not be prepared cognitively.
4 *The context.* Strategies that would be appropriate when learning takes place in a real-world communicative setting involving extensive contact with TL speakers will differ from those that are suitable in a formal mode of learning.
5 *Individual styles.* Language learners remain individuals who differ considerably in terms of personality, background and cognitive style, and, therefore, in terms of their learning preferences.
6 *Cultural differences in cognitive learning styles.* The learning tradition in which learners have grown up can exert a powerful influence on how they will expect learning to be structured and on what they consider to be useful learning activities. (Op. cit.)

These factors will recur in subsequent chapters as poles of variance which need to be explored and accommodated in programme design, a process which constitutes a key feature of a learner-centred approach to teaching. Factors 1 and 4 (*task* and *context*) relate to learning goals and to the context within which learning is being conducted, which will be examined in Chapter 3. Factors 3 and 5 (*age* and *individual styles*) relate to the area of subjective needs, which is the focus of Chapter 4, while factor 6 (*cultural differences in cognitive learning styles*) touches on one aspect of the contextual dimension of teaching, which is considered in Chapter 5. Factor 2 (*learning stage*) lies at the interface between the establishment of learning objectives and the choice of the means by which these goals can most appropriately be achieved, a process which is considered in Chapter 6 in terms of self-assessment. This complex array of factors needs to be taken into consideration in the staging of learners' involvement in the shaping of their study programme, which will be examined at a number of points in the subsequent chapters, and specifically in Chapter 7. Within this framework of goals, strategy development and, in a general sense, learner training, should not be seen simply as a matter of teaching specific skills or techniques. It has more to do with fostering learners' understanding of language, of language learning and of their own subjective interaction with the processes of language use and learning. Indeed, to achieve its goals, learner training needs to acknowledge and help learners themselves to discover what Fröhlich and Paribakht (1984: 71) describe as 'the uniqueness of each language learning career ... and the multitude of ways which can lead to success'.

DAT. Using Rubin's seven good learner strategies as a reference point, interview a number of language learners of different ages and backgrounds to draw up a profile of their learning strategy usage. Analyse:
– the learning strategies each learner uses;
– the interaction between these strategies and the factors Rubin identifies as influencing strategy usage (task, learning stage, age of the learner etc.).
Alternatively, conduct a similar analysis of your own learning of a second language, paying particular attention to your learning goals, the context of learning and your individual learning preferences.
What insights does this give you into the complexities of language learning, and how could you use these insights to influence your own teaching?

2.3 Learner training and the teacher

Learner training, as we have already seen, has an enabling function within a learner-centred approach to teaching by helping learners to acquire the knowledge and skills they need in order to assume a self-directive role in their language study. Learner training has another function, however, one which is no less important to the ultimate success of a learner-centred mode of teaching. This is to create a forum within which the teacher can get to know her students as language learners and thereby initiate the sharing of knowledge and insights between teacher and learners out of which the learners' subsequent involvement in the shaping of their study programme will grow.

A key feature of a learner-centred approach to teaching is that it explicitly caters for a two-way flow of insights between teacher and learners. In other words, it assumes the development of a more equal relationship between teacher and learners than is the case in traditional approaches to teaching. Any relationship, however, is based on mutual knowledge and understanding, and on respect of the other's individuality. Such a relationship must start somewhere, and within a learner-centred approach to teaching, learner training offers the most fruitful forum for initiating this sharing of knowledge and insights.

Many learners may be relatively ill-prepared for assuming a self-directive role in their language study, either because they lack the necessary knowledge and skills, or quite simply because their prior learning experience or their culturally-based expectations of language study have led them to assume that language learning is an essentially teacher-driven undertaking. Learner-centred teaching can also represent a significant challenge to teachers. On the one hand, some teachers may find it difficult to let go of what they have been trained to see as their role of decision-maker, and may feel uneasy about transferring responsibility for pedagogic decisions to their students. Equally well, however, a teacher who is strongly committed to fostering self-direction may find that her students are resistant to assuming an independent role in their learning, and may want the teacher to play a more directive or possibly even a more authoritarian role than she might wish to. The teacher therefore needs to get to know and to understand her students' learning goals (what these goals are in objective terms, and also the learners' subjective perceptions of these goals), their beliefs about language learning and the type of learning strategies they are working with. Whatever learners' attitudes may be, and whether they coincide with the teacher's own views of language learning or not, they constitute the basic material the teacher has to work with and from. From the teacher's point of view, then, finding out where her students stand with respect to these points is one of the main functions of learner training.

Dickinson cites the case of Mahmoud, an imaginary but not unrepresentative student, to illustrate the importance of understanding learners' current approaches to learning, the factors which have given rise to these approaches, and the subjective reality they have for the learners in question. For Dickinson, doing this is an essential first step in planning learner training activities:

> Mahmoud al Shamiry is an imaginary member of a real group of students from an Arab country. Like many of his fellow students, when he is engaged in a reading task in which he is supposed to be reading for global meaning he looks up every unfamiliar word in a bilingual dictionary and writes a mother tongue equivalent against the word in the text. The teacher attempts to get Mahmoud to change to three well-known alternative strategies; these are that he should attempt to guess the meaning of unfamiliar words from the context; secondly that he should postpone looking up words until he has read to the end of the text; third that he should only look up words that he judges to be essential to his purpose for reading the text. (1990: 203)

Dickinson observes that he had in the past tried to persuade students with a similar background to Mahmoud to change their strategies, but frequently with limited success. Dickinson then analyses Mahmoud's strategy usage in two stages. The first involves an assessment of the origins of Mahmoud's approach to reading; the second evaluates what Mahmoud would have to do in order to accommodate the approach to reading recommended by his teacher:

Stage 1: *Possible origins of Mahmoud's approach to reading*
1 It is likely that part of the teaching he has experienced in the past has inculcated these behaviours. That is, the teacher would have approached the text by translating – with the class – all the words he predicted the students would not know, and he would have instructed or encouraged them to write the translations on the text. And maybe – as with Jesuitical beliefs – learners who are trained as children to do this retain the inclination for life!
2 Notwithstanding the declared purpose of the reading exercise, Mahmoud is a 'word collector'; he values foreign language words for their own sake.
3 I am told by my colleagues that cultural values derived from Arabic require the understanding of every word of the text. This apparently relates to reading the Koran.
4 The student's strategy appears to be based on the assumption that the meaning of a text is the sum of the meaning of the words in the text. This is not unreasonable, and I suspect would be the view held by many educated lay people.

Stage 2: *Changes required of Mahmoud to adopt the recommended approach to reading*

a He would need to reject what his early teacher had taught him and adopt what he is now being advised to do.
b He would need to suppress his desire to collect words on all possible occasions. That is, he would have to be persuaded to focus on the teacher's objective in favour of his own in some lessons at least.
c He would need to learn to tolerate ambiguity/uncertainty about meaning until the end of the passage.
d He would need to adopt/change to another cultural attitude that understanding all words may not be necessary for all reading tasks or purposes. In other words he needs to understand, or at least accept a goal of fluent reading rather than 'understanding every word'.
e He needs to understand that the meaning of a reading text results from a negotiation between the reader and the text. In other words he needs to adopt a different mode of reading.
f He has to adopt a more 'risk-taking' attitude in that the recommended reading strategies may lead – at least initially – to him making more errors, and may result in him being less successful in such exercises as answering comprehension questions. (Op. cit.: 203–5)

Without suggesting that Mahmoud simply be left in peace to pursue his reading in the manner to which he has been accustomed, Dickinson rightly points out how deeply rooted Mahmoud's reading strategies are in his prior learning experience and in the views of language study current in his home culture, and how much re-learning would be involved in changing these strategies. A thorough and non-judgmental understanding of learners' current approach to learning therefore constitutes an essential basis for the planning of strategy training. Without this initial stage of discovery and evaluation, attempts to encourage learners to experiment with alternative approaches can prove ineffective either because they fail to link in with the learners' current beliefs and strategies in a positive and constructive manner, or because they place excessive demands on their adaptiveness. Worse still, they may alienate learners by seeming to denigrate aspects of their prior learning experience which may arise out of and have strong affective associations with their home culture.

As we will see in 2.7, learner training is a process which, over time, merges into learners' ongoing involvement in the practicalities of programme development. The areas dealt with in the next two sections, learning goals and motivation, and beliefs about language learning, set the bases for subsequent and more detailed learner training work. 2.4 looks at learners' reasons for learning the TL, their understanding of and affective reactions to these reasons; 2.5 looks briefly at some of the beliefs about language learning learners may bring with them to their course of study, and the way in which these beliefs can influence their learning preferences and approach to language study. In line with what has been said here, the points raised in the next two sections have a dual purpose. The first is to provide the teacher with guidelines for planning more specific awareness-raising activities with her students with respect to their learning goals and motivation, and their beliefs about language learning. The second is to offer a framework within which the teacher can get to grips with these very basic aspects of her students' learning agendas so that she can plan subsequent learner training activities and make an assessment of what seems to be a realistic pace for learner involvement in course development.

REF/DAT. In order to gain an insight into the kind of difficulties your students might experience in planning their language learning, select a learning task which is unfamiliar to you (e.g. driving a car; horseriding; computer programming; tailoring; accountancy; orienteering) and then analyse:

– your strengths and weaknesses vis-à-vis the target activity,
– the learning strategies you would adopt: list both macro-strategies (e.g. joining a class or studying an introductory textbook) and micro-strategies (i.e. the detailed practice and learning activities you would engage in).

If it is feasible, discuss your learning programme with someone who has already mastered the activity in question. How does your programme compare with the informant's views? What differences exist and how can they be explained?

2.4 Learning goals and motivation

Chapter 3 will argue for a learner-based approach to the establishment of objective learning goals involving the shared exploration by both teacher and learners of the communicative agendas which learners bring with them to their language study. This can be a relatively complex educational process which calls for a serious personal commitment from the learners concerned (not to mention the teacher). It is therefore advisable for the teacher to foreground the process in two ways. The first is to investigate her students' learning goals in relatively general terms, either to fix the general terms of reference within which more specific objectives will be defined (this is necessary if little prior information is available on the learners in question) or to confirm the reliability of the information she may have received. The second is to assess her students' subjective perceptions of and affective reactions to these goals, as well as their overall level of commitment to the learning process, factors that are likely to exert a significant influence on learners' willingness to make the necessary personal investment in the learning process. In other words, the teacher needs to make an initial assessment of her students' motivation. This having been said, it is only fair to recognise that the concept of 'motivation' is both complex and difficult to define precisely, and Wall (1958: 23) goes as far as to describe motivation as 'perhaps the most obscure and difficult of all issues in general and educational psychology'.

The best known categorisation of motivation in language learning is the distinction between integrative and instrumental motivation proposed by Gardner and Lambert (1972). *Integrative* motivation is typically found in students learning a language out of an affective interest in or attraction to the TL community, and who may wish ultimately to be assimilated into this community. *Instrumental* motivation characterises students whose desire to learn a language is utilitarian in nature, based on factors such as professional or academic advancement or the need to gain access to specialised information in the TL. Gardner and Lambert also suggest that integrative motivation has a stronger effect on success in language learning (cf. Au 1988, for a review of studies on this point). Gardner and Lambert's integrative-instrumental distinction certainly does capture two aspects of motivation. It is also plausible that integrative motivation may correlate with higher levels of achievement – though this may simply be that learners who wish to be assimilated into a community set themselves more comprehensive learning goals. The main problem with Gardner and Lambert's view of motivation, however, is that it is too narrow to account for the wide range of factors that can influence attitudes to learning a language.

To begin with, one needs to look at the context in which the language is being learned. In this respect, Dörnyei (1990) distinguishes between second language acquisition (SLA) contexts, where the language is learned in direct contact with the TL community or by formal teaching accompanied by frequent interaction with TL speakers, and foreign language learning (FLL) contexts, where the language is studied in a formal setting with little or no direct contact with TL speakers. Much of the research upon which Gardner and Lambert's analysis of motivation was based was conducted in a SLA context, where learners' attitudes (positive or negative) to the TL community are more likely to play a role than in a FLL context, where learners may have insufficient contact with the TL community to form any deeply felt affective reactions to it. This is even more marked in the case of an international language such as English, which is frequently learned as a medium of international communication, with little direct link to any one English-speaking country or community.

On the basis of a study of 134 Hungarian learners of English (i.e. in a FLL context) Dörnyei identifies the seven motivation/attitude variables given in Figure 2. Dörnyei's analysis clearly demonstrates that motivation is a complex construct made up of a variety of factors: these relate not only to the TL community or the uses to which the language may be put, but also to psychological factors such as the learner's intellectual interests and need for achievement. Dörnyei also points to the role that previous learning experiences can have on motivation. In this respect his reference to 'bad' learning experiences may be somewhat restrictive: good experiences can enhance motivation as surely as bad experiences can undermine it. Implicit in Dörnyei's analysis of motivation is that two learners can have a similar global level of motivation, but as the result of two quite separate constellations of factors.

There are two main reasons for investigating motivation. Firstly, it can help the teacher get a feel for the nature and intensity of her students' desire to learn the TL. This can alert her both to positive points that can be built on to promote learning, and to negative points which, if left undetected, can undermine learning and which are likely to manifest themselves in various forms of discontent (dissatisfaction with the teaching method used, with the teacher, or with other students, to name but a few). Secondly, it provides a forum in which learners can reflect upon their own reasons for learning, their attitudes to the TL, and to the process of learning itself. Motivation can be looked into under three headings:

1 *Functional goals*

These are the things learners will want to do in or via the TL – reading specialised literature, using the telephone, participating in business meetings, socialising with foreign colleagues or friends and so on. Learners may have different types of goals which do not necessarily fit together: a learner may *need* to read academic material, but may also *want* to gain access to popular music or films. In addition to discovering her students' functional goals per se, the teacher also needs to evaluate their perception and awareness of these goals. Do they, in fact, see their learning goals in functional terms, or do they see the TL simply as a linguistic system they are learning for some more or less vague future use? Do their perceptions of their goals coincide with those of a possible sponsor (an employer or educational body, for example)? How well are

Instrumentality
e.g. – English can help to get a better job
    – my colleagues speak English / my bosses expect me to learn English
    – English is necessary to obtain a promotion
    – obtaining a recognised exam can help me professionally

Desire to spend time abroad
e.g. – I'm learning English because I'd like to spend a longer period abroad

Interest in foreign languages and cultures
e.g. – I'd like to learn as many languages as possible
    – language learning is a hobby / an exciting activity
    – language learning gives me a feeling of success
    – English proficiency is important to me because it will allow me to get to know various cultures and peoples

Desire for knowledge and values associated with English
e.g. – English proficiency is part of a general culture
    – English proficiency is essential to live a valuable and colourful life
    – everybody should learn English to at least intermediate level
    – most of my favourite actors, musicians, authors are British or American

Language learning is a new challenge
e.g. – studying English is important to me because it offers a new challenge in my life

Need for achievement
e.g. – I would like to take a recognised exam
    – learning English is an important life goal for me

Bad learning experiences
e.g. – I think that language learning is more difficult for me than for the average learner
    – I think I belong to the class of learner who can completely lose their interest in learning if they have a bad teacher
    – I've had some bad experiences with learning languages

Figure 2 Motivation / attitude variables
(taken from Dörnyei 1990)

they able to formulate and express their goals – in the first instance, to themselves?

2 Attitudes to the process of learning

The first point to be considered under this heading relates to the learners' affective reaction to being where they are, learning the TL. Is this something they have chosen to do freely (for whatever reason) or do they feel more or less obliged to do it as a result of their occupation or course of study? If the latter, then is this 'constraint' accepted willingly or tolerated reluctantly? The second point relates to learners' attitudes to the process of language learning itself, and is connected to Dörnyei's last three variables ('Language learning is a new challenge', 'Need for achievement', and 'Bad learning experiences'). A number of questions need to be addressed here:

- Is language learning an interesting challenge or an intimidating burden?
- Does learning a language make the learner feel good; can it raise his self-esteem?
- How far does the learner want to push his knowledge of the TL; what are his achievement goals? (Aiming low can be a sign of a lack of confidence.)
- Has the learner enjoyed previous language learning experiences? (We rarely enjoy what we feel bad at, and so lack of enjoyment may point to a perception of failure or other negative experiences.)
- What does the learner most enjoy in learning a language? (Again, no enjoyment is a bad sign. Positive responses provide a starting point to work from and offer insights into the learner's activity preferences and learning personality.)

3 Practical investment

To be able to plan activities, the teacher needs to get an idea of the intensity of learners' motivation, and of how much time and effort they are willing to invest in their language study. Realism is called for here. Students may have a very strong motivation to learn a language, even if it comes well down the list of their life goals: motivational intensity cannot be neatly quantified in hours. The main questions in this respect are:

- how important learning the TL is to learners within their global set of affective, professional or academic goals;
- how much time they are willing to devote to language study (e.g. in terms of hours per week);
- what form(s) their commitment will take (e.g. attending courses regularly, seeking out contacts with native speakers, studying at home).

The establishment of a realistic *modus operandi* on these points constitutes one of the first forms of 'contract' between teacher and learners (cf. Dickinson 1987).

I want to use English ...	Very Important	Important	Not very Important
1 in shops, offices ...			
2 to speak with new Australian friends			
3 to read newspapers			
4 to understand the news on TV			
5 to understand movies on TV			
6 to study a technical subject			
7 to read stories			
8 to speak with immigrants of other nationalities			
9 to be able to speak by telephone			
10 to explain my ideas			

Figure 3 Functional purpose grid
(taken from AMEP 1989: 40)

- I enjoy learning languages ... (very much, a little, etc.)
- In my English learning this year, I expect to do ... (e.g. well / poorly)
- We waste a lot of time in English class ... (yes / no / sometimes)
- In English class, I understand the lesson ... (what percent of the time?)
- In five years' time, I will know this much English ... (all / half / 20%)
- I like the other people in my English class ... (a lot / a little)
- I want to have Australian friends ... (yes / no / maybe / a few / many)
- I would like to be an Australian ... (very much / maybe / no)
- I would like my children to be Australian

Figure 4 Learning attitudes questionnaire
(taken from AMEP 1989: 32)

DAT. The questionnaires given in Figures 3 and 4 were designed for use with immigrant learners of English in Australia (i.e. in a SLA context), to elicit information on their functional goals and attitudes to learning.

- Using the two questionnaires together trace out and justify two response profiles, one of a learner with a positive motivation to learn, and one of a learner with negative attitudes (the sort of response profile that would set off the alarms bells!);
- Think of how the content and form of the two questionnaires would need to be adapted for use in a FLL context. Where would the changes be made, and why?

2.5 Beliefs about language learning

In Chapters 4 and 5 attention is given to the influence that a variety of factors of an individual or culturally-based nature can exert on learners' interaction with the process of language study and, in consequence, on what will constitute an appropriate mode of study for the learners in question. Exploring this aspect of learners' interaction with language study can take time, especially in the case of learners who have limited experience of language study and who thereby have had little opportunity to get a feel for their learning needs and preferences. The process has to start somewhere, however, and the activities described in this section are meant to provide guidelines as to how this process may be initiated – both by the teacher and by the learners themselves.

Wenden (1986a) suggests that learners' beliefs about language study influence their approach to learning in terms of:

1 the kind of strategies they use;
2 what they attend to;
3 the criteria they use to evaluate the effectiveness of learning activities and of social contexts that give them the opportunity to use or practise the language;
4 where they concentrate their use of strategies.

For Wenden, then, learners' beliefs about language learning constitute a sort of inner logic which directs, consciously or unconsciously, what they do to promote their own learning. Learners' beliefs also influence their reaction to teaching activities. Sooner or later, a teaching method which is based on assumptions about language learning which differ from those held by learners is likely to encounter resistance and discontent. The teacher thus needs to discover what her students' beliefs about language learning are, and to understand how these beliefs influence their approach to learning in terms of both their individual learning strategies and their likely reaction to different teaching methodologies.

On the basis of the belief statements made by a number of ESL learners in the USA, Wenden (1987) identifies three main categories of learner attitudes to language learning, each based on a number of key 'tenets' or beliefs about how a language should be learned:

Category 1   Use the language
This view stresses the role of language as a means of communication and social interaction.
1 *Learn the natural way.* Use social contacts as the main focus of learning. Things should not be forced, however: the learner should exploit communicative situations as and when they arise.
2 *Practise.* Use the language as much as possible.
3 *Think in your second language.* Learners should avoid translating from their first language or planning in advance what they say. They should focus on meaning and try to think in the TL as soon as possible.
4 *Live and study in an environment where the target language is spoken.* Living in the TL community is the best way to learn a language. This allows more scope for practice, improves listening skills, and provides a better understanding of the culture of the TL and its speakers.
5 *Don't worry about mistakes.* Try to use the language to communicate, even if you make mistakes or are sometimes inaccurate.

Category 2   Learn about the language
In this view, the TL is seen as a linguistic system which can be worked out, understood and learned by means of conscious intellectual effort and hard work.
1 *Learn grammar and vocabulary.* Grammar and vocabulary are the basis of learning a language, and must therefore be given priority.
2 *Take a formal course.* Taking a formal course offers a variety of advantages: it is systematic, allows for graded progression, and ensures that 'correct' forms of the TL are learned.
3 *Learn from mistakes.* Mistakes make it possible for learners to obtain feedback and monitor their progress. Paying close attention to what native speakers (or more proficient non-native speakers) say is useful, as is self-monitoring of one's own production.
4 *Be mentally active.* Learning a language calls for alertness and attentiveness. Learners should have an inquisitive mind, be willing to ask questions, and to experiment with the language.

Category 3   Personal factors are important
This view focuses on the affective interaction of the learner with the TL and the process of learning.

1 *The emotional aspect is important.* For language learning in general, or for any specific learning activity to be effective, the learner needs to feel personally interested or involved.

2 *Self-concept.* Learning a language can influence the learner's self-image and how he feels about himself, which, in turn, can either facilitate or inhibit learning. For example, if a learner is unable to express his ideas freely he may feel frustrated and resentful, which can undermine his involvement in (and willingness to use) the TL.

3 *Aptitude for learning.* The ability to learn a language is something inherent, which learners have (or do not have) to varying degrees.
    (Op. cit.: Adapted)

Wenden found that learners who subscribed to a *use the language* view focused primarily on meaning and on the social purposes of interaction: they favoured the use of communication strategies ('speaking clearly', or using explanations) to negotiate meaning, and made active use of contextual clues (pictures, headlines, or background knowledge) to disambiguate meaning. Learners who stressed *learning about the language* focused relatively more on the form of the language used, and made more use of cognitive strategies (using a dictionary, making notes, practising specific constructions) in order to improve their understanding of the TL. Wenden found that learners who emphasised the role of *personal factors* did not have a distinct set of strategies: however, they focused on and remembered their emotional reactions (frustration, embarrassment, etc.) in interactive situations. Wenden's study was limited in size and she says herself that it serves primarily to provide 'an initial set of hypotheses'. Nonetheless, the three views of language learning she identifies and the strategies she found to be associated with each will ring a familiar bell with many teachers.

An understanding of how learners' often unconsciously held beliefs can influence their behaviour is needed not only by teachers, but also by learners themselves. As Wenden puts it:

> It is ... important that the students themselves be given opportunities to 'think about their learning process', so that they can become aware of their own beliefs and how these beliefs can influence what they do to learn. (1986a: 4)

As long as learners assume that their current approach is *the* way to learn a language, there is little likelihood of them developing as learners. Investigating learners' beliefs about language study is a process of (self-)discovery which involves the learners themselves as much as the teacher. This does not mean that learners need to feel pressurised to change their basic learning personality. Both *use the language* and *learn about the language* approaches, for example, can generate a variety of productive learning strategies. It is more a matter of learners becoming consciously aware of what may frequently be passively accepted (and never questioned) assumptions about how to learn a language, being willing to evaluate these assumptions critically, and, finally, being ready to do the same with alternative approaches. The goal, in other words, is to help learners develop what Wenden (1986b: 199) describes as 'a critical and informed awareness' of learning options.

This sort of awareness can arise only out of a long process of experimentation with a variety of learning options. Indeed, it is probably very easy for teachers to underestimate how difficult it is for their students to think innovatively about alternative approaches to language learning. Their beliefs and expectations may result from previous learning experiences, from certain personality traits, or from the un-thinking acceptance of popular wisdom. Learner training in this area should therefore have three components:

a) stock-taking and evaluation of learners' current beliefs;
b) exposure to alternative approaches and options;
c) guidelines as to how learners can explore these options.

In the section of their learner training programme entitled, 'What sort of language learner are you?', Ellis and Sinclair (1989b: 6–7) suggest an activity for the initial exploration of learning preferences based on a nine-point questionnaire where learners score their responses to questions on various language learning skills or activities (e.g. 'Do you have a good memory for new words?', 'Do you hate making mistakes?', 'Do you like to learn new grammar rules, words, etc. by heart?'). Learners' responses place them on a flow chart (Figure 5) geared around two main learner types – 'analytic' and 'relaxed'. This allows learners to identify and evaluate the general orientation of their learning preferences, and also to get an idea of alternative approaches. The flow chart also provides a number of practical suggestions as to how learners might broaden or balance out their approach to learning. From the teacher's point of view, this activity can provide an initial indication of learners' general approach to language learning, which can then be used as a basis for further exploratory work. For instance, the class could be divided into three or four teams on the basis of the profiles they obtained from the questionnaire (analytic, relaxed, mixed, not sure): each team could then draw up a list of their preferred learning activities and present these to the rest of the class and argue for the usefulness and value of these activities. If conducted in a constructive and good-humoured manner, this can lead to a sharing of views among learners and discussion of the type of difficulties (either practical or attitudinal) that might arise in the realisation of the various activities.

Alternatively, the teacher might draw up a list of the learning opportunities which, in her opinion, are available to her students – facilities available in the teaching institution, opportunities to be found in the wider learning environment (contacts with native speakers, radio or television programmes in the TL, visits to local cultural centres such as those of the British Council or Goethe Institut, and so on), and different private study options. Learners could then make an individual selection of their three or four most favoured activities, explain their preferences and indicate how the activities chosen might contribute to their learning goals. The presence of a list of learning options is in itself a form of consciousness-raising, and can serve to open learners' minds to possibilities which they may not have thought of before and create a basis of discussion around which learners can exchange ideas and insights with one another. It also offers to the teacher the possibility of providing advice and guidance to learners on how they might go about exploiting various learning opportunities – in other words, it can create a context for focused learner counselling. Another option is for the teacher to initiate a (guided) brainstorming session in which it is the learners themselves who survey the opportunities that are available to them and draw up (in groups or teams, for instance) their own list of activities. The choice between the two options (relatively more teacher- or learner-initiated) depends on the language learning experience and initiative of the learners concerned: a more supported approach may be preferable with novice language learners, whereas a more open approach might be preferable with those who have more experience of language learning and/or who show a greater propensity for self-direction.

PED. With reference to a teaching situation and students that you are familiar with, draw up a list of the various learning opportunities which you consider to be available. Be as creative as you can in this respect! Then, for each learning opportunity assess:

– its relevance to the learning goals of the students concerned;
– the type of learning skills and attitudinal/psychological preparation that may be required of learners to avail themselves of the opportunity in question.

Be cautious with respect to the second point: there will generally be factors which even the most experienced teacher will not anticipate; equally well, what you do anticipate to be a problem may not be perceived as such by your students.

Score: 23–27 points
Analytic?
You may feel it is very important to be as accurate as possible all the time. You probably prefer the sort of language learning where you need to think carefully: for example, when you are doing grammar exercises, working out the meanings of words, practising pronunciation, etc. This is very often the sort of language learning you do in class or when you are studying alone.
  You may be able to improve your language learning. Look at the following suggestions.

Score
14–22
A mixture?
You may find that you do not fall exactly into either of the categories marked *Analytic?* or *Relaxed?*. Many people are a mixture and learn in different ways at different times depending on the situation and what they are doing.
Suggestion
Look at the descriptions for *Analytic?* and *Relaxed?* You may find that you are more similar to one than the other and this could help you to think about what areas of your learning you might improve. If you can't decide now, try to do this during your course.

Score: 9–13 points
Relaxed?
You seem to 'pick up' languages without really making too much effort and you usually enjoy communicating with people. You may sometimes feel, however, that you should be learning more grammar rules, but you probably don't enjoy this and quickly lose interest.
  You may be able to improve your language learning. Look at the following suggestions.

Suggestions
You could improve your fluency by:
- *trying to speak more*
  For example, try talking to English-speaking friends, tourists, etc. as often as possible.
- *not worrying too much about your mistakes*
  Trying to be correct all the time is hard work and can stop you from communicating well. Although making mistakes is an important part of the learning process, don't always try to correct yourself immediately. Remember that the people you speak to won't be listening for your mistakes, but for what you are trying to say. After you have finished speaking, you can usually remember the mistakes you want to work on, this is a good time to make a note to yourself to do something about them.
- *depending on yourself*
  Outside the classroom you won't always have a dictionary or a teacher to help you, so don't be afraid to depend on yourself: you probably know more than you think.

Score: 0–8 points
Not sure?
Your score does not mean that you are not a good language learner. Perhaps this is the first time you have thought about the way you learn. To know more about this can be very useful in helping you to become a more effective language learner.

Suggestion
You can find out some general information about learning languages by looking at the descriptions marked *Analytic?* and *Relaxed?*. During your course, try to become more aware of the ways you learn. This can help you decide which areas of you learning you might improve.

Suggestions
- *try finding more time to learn*
  You may need to spend more time thinking about and practising things like grammar, pronunciation, etc. Try to organise a regular time for learning.
- *try being more self-critical*
  You probably need to correct yourself more. You may not worry or even notice when you make mistakes, but if you try to become more aware of the mistakes you make regularly, you may find it easier to do something about them.

Figure 5 Learning preferences flow chart
(taken from Ellis and Sinclair 1989b: 8–9)

55

Ellis and Sinclair's questionnaire is one activity designed to initiate the exploration of learners' approaches to language study and is meant to provide a starting point for more detailed discussion work both among learners and between teacher and learners (this is developed in a variety of ways in subsequent chapters of Ellis and Sinclair's book). Wenden (1986a) describes a rather different approach which is built around eight reflection-discussion modules designed to broaden learners' perspectives on language study and help them think creatively about their learning. The modules do, however, call for a level of debate which would be feasible only with students who already have a relatively advanced level of competence in the TL. They also reflect an underlying philosophy of education and debate which might not fit in too well with certain educational traditions (cf. Chapter 5 for a discussion of the cultural implications of certain aspects of learner-centred teaching). The modules begin with a reflection task in which learners are asked to think critically about the nature of learning in general or specifically about language learning. Module 3, for example, *Bicycle riding and the art of language learning*, is based on learners' reactions to the following statements:

Learning a second language is just like
a) learning to ride a bicycle
b) learning to use a computer
c) making friends

This leads into a discussion of the points that are common to all forms of learning, and those that are specific to learning a language. A follow-up activity asks learners to draw up a plan for learning a language 'on the spot' in a foreign country. Other modules take as their starting point accounts of learners' experiences or beliefs, a questionnaire on the affective aspects of language learning, or an account of 'good' learner strategies. Taken together, the eight modules constitute a challenging and potentially self-contained learner training package which places language learning within a broad context of learning and human experience: they therefore merit serious consideration as an imaginative example of how learner training can be approached.

PED. Study Wenden's eight learner training modules carefully and evaluate the approach to learner training which they contain.
- In which type of learning context and with which type of students do you feel they would be most appropriate?
- In which teaching situations do you feel that an alternative approach would be more appropriate, and for which reasons?
- What does this indicate about the design of learner training materials?

2.6   Planning learner training

Learner training is a pedagogical undertaking which, like any other, involves a number of choices with respect to the content, form and structuring of instruction. In what follows, this will be looked at under the four headings of content, explicitness of purpose, integration and evaluation suggested by Wenden (1986c), and in terms of timetabling options.

2.6.1   Content

The main distinction Wenden (op. cit.) establishes in this respect is between cognitive and metacognitive strategies (a distinction that will be examined in more depth in 7.2). *Cognitive strategies* have a closely defined focus, and are linked to a particular learning task. They may, for instance, involve:

a) using background knowledge or contextual clues to infer the meaning of unfamiliar words;
b) making thematically linked word lists to aid learning and recall;
c) reading TL material aloud to improve pronunciation;
d) learning useful expressions such as 'I'm sorry. Could you repeat that, please?' or 'You want me to [WHAT]?' to facilitate oral interaction.

Metacognitive strategies, on the other hand, relate to the way in which a learner plans, monitors and evaluates his learning. Metacognitive strategies are general learning skills, and grow out of a learner's awareness of his learning goals and his understanding of language learning. They will therefore influence the array of cognitive strategies that will be employed. A few examples might be:

a) periodically monitoring one's abilities against one's learning targets;
b) developing one's range of expression and spoken fluency as a priority, without paying too much attention to accuracy;
c) reading (or listening) extensively to get a feel for the language before attempting to develop productive skills;
d) joining a social or sports club in order to get into contact with native speakers.

Cognitive and metacognitive strategies play a complementary role in language learning. For example, to implement the metacognitive strategy of 'reading extensively to get a feel for the language', a learner needs to use a range of cognitive strategies such as 'using background knowledge to infer meaning and predict outcomes', 'reading for general meaning without checking up on every unfamiliar word' or 'choosing materials you enjoy reading'. Cognitive strategies are used in the light of the learner's overall goals and are therefore driven by the relevant metacognitive awareness and strategies. Learner training should thus aim at helping learners to develop an integrated package of both general (metacognitive) and specific (cognitive) learning skills.

2.6.2 Explicitness of purpose

Recent language teaching materials (particularly in the fields of reading and listening) quite frequently incorporate strategy work as a means of helping learners to perform their target tasks more effectively. This, however, should not be seen as being synonymous with strategy training, as learners may not be able to perceive the relevance of these strategies within the broader context of their language study, and may thus fail to transfer the strategies in question to their independent study. For learner training to perform a genuinely educational function there needs to be clarity and explicitness with respect to the role and interrelatedness of the strategies being suggested. Wenden refers to this as 'informed' in opposition to 'blind' training:

> ... informed training tells students that a strategy can be helpful and why. Students are not instructed in the use of the strategy but in the need for it and its anticipated effects. (Op. cit.: 316)

This allows learners to assess the strategy in question with respect to their learning objectives, and also to evaluate their ability to use it effectively, together with any personal reactions they might have to it.

In addition to this, learner training is the starting point for the reflective involvement of learners in their language study. This process will be in part personal to each learner as an individual, but will also involve dialogue and debate with fellow students and with the teacher. For this process to be feasible, participants need to be able to formulate their thoughts and communicate in a mutually comprehensible manner. Initial learner training is partly about achieving this, and serves to set the bases for subsequent discussion by establishing a common language and a stock of shared concepts among participants. With this goal in mind, clarity and explicitness of purpose in learner training are essential.

2.6.3 Integration

The goal of learner training is not to impart a body of knowledge, but to help learners develop a personalised understanding of language learning and of the options that are available to them. For this reason, learner training must inevitably be integrated with language study activities:

various possibilities exist, however, with respect to the nature and degree of its integration. At one end of the continuum, learner training can be fully linked to day-to-day teaching activities; at the other, it may be concentrated into a slot on the timetable along with others. Wenden makes the following points about the pedagogical implications of more and of less integrated approaches to learner training:

> ... it is generally acknowledged that learning in context is more effective than learning that is not clearly tied to the purposes it intends to serve. The former enables the learner to perceive the relevance of the task, enhances comprehension, and facilitates retention. Seen from this perspective, for learners who do not immediately appreciate the relevance of learner training, the more integrated the learner training, the more effective it should be. On the other hand, such an approach does not encourage the learner to be autonomous in the use of these skills, for learner training, like language training, becomes a teacher directed activity. (Op. cit.: 318)

The decision whether to opt for a more or a less integrated approach to learner training should thus be made in the light of the experiential and attitudinal characteristics of the learners involved and also, of course, within the constraints imposed by considerations of staffing and time-tabling. The less integrated the learner training, the greater the effort learners must make to transfer the insights potentially available in the learner training materials into their own language study. As a general rule, then, it would seem advisable to adopt a more integrated approach with learners who show less cognitive or personal maturity, and/or who are less motivated in their language learning. On the other hand, more mature learners, especially if they have an existing propensity for self-direction, may feel more at ease with a less integrated approach, one which allows them greater scope for personal reflection and exploration.

2.6.4 Evaluation

Learner training is an activity which takes up (possibly limited) time and resources. The teacher should therefore be able to evaluate, and possibly to justify, its usefulness – in the first instance to her students, but also to parents, sponsors or educational authorities. Wenden suggests the following reference points for the evaluation of learner training activities:

- Learner attitudes: has learners' appreciation of learner training changed?
- Skill acquisition: has the learning skill been learned?

  - Task improvement: does the skill facilitate performance of the language task?
  - Durability: does the skill continue to be utilised?
  - Transfer: is the skill utilised in similar contexts? (Op. cit.: 323)

These are all valid questions. However, it needs to be borne in mind that learner training is not an end in itself and cannot be evaluated separately from the wider process of which it is part, namely the development of learners' ability to assume an informed and self-directive role in their language learning. Thus, the essential question to be addressed is whether learner training seems to be helping students to grow and develop their insights as language learners. If this does not seem to be the case, the teacher may need to reconsider the approach she has adopted and assess whether inappropriate choices have been made with respect to one or more of the points raised here. For example, there may be mismatches between the approach adopted and certain learner character-istics such as motivation, cognitive maturity or learning style preferences. There may also be conflicts between the views of language learning implicit in the learner training materials and the beliefs about language study and the roles of teacher and learners which the learners have brought with them from their home culture or their previous language learning experience. Mismatches of this nature do not mean that learner training should be abandoned: one of its goals is, precisely, to bring implicit beliefs to the surface so they can be discussed openly. They may, however, require the teacher to modify or re-orient her approach to make it more accessible to her students' current level of awareness. Learner-centredness should start in the planning of the learner training component, and learners should not be made to feel overwhelmed or threatened, either as individuals, as language learners, or as members of a given cultural group. Indeed, in an appraisal of work on learner training, Rees-Miller (1993) stresses the importance of flexibility and responsiveness to learners' cultural background, prior learning experi-ences and expectations in the planning of learner training activities. The teacher therefore needs to keep the *goals* of learner training clearly in mind and then adopt the *approach* which seems most appropriate in her own teaching context and with the learners concerned.

If learner training is being evaluated together with students, collea-gues, sponsors or other participants in the teaching-learning process, the teacher may need to be attentive to what precisely is being evaluated. Is it the effectiveness of a given set of learner training procedures, or is it the idea of learner training itself? Learner training is an essentially educational undertaking, and its effectiveness must therefore be assessed in educational terms. If, however, other participants view the goals of language teaching essentially in terms of the assimilation of a given body of linguistic knowledge or of the development of a discrete set of functional skills, it is not unlikely that the whole idea of learner training may be seen as an optional extra, if not as a superfluous waste of time. This is a matter of the teacher who is committed to an educationally-based approach to language teaching being attentive to the beliefs and expectations of other participants and, if necessary, being ready to argue the case for such an approach in a constructive and sensitive manner.

2.6.5 Timetabling

Three main approaches exist with respect to the practical organisation of learner training, though they should not be viewed rigidly, and can be adapted to suit the demands of the target teaching context.

The first is the *training block*. In this option, learner training is concentrated in a (semi-)intensive series of classes at the start of a course. This is most suitable in brief, intensive courses, where the learner training component can provide learners with a basic baggage of awareness and strategies to launch them into the course. If learner training is organised in this way, however, learners will have little time to experiment with the TL and get a feel for their learning preferences during the learner training programme itself. This can be overcome, in part, if there is close coordination between the learner training and main course materials in terms of orientation and exploitation. Naturally, in brief courses, language learning goals have to be scaled down to what can feasibly be achieved in the time available, and the same degree of realism is called for with respect to learner training. This is particularly the case if learners might perceive time allocated to learner training as time lost for language learning purposes. Learner training should there-fore be geared to:

a) the finalities of the course;
b) the time available (and also what the teacher feels to be the learners' tolerance levels for learner training, as opposed to language develop-ment activities *per se*);
c) the learners' ability to assimilate and transfer into their language study the insights provided by what is a less integrated form of learner training.

The second main option is that of the *ongoing slot*. This involves learner training being allocated a regular slot in the timetable alongside other teaching-learning activities. This approach is feasible in both intensive and extensive courses, and has the advantage of allowing more time for reflection and experimentation. It also provides shared input for reflection tasks in the form of the activities learners are involved in during their other classes. Naturally, this assumes a sharing of information among teachers, as well as a consensus about the goals and methodology of the course as a whole. The ongoing slot option can, of course, be combined with a brief initial training block. The initial block could cover certain basic points, such as those dealt with in 2.4 and 2.5 above, while the regular sessions could explore the practical implications of these issues and develop the learners' repertoire of learning strategies on the basis of day-to-day teaching activities. Readers may find it interesting to consider the timetable for a one-week intensive course (30 hours) reproduced in Figure 6. This illustrates two forms of learner training – one which appears as a distinct feature on the timetable in separate sessions, and one in which learner training activities are integrated into classwork.

The last two options (the training block and the ongoing slot) assume regular contact between teacher and students. When, however, the learner is working primarily on his own and sees the teacher only occasionally for advice and counselling, the teacher's main role is that of learner trainer and learner training assumes the form of *consultancy*. In such cases the teacher needs to work as closely as possible around the practical options available to the learner and the attitudinal or strategic difficulties that arise. This calls for considerable flexibility and intuition, as the teacher will have to respond to the student's development as a learner on the basis of limited direct contact.

PED. With reference to a teaching situation and students you are familiar with, assess the orientation you would give to learner training in terms of content, integration and timetabling. Explain your choices in the light of the learning goals and characteristics of the students and the pragmatic constraints operating in the target learning context.

2.7 From training to involvement

The role of learner training is most obvious at the start of a course of study: learner training should not, however, be seen as something that can be dealt with once and for all within a given number of hours, nor can it be equated with any one set of materials. Learner training will be an ongoing strand running throughout the learning career of most (if not all) learners. There are a number of reasons for this. As learners' language competence develops, they will be able to undertake a wider

One week intensive English language course (30 hours)   Level: lower-intermediate

Time	Monday	Tuesday	Wednesday	Thursday	Friday
8.30–10.00	'Breaking the ice!' (Getting to know each other)	How to improve your discussion techniques Stage 2: 2.4 *Speaking* Step 2 *	How to talk about the past: Stage 2: 2.2 *Grammar* Steps 3, 4 *	How to improve your social skills	Language recycling (Video)
10.15–11.30	Preparation for language learning Stage 1: 1.1, 1.2, 1.5 †	Practising your discussion techniques: role play	Role play and feedback	Role plays and feedback *	It's your choice (Self-access revision) Stage 2: 2.2 *Grammar* Step 4 2.3 *Listening* Step 4 2.4 *Speaking* Step 4 *
11.45–12.30	Grammar: Typical mistakes of German speakers Stage 2: 2.2 *Grammar* Steps 1, 2, 3, 4 †	Assessment and feedback Stage 2: 2.4 *Speaking* Steps 3, 4 *	Grammar clinic *	Grammar clinic	Feedback and 'round-up'
14.00–15.15	How to talk about the future: plans, intentions, business appointments	How to improve your listening techniques Stage 2: 2.3 *Listening* Steps 1, 2, 6	How to be more fluent Stage 2: 2.4 *Speaking* Step 6 *	Be creative in English! (Radio or TV programme) †	
15.30–16.30	How to improve your telephoning Stage 2: 2.4 *Speaking* Steps 1, 2, 3, 5 *	How to extend your vocabulary techniques Stage 2: 2.1 *Vocabulary* Steps 1, 2, 5, 6 †	Let's debate! †	Feedback and assessment *	

Learner training = approximately 9 hours (30%)

* = Learner training integrated into classwork
† = Learner training in separate sessions

Figure 6 Learner training on the timetable: one possibility
(taken from Ellis and Sinclair 1989a: 21)

range of learning activities and make use of different input sources in the TL; their learning goals may change, or new needs may arise; they may also find that new learning opportunities, such as a visit to the TL country or social contacts with TL speakers, become available. These, or many other possibilities, can present the learner with new choices and make it necessary for him to acquire new learning skills: in this way, a further cycle of learner training may be necessary to help the learner to respond to these circumstances creatively.

Over time, however, as learners' understanding of language learning increases, learner training will give way to learner involvement, viz. the negotiation and joint selection of learning content and form which is the essence of a learner-centred approach to course development. There is, however, no hard-and-fast crossover point between learner training and learner involvement. Learners clearly need to be helped to acquire the basic insights into language study which will allow them to discover their own path to learning, and this is the goal of learner training. At the same time, this goal may often be best achieved by involving learners in decisions relating to specific aspects of their study programme, which is in itself a form of learner involvement. Learner training and learner involvement are thus related processes which will co-exist in varying degrees throughout most learners' language study. As learners acquire more knowledge about language learning, however, one would normally assume that their learning-how-to-learn will become more self- than other-initiated, and that this will be realised increasingly through their direct involvement in decision-making.

There are ambiguities in the literature as to the precise relationship between learner training and learner-centredness. The activities described in the following chapters would be classified as learner training by some authors, whereas the present writer would see them in terms of learner involvement in that they relate to the shaping by learners, at whatever level of the decision-making hierarchy, of their study programme. The general framework of reference that will be followed in this book was presented in 1.4.2 in terms of the goals of language education (which includes both learner training and learner involvement) and learner empowerment – the latter being the ultimate goal of a learner-centred mode of teaching. In what follows, then, *learner training* will refer principally to the initial sharing of perspectives between teacher and learners and among learners themselves – whether this takes place at the start of a course or as a means of initiating a new learning cycle; *learner involvement* will refer to the participation of learners in the development of their study programme at levels varying from the provision of study materials for a given class or activity slot to the collaborative establishment of learning goals and the negotiation of study mode.

2.8 Summary

a) Learner-centred teaching entails an active and reflective involvement of learners in their language study. However, as a result of a lack of experience of a participative approach to learning and/or of their expectations about language study, not all learners may be prepared for this role in either strategic or attitudinal terms.

b) Learner training has an enabling function in a learner-centred approach to teaching by helping learners to deepen their understanding of language learning and to acquire the knowledge and skills they need in order to pursue their language study in an informed and self-directive manner.

c) Learner training does not, however, simply involve a one-way flow of information, from teacher to learner. It also creates a forum within which teacher and learners can exchange their knowledge and insights and thereby initiate the process of consultation and negotiation upon which a learner-centred approach to teaching is based.

d) Two main areas were identified for initial learner training – learning goals and motivation, and learners' beliefs about language learning. A number of exploratory awareness development activities were discussed under each heading.

e) Learner training (the initiation of learners into the processes of language study) is one part of language education. The other is learner involvement (the active shaping by learners of their study programme in any way from the provision of study texts to the joint setting of learning goals or the choice of study mode). The two processes will be present throughout the study careers of most learners, but the general trend will be from training to involvement, as learners deepen their understanding of language learning and are thus able to operate in a more self-directive manner.

3 Objective needs analysis

3.1 Trends in needs analysis

The trends reviewed in 1.2 (the humanistic and communicative movements, learning strategy research and individualisation) all reflect, in one way or another, the concern felt in the 60s and 70s with making language teaching more responsive to the needs of language learners and, in this way, more learner-centred. Logically enough, this led to increased interest in the concept of learner needs – what they are, how they may best be defined and identified, and how they may most appropriately be incorporated into course design. Of the four formative trends reviewed in 1.2, CLT has received the most widespread attention since the 1970s, and for this reason it is the perspective on needs developed within CLT that has had the most pervasive influence on needs analysis work during this period of time. The main emphasis in needs analysis within CLT was on the identification of the objective or functionally-oriented communicative needs of learners in their target situations of use.

The goals of needs analysis in CLT thus revolved around identifying learners' real-world communicative requirements so that course designers and teachers could construct courses whose content reflected and prepared learners meaningfully for their intended uses of the TL. This could, for instance, involve concentration on a given skill (e.g. reading) as practised in a given domain (e.g. academic writing) and a given subject area (e.g. veterinary medicine). Alternatively, a course could be defined in terms of the performance of certain functions via the use of a given skill or grouping of skills such as using the telephone to provide information to clients, negotiating business agreements, finding accommodation and settling into life in a foreign country. In either case, the specification of learners' intended uses of the TL allows the teacher to concentrate on those skills, language functions and linguistic forms that relate most closely to their real-world communicative requirements. The analysis of learners' real-world functional needs thus assumed a central place in CLT course design, and especially in LSP.

The model which embodies this approach to needs analysis in its most coherent form is that of Munby (1978), and the Munby model has become an unavoidable reference point in any discussion of needs analysis since its appearance. West, however, comments that:

> The rigour and complexity of the Munby model tended to halt rather than advance development in the field of needs analysis ... However, it is now possible to see that the subsequent developments in needs analysis have either derived from Munby ... or in many ways been a reaction to the shortcomings of Munby's model. (1994: 9)

The shortcomings of the Munby model may be seen on two main levels. The first relates to the manner in which it approaches the identification of learners' objective or functionally-oriented needs, i.e. the explicit purpose of the model itself. These will be examined in 3.3 below. The second shortcoming relates to the usefulness of the Munby model as an instrument for course design, rather than simply for the analysis of learners' objective needs, and these points will be looked at briefly in this section.

To begin with, the title of Munby's book, *Communicative Syllabus Design*, is in itself somewhat misleading. In reality, it deals with the analysis of learners' target situations of use, and while target situation analysis (TSA) is clearly an important factor, course and syllabus design involve far more than simply an accurate specification of learners' target uses of the language. The title of Munby's work, combined with its undeniable thoroughness, has thus tended to distract attention from other aspects of course design which are as important as TSA in producing courses which are genuinely learner-centred and likely to satisfy the communicative needs of learners in an effective manner. West (op. cit.) mentions three areas of needs analysis (in a broad sense of the term 'needs') which merit attention in course design in addition to TSA – deficiency, strategy and means analysis.

Deficiency analysis, or *present situation analysis* (PSA) (cf. Allwright 1982; Robinson 1991), is a logical counterpoint to target situation analysis in that it involves the analysis of learners' current abilities with respect to their intended uses of the language. This can involve two processes. The first is the prioritising of activities identified in the TSA. For instance, a group of learners may need to read academic articles and also to write academic reports in the TL: if, however, the learners already have adequate reading abilities, there is little purpose in spending course time on this skill when it could be devoted to the writing skills component, where they may still be experiencing difficulties. The second process involves the detailed evaluation of learners' abilities in the relevant skill domain. This can be achieved either by the use of tests, or by means of self-assessment. Within a learner-centred approach to teaching, self-assessment and goal-setting are intimately related activities which lead into the strategic selection of learning activities. (Self-assessment will be discussed in Chapter 6 as a pivotal activity in learners' involvement in their language study.) PSA is thus complementary to TSA in that the two have to be used in conjunction in order to establish and prioritise learning objectives. Henceforth, the term 'needs analysis' will be used to refer to the analysis of learners' objective needs and will be taken as including both TSA and PSA. The addition of PSA to a Munby-type approach to needs analysis is relatively uncontroversial. The incorporation of strategy and means analysis, on the other hand, involves the addition of levels of concern which are absent from or only marginally present in Munby's perspective on course design.

Both TSA and PSA relate to the product of learning and learners' objective needs. The concept of *strategy analysis*, on the other hand, arises out of the interest shown in the 70s and 80s in the process side of language learning and in the role of subjective needs as seen in work on learning strategies, learner autonomy and learner training. Strategy analysis is designed to assess learners' current awareness of the processes of language study, the learning strategies which they use, and the expectations with which they approach their language study. In this way, it provides the essential basis for the joint exploration of learning options and, in time, the negotiation of methodology and study mode between teacher and learners. West (op. cit.) suggests that strategy analysis is of particular importance in course design when teacher and learners come from cultures with different educational traditions which are likely to generate differing expectations with respect to the process of language study. If language teaching is to be learner-centred in form as well as content, some form of strategy analysis is unavoidable in that it represents the means by which teacher and learners can start to exchange perspectives on what language learning means to them and how they feel it should best be approached. Oxford (1990: 283–291) provides a detailed strategy analysis instrument, the Strategy Inventory for Language Learning (SILL), which can be used to explore learners' activity preferences and thus form a basis for further discussion and negotiation of learning procedures. The activities proposed by Ellis and Sinclair and by Wenden (2.5) also constitute forms of strategy analysis in the sense that they acknowledge the importance of learners' current strategy usage and their subjective perceptions of language study as constituent features in course design. These factors will be considered further in Chapter 4 in terms of the topic of subjective needs, which involves consideration of individual differences (4.2), learning style (4.3), and the interaction between learning style and methodology (4.4).

Another element absent from Munby's model is explicit consideration of contextual factors, or *means analysis*. In the epilogue to *Communicative Syllabus Design*, Munby (1978: 217) does mention a number of variables which he views as 'constraints upon the implementation of the syllabus specification'. These include sociopolitical variables (e.g. the attitude of the government or the status of the TL), logistical variables (e.g. the number of trained teachers, accommodation, materials available), administrative variables (e.g. mode of instruction, timetabling), as well as psychopedagogic (e.g. learners' motivation and expectations, traditional learning styles) and methodological variables. While Munby (op. cit.) acknowledges that these 'constraints' are 'significant in the modification of syllabus specifications and production of materials', he views them as playing a role only once the needs analysis has been completed. He thus allocates to these factors a secondary role in course design, one that intervenes only at the implementation stage. In reality, of course, such factors, relating to the attitudinal and pragmatic context in which teaching is conducted, are crucial to the successful realisation of any language teaching programme. The considerable influence of the Munby model has thus led to a neglect of contextual factors – Munby viewing as 'constraints' what are in fact integral aspects of the sociocultural context of language teaching and which therefore merit explicit consideration in course design. Indeed, Holliday (1984: 37) suggests that this has 'allowed the practitioner to unconsciously evade responsibility for judging when, where and how, and whether'. Means analysis involves the study of the contextual factors which are present in the target teaching situation and the attempt to incorporate them in a constructive manner into course design. This will be examined in Chapter 5 in terms of means analysis (5.2) and classroom culture (5.3), and the implications these factors have for the realisation of a learner-centred approach to teaching (5.4).

The whole concept of 'needs' in language teaching is thus far more complex than is represented in the Munby model or similar approaches to needs analysis. This having been said, TSA is undeniably a key component in objective needs analysis and therefore merits explicit treatment. 3.2 will therefore examine the Munby model and another similarly-oriented needs analysis model proposed by Tarone and Yule (1989); 3.3 will then consider a number of needs analysis procedures and will argue for an approach to needs analysis which is developmental and experiential in nature. 3.4 and 3.5 will examine the knowledge structures which learners bring with them to their language study and the way in which these structures shape the communicative agendas which the learners will wish (or need) to realise via the TL. To conclude, 3.6 will suggest a few practical activities involving the integration of learners' existing knowledge into needs analysis and goal-setting.

> *REF.* You will certainly have encountered the term 'learner needs' quite frequently in your reading and in discussion with colleagues. Have you ever felt any confusion with respect to
>
> – what the term was meant to refer to?
> – its implications for your own teaching?
>
> Has the brief discussion of the term in this section served to clarify any of the uncertainties which you may have felt about it?
> If not, make a note of the points which remain unclear (or which you disagree with) and keep them in mind during your reading of this and subsequent chapters as part of your personal reading agenda.

3.2 Communicative goal-setting

As pointed out in 1.2.2, CLT may be seen as being learner-centred by having accorded centre-stage in programme design to the messages learners wish to convey and the communicative goals they need to pursue in real-world situations of use. The communicative movement thus saw language teaching as having a mediating or enabling function between learners' communicative intentions and the demands of the situations in which they need to use the language.

There is, of course, vast scope for variation in terms of both the communicative intentions which learners will wish to express and the situations in which they will need to use the language. As a result, a key role is played in CLT by needs analysis, or the process by which the communicative needs of one learner are identified and described in a manner which distinguishes them from the potentially vast array of needs which exist. The usefulness of a needs analysis based approach to course design is most apparent when learners' needs relate to a more or less discrete set of communicative situations – those of a tourist guide, an air traffic controller, or a mechanical engineer working in an oil field, for example. However, even when learners' needs are less specific, choices still have to be made. Should learners' competence be geared primarily round the written or the spoken language? If the former, then which type of written material should be dealt with – literary, journalistic or scientific, or a combination of all three? If the main focus is on the spoken language, then in which situations and in which register? In both 'general' and specific purpose language teaching, therefore, course content should be based on an analysis of the situations in which the learner will be required to use the language, whether these situations and the language needs which arise out of them can be specified with precision or only in terms of a general orientation.

A TSA is designed to gather as much information as possible on learners' intended uses of the language. As pointed out in 3.1, the best-known needs analysis (or, to be more precise, TSA) model is that developed by Munby. Munby's instrument operates in two stages. The first of these, the Communicative Needs Processor, has nine components, each of which relates to one aspect of the learner's communicative requirements. The nine components and the information they focus on are as follows:

1 *Participant*: basic information on the learner, such as age, sex, nationality, L1, other languages known, level in the TL, and educational background.
2 *Purposive domain*: the purposes for which the language is being learned (e.g. educational vs. occupational, together with further specification in terms such as occupational/post-experience/managerial/in commerce or industry).
3 *Setting*: the environment, both physical and psychosocial, in which the learner will use the language.
4 *Interaction*: the people with whom the target interaction will take place.
5 *Instrumentality*: the medium of communication (e.g. spoken or written language), the mode of communication (e.g. monologue-spoken to be heard; monologue-written to be spoken), and the channel (e.g. face-to-face interaction, written exchange, use of the telephone).
6 *Dialect*: the variety of language required (e.g. British or American English, or English as an international language used by speakers of a variety of L1s).
7 *Target level*: the level of command of the TL the learner needs to attain.
8 *Communicative event*: what the learner will have to do (e.g. take part in business meetings, provide information by telephone on the services offered by a firm).
9 *Communicative key*: the attitudinal tone in which the activities identified under communicative event will need to be carried out (e.g. participating in business meetings may call for a mastery of a range of attitudinal options, from polite agreement to forceful disagreement, whereas providing information to potential customers might require a polite and courteous tone come what may).

The communicative needs profile derived from these nine points is then fed into the second stage of Munby's model, which deals with syllabus specification, and is analysed in terms of language skills (e.g. using intonation patterns to express attitudinal meaning), micro-functions (e.g. agreement, approval, concession), and the language forms required for their realisation.

Tarone and Yule (1989) propose an alternative framework which operates with four levels of information:

Global level: the situations in which the learners will need to use the language, the participants, the communicative purpose pursued and activities undertaken.

Rhetorical level: the organisational structure of the communicative activities identified at the global level, this generally being expressed in terms of language functions (participating in university seminars, for example, might involve learners interrupting, asking for clarification, or making suggestions).

Grammatical-rhetorical level: the linguistic forms required to realise the language functions identified at the rhetorical level ('making suggestions', for example, may require the learner to command modal verbs, the use of intonation to mark attitudinal tone, and the appropriate register).

Grammatical level: the final level of analysis is quantitative in nature, and involves study of the frequency with which grammatical and lexical constructions occur in the target situations of use (generally on the basis of a corpus of data drawn from these situations).

Tarone and Yule concentrate into their first, global level much of the information dealt with in the first part of Munby's model, the Communicative Needs Processor. The three remaining levels correspond to the second part of Munby's model, focusing on the detailed realisations of learners' communicative activities that feed into syllabus design.

Although they differ in structure, these two models cover very much the same ground. Condensing the main points of the two models, then, it would seem that a needs analysis should move from an identification of learners' target *situations of use* (setting, participants and mode of interaction) and the *functional goals* they will be pursuing in these situations, to an analysis of the *communicative activities* learners will need to perform in order to achieve their goals, and the *linguistic forms* by which these activities will be realised, together with an assessment of the *performance parameters* operating in the target situations.

DAT. Using both Munby's and Tarone and Yule's models, conduct an analysis of one or two specific domains of your own language use. If you are actively involved in the use of an L2, focus on this language. If not, do the same with respect to your L1.

- Which framework do you find more useful, and why?
- Did you find any difficulties in using either model? If so, what were they?
- Finally, on the basis of your own personal experience of the domain(s) in question, how close does either model bring you to a satisfactory assessment of your own communicative needs?

3.3 Needs analysis procedures

The needs analysis models considered above are, of course, only checklists for the information that is required to specify learners' communicative needs which, in conjunction with an assessment of the learners' current abilities, provides the basis for the selection of course content. They therefore rely on the use of research techniques designed to gather the relevant information. Robinson (1991) lists seven such techniques, four of which derive information primarily from learners, and three that focus on the learners' target situations of use.

Questionnaires and *interviews* elicit information directly from learners. They are probably best used in conjunction with each other, the questionnaire providing basic information that can then be discussed in more depth in a one-to-one interview with the teacher. *Tests* can provide information on learners' general abilities in the TL and, if the learners' target needs are already known in part, on their abilities within their target domain of use (e.g. academic reading skills, or aural comprehension). Robinson also mentions a technique she refers to as *participatory needs analysis*, where learners engage in a more open-ended discussion of their needs and of what they would like to get out of their course of study, either one-to-one with the teacher, or as part of a group activity.

Information on the characteristics and demands of learners' target situations of use can be elicited by *observation* of the behaviour of proficient native speakers functioning in these situations: this technique can set an 'ideal agenda' for learners' ultimate performance in these situations. Alternatively, *case studies* can be conducted by shadowing and observing a learner in his day-to-day uses of the TL: this technique can provide insights into the learner's abilities *vis-à-vis* the target situations, which observations of native speakers clearly cannot yield. Another option is *authentic data collection*, which involves the collection and analysis of data from the target situations, possibly by means of audio or video recordings of interactive exchanges, or the gathering of written materials learners will need to consult or use as a basis for interaction.

A potentially useful research technique not mentioned by Robinson is consultation of *qualified informants*. These are individuals who, for one reason or another, are able to provide insights into the learner's future needs – either in terms of the demands of the target situations themselves, or on the basis of the observed difficulties of previous learners in the same situations. Informants might be sponsors (employers or educational institutions), individuals involved in the learner's target fields of activity, fellow teachers who have experience with similar categories of learner, or former students.

Robinson (op. cit.:15) suggests that 'as much as possible of the needs analysis should be completed before any course ... starts'. This is obviously desirable, and if thorough use is made of a range of elicitation techniques, a considerable amount of information can be gathered on learners' needs before a course begins. So far so good, it would seem. However, it is difficult not to feel uneasy about the feasibility of conducting a thorough pre-course needs analysis amid the practicalities and pressures that face many teachers. These doubts have at least four sources.

3.3.1 Access to linguistic realisations

Both Munby's and Tarone and Yule's models assume knowledge not only of learners' target situations of use, their interlocutors and functional goals, but also of the details of the communicative acts to be performed and their linguistic realisations. A number of studies such as Barber (1962), Dudley-Evans and Henderson (1990), Ewer and Latorre (1967), Gustafsson (1975), Huddleston *et al.* (1968), or Swales (1981), have looked in detail at the language used in various domains. However, these studies are not always easily available, and frequently do not lend themselves readily to being pedagogised for syllabus development. Furthermore, given the range of learning needs that can arise, very few areas have, in fact, been investigated in enough detail to provide meaningful input to syllabus specification. In other words, there is a serious lack of detailed information on the linguistic forms actually used in different situations, and which is required in the syllabus specification part of Munby's model, and the grammatical level of Tarone and Yule's model.

3.3.2 Difficulties in direct observation

In the absence of hard evidence in an already existing form on the details of the language used in a given area, the teacher can have recourse to the three hands-on elicitation techniques mentioned by Robinson – observation, case studies and authentic data collection. Such work, however, is extremely time-consuming, and calls for greater investment of time and resources than many teachers can afford. This is particularly the case in situations where the language used is more complex and/or subject to individual variation. For example, it may be feasible for a teacher (or a small team of teachers) to conduct a hands-on needs analysis of the language required by a waiter in a restaurant, or by customers in a post-office or shop. Doing the same in the case of business meetings or presenting papers at an academic conference is a very different matter – in practice, if not in theory. Furthermore, in special purpose language teaching, it can sometimes be difficult for a teacher who is not a specialist in the target field to prioritise learning points.

3.3.3 Coursebooks

Coursebooks can be a very valuable teaching resource in a number of ways. When they do not have access to data based studies or hands-on data, teachers therefore tend to turn to coursebooks for ideas or information on the content of teaching. Coursebooks, however, are a resource which needs to be treated with caution. Williams (1988), for example, compared the structures and functions which a corpus of 30 coursebooks put forward as being relevant for business meetings with the language which was actually used in about three hours of business meetings conducted by native speakers of English in Hong Kong. Firstly, there was very little agreement among the coursebooks about what was to be taught. Secondly, of the 135 expressions found in the coursebooks, only seven actually occurred in the meetings recorded. In a similar study, Burkhalter (1986) looked at the language presented as relevant to discussion skills in 11 ESL coursebooks. Like Williams, Burkhalter found little consensus about what was to be taught. Furthermore, of the 56 expressions given in five coursebooks as exponents of 'expressing an opinion', only three were used in a 45 minute discussion among native speakers at an American university. The language presented in coursebooks may well be 'useful', but it is often unclear whether the forms presented are derived from observation of the target situations, or simply from the intuitions of the writer – intuitions which may or may not be valid.

3.3.4 The role of specialist knowledge

A theme which recurs in several forms in Robinson's survey of language analysis in English for Specific Purposes (ESP) (Robinson, op. cit.: 18–32) is the importance of the conceptual content of communication. Referring to the work of Sager *et al.* (1980) Robinson (ibid.: 21) suggests that '... what is important first of all for the ESP researcher is the content of students' specialist disciplines: the knowledge and the conceptual networks involved'. With the best will in the world, teachers cannot be expected to possess this knowledge – other than by a chance coincidence of personal experience or extensive contact with a given category of learners. It is the learners themselves who possess this knowledge, even if they may lack the insights or metalanguage to express it in a pedagogically usable form. If they can be tapped, however, the knowledge and expectations that learners bring with them to their language study represent an extremely valuable resource in identifying their communicative needs. This is true not only of domain-specific knowledge. All learners have their own learning agenda based on the ideas and intentions they would like to communicate. Whether they can express this agenda explicitly or not, it will still be there, and learners' perceptions of the relevance of a course will depend a lot on how far it allows them to fulfil their individual learning agenda.

As it is the learners who will ultimately use the language, they should, at very least, have something meaningful to say about what they need to learn. This relates to the situations in which they will use the language, the functional goals they will pursue, and the communicative activities they will engage in, all of which sets a framework within which the relevant linguistic forms can be identified and the appropriate performance parameters fixed. This knowledge may be unconscious and may not be easily accessible at the start of a course. Helping learners to gain access to this information and to be able to formulate it in a manner which can be channelled into goal-setting is one of the tasks of learner training. Once learners have begun to acquire this ability, they can become directly involved in the shaping of this aspect of their study programme. The next two sections look at the conceptual bases for learners' participation in goal-setting, and the final section suggests a few activities by which this participation can be realised in practical terms: these activities combine elements of both learner training and of learner involvement (2.7).

Such an approach implies that initial or pre-course needs analysis would be seen as providing a framework which has to be refined by a form of needs analysis that is *developmental* and *experiential*, and arises out of an ongoing exploration of the learners' needs, both by the teacher and by the learners themselves. Teachers may or may not have access to detailed descriptive studies of learners' target situations of use; they may or may not have time and resources for hands-on observation of these situations. But, over time and with appropriate preparation,

> *DAT.* Use Figure 7 to help you analyse the ways in which the learning goals of a group of students you are familiar with were arrived at. Identify the techniques or sources of information which were used to decide on the learners' target situations of use, their functional goals, the communicative activities they will need to perform, the target linguistic forms, and the relevant performance parameters.

needs analysis component / elicitation technique	situation(s) of use	functional goals	communica- tive activities	linguistic forms	performance parameters	current abilities
questionnaires						
interviews						
tests						
observation						
case studies						
authentic data collection						
participatory needs analysis						
qualified informants						
other (specify):						

Figure 7 Needs analysis breakdown: components and information sources

they can have access to the conceptual and expressive agendas that their learners bring with them. This will be examined in the next two sections in terms of the networks of conceptual and pragmatic knowledge that underpin communication (3.4) and the ways in which these aspects of knowledge are realised in different domains of communicative activity (3.5).

3.4 Conceptual and pragmatic knowledge

In the last section it was suggested that there are limits on how far an 'external' or expert-driven approach to needs analysis can go in identifying learners' objective needs, and that such an approach should be complemented by a learner-based form of needs analysis involving the exploration of the communicative agendas which learners bring with them to their language study. The belief that learners are able to make a meaningful contribution to the establishment of their objective learning goals underlies a number of the activities discussed in 1.3.1 in terms of learner-centredness as a principle for activity organisation, and is a key component of the learner-centred curriculum (1.3.3). So far so good, it would seem. An active exploitation of learners' communicative agendas, however, involves an understanding of the type of knowledge which learners possess and of how this can contribute to goal-setting. This section examines the underlying knowledge structures which shape learners' communicative agendas, and which are seen as falling into two main categories – conceptual and pragmatic. The following section is more practical in orientation and presents an analysis of three domains of language usage (occupational, interactive, and cultural/affective) which arise out of the knowledge structures presented in this section. These three domains of usage can help the teacher to explore learners' communicative agendas in pedagogically usable terms as a means of channelling their input into goal-setting.

The first category, *conceptual knowledge*, relates to what learners know about events, people, entities and phenomena in the world, and the relationships that exist between them. There are two components of conceptual knowledge, factual and relational. *Factual knowledge* is 'knowledge that', and includes all the information that goes to constitute a learner's general knowledge of the world, as well as any specialist knowledge he may have. A learner's general knowledge includes elements such as:

– historical events and personalities;
– geographical information;
– national traditions, political parties and social trends, or cultural events and practices;
– current affairs in the learner's home country and in the world in general.

Specialist knowledge derives, for example, from a learner's:

– academic or vocational studies;

- occupational or professional life and experience;
- personal interests pursued in an area not generally considered part of 'general' knowledge (do-it-yourself, classical music, a sport, or classical music – to mention just a few).

Relational knowledge is composed of the network of logical relations that a learner establishes between the personalities, events, actions or entities that make up his factual knowledge. A learner's relational knowledge is thus linked with his beliefs and value system and, in general terms, with the way in which he sees and interprets the world around him. While factual information may be relatively unambiguous (e.g. an international coalition of forces under the auspices of the UN initiated military action against Iraqi forces in Kuwait and southern Iraq in the spring of 1991), relational knowledge frequently varies between individuals, depending on their interpretation of the events or actions in question (e.g. the military action against Iraqi forces was: in defence of democracy and the independence of a sovereign state/to deter international aggression/to protect the West's economic interests/an example of Western interference in Middle Eastern affairs, etc.). A learner's relational knowledge comes into play in his beliefs and opinions about subjects as varied as:

- religion and moral questions;
- social norms and the organisation of society;
- historical and political events;
- economic decisions and policy;
- the norms of scientific investigation;
- the nature and goals of education.

A learner's factual and relational knowledge underpin virtually any communicative event he will be involved in, either productively or receptively. They constitute the knowledge base and world view that will shape the messages that the learner will wish to convey, and they form the framework within which the learner will interpret the messages he receives. In this way, they constitute a central component of the communicative agenda learners bring with them to their language study. They will play a significant role in both the occupational and the cultural/affective domains of input discussed in 3.5.

The second category, *pragmatic knowledge*, includes elements of conceptual knowledge, but relates principally to the way in which language is structured and used to achieve communicative goals. Faerch and Kasper (1984) identify two types of pragmatic knowledge. The first, *declarative knowledge*, contains the speaker's knowledge of the components and rules of use present in one or more languages: this knowledge is static or taxonomic and is independent of any specific communicative goal or the use of language in real time. The second, *procedural knowledge*, is dynamic and 'selects and combines parts of declarative knowledge for the purpose of reaching specific communicative goals, observing constraints imposed by language processing in real time' (op. cit.: 215). Faerch and Kasper recognise a number of sub-parts in each of these two categories of pragmatic knowledge.

Components of pragmatically relevant declarative knowledge
1 *Linguistic knowledge* of the rules and components of the phonological, morpho-syntactic, and lexical systems of one or more languages.
2 *Speech-act knowledge* of which verbal acts are possible within a given speech community and its institutions, as well as their constituting conditions.
3 *Discourse knowledge* as to how to establish coherence, and of how different discourse phases are structured (e.g. openings and closings, and the structure of different discourse types), and speech acts modified.
4 *Sociocultural knowledge* of the social values, norms, institutions and patterns of relations between individuals in a given social group.
5 *Context knowledge* of those features potentially present in a given communicative situation which are 'context-determining', i.e. the factors that determine which actions are possible in a given situation and how these actions are interpreted.
6 *Knowledge of the world* contains knowledge about facts, objects, relations, and so on, other than the communicative knowledge covered by the last five categories.

Procedural knowledge used in the production of speech
1 *Goal-formulation and context analysis* involves the speaker establishing a communicative goal in the light of the target context (e.g. the other participants and their relation to the speaker, or the content of foregoing speech acts). This is based on a strategic selection and combination of knowledge from the six areas outlined above.
2 *Verbal planning* involves the conversion of the communicative goal specified at the last stage into an appropriate linguistic form. This entails choice of syntactic structures and lexical elements and, as required, set formulae, for the expression of certain speech acts (e.g. 'I'm sorry').
3 *Monitoring execution* involves comparing the outcome of a given speech act with the speaker's intention, i.e. assessing whether one has achieved the goal one had set out to achieve. A key part of this process is monitoring the reactions of one's interlocutor.

Faerch and Kasper's analysis of pragmatic knowledge brings out very clearly how powerful a role is played in language use by factors which are independent of the linguistic system of any one language. Of course, a language learner will not possess the same linguistic or speech-act knowledge as a native speaker; the learner's L1 may also have different discourse and sociocultural conventions from the TL. Nonetheless, language learners (adult learners at least) will possess well-developed systems of pragmatic knowledge in their L1 which constitute a powerful body of communicative expectations underpinning their learning of the TL. This will be discussed in 3.5 with respect to learners' awareness of communicative goals and conventions in the occupational domain of input, and will play a crucial role in the interactive domain of input.

Learners' conceptual and pragmatic knowledge feed into and inform their language study in two ways:

1 by setting the meaning agenda and communicative goals they will wish to pursue by means of the TL;
2 by providing a framework for the production and reception of language on the basis of the learner's existing knowledge of the conventions and goals of language use.

In this way, they underpin the contribution which learners can make to goal-setting – the focus of the rest of this chapter – as well as the related area of self-assessment (which is considered in Chapter 6).

DAT. Select a few situations you will find yourself in over the coming week, such as having a meeting with colleagues, discussing politics with friends over lunch, or practising a sport with other club members.

Then, analyse the networks of both conceptual and pragmatic knowledge you and your interlocutors are working with in each situation. Think in particular about:

– the networks of conceptual knowledge (both factual and relational) that underlie what is said in the target situation;
– the norms and conventions of interaction that govern what is (and is not) considered to be acceptable behaviour in this situation.

Focusing on one specific group of learners you are familiar with, make an assessment of the conceptual and pragmatic knowledge that these learners are likely to possess, and how this knowledge might be used to inform the choice of teaching-learning content.

3.5 Domains of learner input

In his study on L2 learning motivation referred to in 2.4, Dörnyei identifies four 'language use fields'. *Instrumental language use* relates to language use for occupational purposes, with goals such as gaining access to specialised literature in the TL, or using the TL to facilitate contacts with foreign colleagues. *Communicative sociocultural language use* refers to the use of the TL as a means of establishing and maintaining personal social contacts, for example by making friends with foreigners, keeping in touch with friends and acquaintances, or travelling abroad as a tourist. In Dörnyei's last two categories, *passive sociocultural language use* and *reading for non-professional purposes*, the TL is seen as a medium for gaining access to films, broadcasting or music, learning about world events, and reading literature or magazines. This produces three main categories of learning purpose, or target domains of language use – occupational, interactive and cultural/ affective. The *occupational* domain yields learning goals related to the learner's work or professional advancement; the *interactive* domain provides goals related to the establishment and maintenance of social contacts; the *cultural/affective* domain yields learning goals which arise out of the pursuit of knowledge for reasons of personal interest, enjoyment or self-advancement. This section will examine the contribution learners can make to the specification of their learning goals under each of these three headings on the basis of their domain-specific conceptual and pragmatic knowledge.

3.5.1 Occupational domain

It is probably in the occupational domain that learners can most clearly make a contribution to goal-setting (when, at least, their learning goals are related to their working lives). With the best will in the world, it can be very difficult for someone not actively involved in a given area of professional activity to reach as close an understanding of the relevant communicative goals and performance parameters as someone involved in this area on a daily basis. What learners have to say in a given situation (and, therefore, what they will need to learn) depends on what they have to *do*, and it is the learners themselves who are likely to have more insight into this than the teacher. This relates to the role of specialist knowledge discussed in 3.3, and involves elements of both conceptual and pragmatic knowledge (3.4).

In a talk which pointed out a number of weaknesses in current business English teaching, Holden (1990) suggested that some of these weaknesses were a result of a lack in the language teaching community of direct, hands-on experience of the realities of business life. One example given by Holden is the frequent attention given by language teaching materials to the skills of selling and negotiating. Without denying the importance of these skills, Holden suggested that socialising and the ability to build up and maintain contact networks are far more pervasive requirements, especially at senior levels. Holden explained this mismatch between what is frequently taught and what learners actually need in two ways. The first is the tendency to teach what is easy to teach. The second and more fundamental reason is reliance on an analysis of target situations which is too general and too linguistically oriented – with insufficient understanding of the underlying communicative goals, and inadequate consultation of participants.

The studies by Williams (1988) and Burkhalter (1986) referred to in 3.3, although both limited in scale, indicate how marked the difference can be between what is taught for use in a given field and the language that is actually used. With the best of intentions, we may sometimes be teaching our students things they simply do not need, and thereby not making the best use of their learning time. Worse still, we may even be teaching them inappropriate forms, inappropriate in that they are over-correct or over-explicit. These difficulties may be addressed, in part at least, if we make more use of learners' own intuitions and feeling for the communicative requirements of their target situations of use. Three areas of knowledge merit consideration in this respect.

Conceptual content: This relates to the content or subject matter that has to be dealt with in the learners' field of activity and, in particular, in their target situations of use. In a business context, for example, this could include the structure and goals of the learner's firm, the specifications and advantages of the products it offers, how they compare with those of rival firms, or the relative advantages of two production methods. It is this sort of knowledge that forms the substantive basis for communication in a given field of activity, and is most readily available to individuals working in this field.

Communicative goals and conventions: In addition to the conveyance of factual information, professional communication involves the establishment and maintenance of a variety of interpersonal relationships. In her study of business meetings, Williams observes that:

> ... the speakers' use of language was far more complex than simply realising functions with suitable exponents. There was evidence of care being taken by speakers in selecting strategies and planning their tactics in order to achieve their purpose in the

most effective way. Speakers tended to build up arguments and support their information and views in consistent ways. They appeared to exhibit an awareness of the needs of the listeners and of how the listeners might react, and select their strategies accordingly. (Op. cit.: 53)

In other words, Williams found that the speakers' awareness and use of the pragmatic conventions specific to their domain of activity were the main source of communicative dynamism in the meetings she observed. This is likely to be the case in most domain-specific interaction, and it is the learners themselves who (albeit implicitly) will best understand the nature of the communicative goals they will be pursuing and the interactive conventions they will have to respect.

Textual component: Communication, especially in professional and educational fields, frequently turns on a set of textual materials. These materials provide a conceptual reference point and thus play a role in the target interactive situation. Textual material can take a variety of forms, depending on the professional domain and on the goals of the interaction – product descriptions or contract forms in a business setting, medical reports in health care, or the text of an article and experimental results in academic life. Learners actively involved in a given profession will obviously have more direct access to such materials (either in the TL or in their L1) than language teachers. Using these materials, albeit alongside standard language teaching materials, can enhance the relevance of learning activities and increase learners' involvement, both real and perceived, in shaping the content of their study programme.

3.5.2 Interactive domain

For many learners, the TL is seen as an enabling medium which will allow them access to a potentially wide range of interactive situations. In broad-focus learning programmes of this type, the contribution learners can make to goal-setting will be based on their familiarity with the conventions of social interaction and on their interactive intentions. This domain of input relies heavily on learners' pragmatic knowledge, as discussed in 3.4. Two main points merit consideration.

Communicative awareness: The ability to use a language to achieve one's communicative goals involves knowledge not only of the grammatical and lexical systems of the language, but also of the sociopragmatic conventions of the TL community. These conventions certainly do differ between speech communities, but such differences should be kept in perspective: learning a second language does not involve a re-learning of the whole process of socialisation. Adult learners, as we have seen from Faerch and Kasper's analysis of pragmatic knowledge, have a powerful (even if implicit) knowledge of the goals and conventions of social interaction. The development of interactive skills in a L2 should thus be seen as the channelling of an existing awareness into the linguistic and pragmatic forms appropriate in this language. In this way, differences on the sociopragmatic level, and their linguistic realisations, can be dealt with as alternative manifestations of known phenomena.

Interpersonal intentionality: Beyond a relatively conventional level of social interaction, communicative exchanges involve a more or less marked degree of individual psychosocial investment: L2 learners will generally wish to function in the L2 as themselves, i.e. as individuals whose communicative intentions will grow out of their own personality and experience. This influences the type of interactive situations they will seek out and the nature of the interpersonal relationships they will try to establish. It also affects the social persona and self-image they will wish to project in their dealings with others. Naturally, not every desire or need of every student can be accommodated, except perhaps in one-to-one or small-group instruction. Nonetheless, this level of interpersonal intentionality, the desire to 'be oneself' in the TL, constitutes a very powerful source of motivation for many learners. Channelling this intentionality into the content of language teaching can increase the communicative dynamism and authenticity of learning activities, and thereby help learners to personalise their study programme.

3.5.3 Cultural/Affective domain

Our students do not cease to be themselves simply by being in the process of learning a language. Their opinions and beliefs, the things they enjoy or are interested in remain just as important to them in their capacity as language learners as they do in the other aspects of their life. Allowing learners to inform their language study with the ideas and interests that are important to them as individuals can help them to personalise learning content and (as in the interactive domain) 'find themselves' in their language study. Furthermore, it is difficult to underestimate the communicative energy which can result from the genuine personal involvement of learners in what they are communicating. This can make learners more ambitious in terms of both the communicative goals they will set themselves and their willingness to experiment with means of attaining these goals. Positive energy also tends to be contagious: a learner with a strong personal involvement in what he is saying will generally manage to arouse richer interaction with fellow students than one whose communicative desire is less personally felt. Two main types of cultural/affective input call for consideration.

Opinions and beliefs: These derive from learners' conceptual knowledge, both factual and relational, though particularly the latter. What do learners know about the world, and what is particularly important to them? What are the topics or ideas that they feel strongly about, and which they most wish to investigate or discuss? What are their likes and dislikes? What do they consider to be good or bad, right or wrong? These questions touch on what learners think and believe as individuals and, in this way, tell us a great deal about what they would like to be able to express in the TL – in other words, about their communicative agenda as individuals.

Personal interests: These are, very simply, the things that learners enjoy or are interested in – their preferred activities, cultural interests, pastimes or hobbies. They can vary widely, both among individual learners and between categories of learner, from classical music through an enjoyment of detective stories to a passion for water sports or karate. Few learners will not have at least one or two activities they particularly enjoy or have some special interest in. As in the case of opinions and beliefs, these concerns form part of the personality of the learner and of his personal communicative agenda.

The language teaching profession has long recognised the importance of the authenticity (and, therefore, the interest value) of learning activities and materials. The question is whether the creativity of language teachers and materials writers is best used in trying to generate this authenticity themselves, or in developing pedagogical frameworks within which students can enrich learning activities with their own intentions, concerns and interests – in other words, create their own authenticity. Holec sets this challenge in the following terms:

> The choice of a communicative approach entails dealing with the many implications of communication. Among these is the necessity to allow each learner to develop his own competence. Indeed, if we fail to do this we will, at best, succeed only in providing learners with an elementary, static and stereotyped form of competence. (1980: 32)

DAT. Look at the four learner profiles which follow and make a provisional assessment of the way(s) in which each of the four learners might be able to contribute to a specification of his or her learning goals in the light of the three domains of language use discussed above. What sort of information would you look for, and how might this be used to inform the choice of learning content?

Profile 1: John

Biographical data: 40 years of age; British; L1 English; TL German; some German at school.

Occupation: Lecturer in mechanical engineering.

Learning goals: John needs to learn German in order to gain access to academic material in German in his field of specialisation. He has no particular desire to acquire spoken proficiency in German. He has not yet decided what the best means of attaining his goal would be, joining a class or self-study.

L2 Level: False beginner.

Interests: Gardening; football; country walking.

Other information: John has a reading knowledge of Russian for academic purposes which he acquired from a specialised reading skills course in Russian a few years ago.

Profile 2: Marc

Biographical data: 43 years of age; French; L1 French; TL English; some English at school, and a couple of short courses in English since (which he claims to have been of little help).

Occupation: Sales manager in an engineering firm.

Learning goals: Marc has to follow an intensive 30 hour course in negotiating skills in English with two other students of similar backgrounds, before going to Sweden to negotiate an important contract for his firm.

L2 level: Somewhere between false beginner and low intermediate. Marc's command of English is limited in both range and accuracy. Although he has quite a range of set phrases and conversational gambits, his ability to string ideas together coherently is rather poor.

Interests: Football; current affairs; eating out and socialising with friends.

Other information: Despite his clearly limited English, Marc was chosen to go to Sweden because he is considered to be one of his firm's best salesmen and negotiators: it is assumed his personality and experience will be enough to compensate for his weak English.

Profile 3: Moira

Biographical data: 33 years of age; Scottish; L1 English; TL Italian; evening classes twice a week for three years.

Occupation: Housewife, and frequently helps (her terms!) in aspects of the running of her husband's firm, which produces tartan materials.

Learning goals: Moira has a very strong interest in Italy and Italian culture. She and her husband spend most of their holidays in Italy, and it was this contact with Italy that gave her the desire to learn the language. Also Italy is one of the main markets for the tartan materials produced by her husband's firm. The visits she and her husband make to Italy frequently combine relaxation and business. However, Moira says she feels no need for 'business Italian' as most contacts with clients are informal, and involve more socialisation than business *per se*.

L2 level: Upper intermediate to advanced. Although there are inadequacies here and there, Moira can express herself on a wide range of topics fluently and accurately. Her reading and listening skills are excellent.

Interests: Italian art and culture; history of art; cooking; travel.

Profile 4: Hans

Biographical data: 18 years of age; German; L1 German; TL English; seven years English at secondary school.

Occupation: Secondary school student preparing his *Abitur* (school leaving examination).

Learning goals: Hans' main goal is to achieve a sufficiently high grade in his *Abitur* (of which English is part) to be able to gain admission to study medicine at university.

L2 level: Upper intermediate with a solid basis in all four skills.

Interests: Music: recent trends in music *per se*, but also the technological side of music production.

Other information: Outside his English classes, Hans' main contact with English is via music. A large part of the music Hans enjoys has lyrics in English, and is by British or American artists. He is also an ardent viewer of MTV (Music Television, an English language channel devoted exclusively to popular music and trends in the music industry).

3.6 Learner-based needs analysis

A learner-centred approach to needs analysis rests on the belief that a full specification of learners' needs can emerge only over time, as learners gradually come to understand their needs and acquire the ability to express them in a pedagogically useful manner – a process of (self-) discovery that involves learners in an ongoing exploration of their communicative intentions conducted in collaboration with their teacher. This means that pre-course and initial needs analysis sets a framework which will then be filled out and refined over time *on the basis of ongoing teaching-learning activities*. The activities outlined below provide a few ideas as to how this can be realised. Most of these activities include both TSA and PSA: in other words, they involve learners in assessing both the objective demands of a given situation of use and also their current abilities with respect to these demands. This will be looked at further in Chapter 6 in terms of self-assessment. Numerous other activity types clearly do exist, and the options presented here should be seen primarily as stimulus for reflection and experimentation.

3.6.1 Sharing goals and experiences

Learning a language is a social activity and most learners will wish to enjoy their contacts with fellow students, get to know each other and exchange their experiences. This natural human curiosity can be exploited in a number of ways to:

– establish group dynamics and the sharing of knowledge and insights upon which a learner-centred approach is based;
– open learners' eyes to different communicative goals and attitudes to learning;
– elicit information from learners on their communicative goals in a non-threatening and non-technocratic manner.

Example 1: Why are we here?
This would be relevant in a general purpose class, and relatively early in the course:

Stage 1 Each learner works with a partner to fill in a checklist on the partner's interests and learning goals. The checklist could contain points such as,
 – 'I'm learning (English) because ...'
 – 'My interests/hobbies/likes are ...'
 – 'My dislikes are ...'
Stage 2 The 'interviewer' moves around the class trying to find other learners with a profile similar to that of the person he interviewed, and sending them to see his initial partner (a degree of disorder in the classroom is likely at this stage!).
Stage 3 Once a few interest groups have been formed (the learners

themselves have to decide on this), each group can present itself to the class. Together with the other class members, they can then suggest how they can:
- pursue their personal interests as part of their learning of the TL;
- use these interests to inform or animate class activities.

Example 2: Discussing difficulties: using the telephone

This version would be suitable in a specific-purpose learning context where learners' functional goals include the use of the telephone. The same approach could, of course, be used with a wide range of other learning tasks:

Stage 1   Learners establish groups based on similarity of needs in terms of:
- place of work/type of company
- why they need to use the telephone
- the sort of information they have to handle, both productively and receptively

Stage 2   In each group, learners list and prioritise the difficulties they have experienced in their use of the telephone. These might include speed of speech received, difficulties in responding to the unexpected quickly enough, accents, names, numbers etc. (depending on the individuals).

Stage 3   Each group presents and discusses its list of priorities. The class, working with the teacher, would then draw up a learning agenda and plan how the necessary language skills and strategies could be developed.

3.6.2   *Simulation-based needs analysis*

Simulations have a variety of functions in language teaching – fluency practice, increased motivation, strategy training and the activation/consolidation of resources, being just a few. They can also, however, be a means of promoting learners' understanding of their communicative goals and intentions (consciousness-raising), or identifying the problems learners have in fulfilling these goals and intentions and, on this basis, of setting learning objectives. In this function, there are two main types of simulations. *Projective* simulations look forward to the learners' target situations of use and try to prepare them to operate in these situations. *Remedial* simulations relate back to situations learners have already found themselves in and which have caused problems in one way or another; the simulation then offers the learner the possibility to re-enact the situation and identify where and why the problems arose, and how they might be resolved – either strategically, or by the acquisition of specific skills and resources.

For this to be effective, of course, the simulation has to grow out of the learners' own communicative intentions and experience of life, and allow them to make active use of their own situation-relevant knowledge (both conceptual and pragmatic). In practice, this means that it is the learners who should decide on the setting, the interactive goals pursued, the role and personality of the other participants, and how the target interaction should be structured. It may also involve the learners supplying relevant reference materials or documents. In other words, the simulation should involve learners (or the main participants, at least) functioning more or less as themselves, and not in an assumed role.

Example: Developing negotiating skills in German

The following activity sequence was described by Sabine Münkle, of Industrie-Sprachen-Dienst (ISD), Stuttgart. The learners were two Japanese businessmen with an already good level of competence in German who needed to improve their German further, with specific reference to negotiating and participating in meetings:

Stage 1 The learners were shown a video sequence from a business English course which showed a business meeting in Japan involving an American manager whose behaviour (promotion of a junior employee, demonstrative praise of the employee in question, and physical contact to indicate approval) clashed with the interactive norms current in this situation in Japan. Although the sequence was shown picture-only (the video was in English, whereas the TL was German), the learners immediately identified how the American manager had violated Japanese interactive norms in a business context. This led into a discussion of Japanese interactive conventions and of how they differed from what the learners had noticed around them in Germany.

Stage 2 The learners were then shown a video sequence of an authentic German business meeting. After initial language work to facilitate comprehension, the learners' attention was drawn to the interactive conventions being used in the German business meeting. These were discussed and compared with Japanese practice. The learners' attention was then focused on the linguistic and communicative forms used in the German meeting.

Stage 3 Together with two other learners of German (also practising businessmen), the two Japanese students then prepared, scripted and enacted a business meeting in German, trying to approximate as closely as possible to German norms both interactively and linguistically. The simulated meeting was videoed, and this served as a basis for subsequent feedback and remedial work. In addition to her role as language advisor, the teacher acted as a consultant on interactive conventions in German.

This activity sequence is interesting in at least two main ways. The first is that it takes the learners' existing knowledge as the starting point for the development of their interactive skills in the TL: in this way, the TL norms can be seen as alternative manifestations of known phenomena and integrated more easily into the learners' interactive repertoire, together with their linguistic realisations. The second is that the simulation was prepared by the learners themselves on the basis of their own professional knowledge and experience. This allowed them to inform their roles with their own personalities, which presumably made the feedback stage more relevant to their subsequent uses of the language.

The use of simulations as an instrument for needs analysis and goal-setting involves a *performance-based* approach to syllabus design. This does not preclude the pre-selection and teaching of structure and vocabulary likely to facilitate communication. It does, however, assume that a large part of the language content of a course will be derived from the observation of learners' attempts to communicate in the TL, teaching points being selected on the basis of observed shortcomings or breakdowns in learners' communicative abilities, both productive and receptive.

3.6.3   Learner diaries

Learner diaries are records kept by learners themselves of their use and learning of the TL. The simplest form is the 'difficulties diary' which, as the name suggests, records the problems learners have experienced in their use of the language over a given period of time. This is probably the easiest form of diary for learners to keep as it focuses on those situations which have caused them difficulty, and with which they therefore most want to have assistance. A form such as the following (adapted from AMEP, 1989: 79) may be used to help learners keep track of their problems.

The difficulties diary can be exploited in a number of ways, depending on class size. In a small learning group, the teacher can discuss each learner's diary individually, or as part of a group activity. In larger groups, the learners themselves can form study groups and devote a part

My difficulties with (English) this week			
Where?	With whom?	What for?	What was the problem?

of their weekly class time to discussion and brainstorming of each other's diaries, with the teacher moving from group to group to offer suggestions or provide advice. Whatever the mode of exploitation adopted, however, the debriefing on each learner's diary should involve:

- an analysis of the nature and causes of the communicative, linguistic, or strategic problem identified;
- as assessment of the learner's current abilities with respect to the target situation or task;
- the development of an action plan involving concrete learning activities to help the learner cope better with the target situation or task the next time round.

It should also be noted that linking the 'difficulty' with the setting (where?), participant(s) (with whom?), and communicative purpose (why?), is a means of helping learners to view their language use in situational and functional terms. In other words, it is a form of awareness development or learner training which links instances of language use to their pragmatic and communicative context.

A second and more demanding form of learner diary involves learners recording their own language use over a period of time. In a SLA context, where the learner is in regular contact with the TL, this could be adapted from the difficulties diary form given above. It can, however, also be based on the learner's use of his L1. For example, if a learner will have to move to a foreign country to perform more or less the same professional functions he now performs in his L1, his current language use is the best starting point for a specification of his learning goals in the TL. In this case, even while he may be following a basic preparatory course in the TL, the learner can monitor and record his language use over a few weeks noting, in particular:

- situations;
- participants (including their hierarchical relationship to the learner);
- communicative goals (including the type of interpersonal relationships and atmosphere the learner wishes to establish);
- conceptual content of the interactions;
- pragmatic norms and conventions in operation;
- textual materials discussed or referred to.

This is not an easy task, and will generally need to be carried out in close collaboration with the teacher, whose task it is to provide the learner with guidelines within which he can analyse and interpret his experience, and then express it in a pedagogically usable manner.

PED. Look back over the techniques for learner-based needs analysis outlined above and assess which could be used in a teaching situation that you are familiar with (as they stand, or with adaptations).

- In which way could they complement the needs analysis and goal-setting procedures that are currently used?

3.7 Summary

a) The approach to needs analysis developed in CLT fails to take account of the full range of factors which are required for effective course design. Furthermore, even with respect to objective needs analysis, it has two weaknesses: One is that its data collection procedures are, in practice, very difficult to realise, and the other is that it makes insufficient use of the learners' own knowledge and insights into their learning goals.

b) A two-stage approach to needs analysis was suggested. The first stage involves the gathering of as much information as possible on learners' intended uses of the language prior to or at the start of a course. This sets a general framework of goals which is then filled out in the second stage, which involves the collaborative exploration by both teacher and learners of the communicative agendas which learners bring with them to their language study. This stage is experiential and developmental in nature, and arises out of the learners' exploration of their own communicative intentions and of the process of language learning.

c) Learners' communicative agendas are based on their networks of

conceptual and pragmatic knowledge. Conceptual knowledge includes what learners know about events, people, entities, etc. and the
relations that exist between them. Pragmatic knowledge relates to
what learners know about the way in which language is structured
and used to achieve communicative goals.

d) These two knowledge networks are realised in three domains of
language use which can be effective in channelling in a pedagogically
manageable manner the knowledge learners have of their communicative goals and intentions. These are the occupational domain
(which relates to learners' professional or academic fields of interest),
the interactive domain (which relates to the interpersonal relations
learners will wish to establish via the TL), and the cultural/affective
domain (which relates to the opinions and beliefs learners will wish
to express, or the personal interests they will wish to pursue). The
knowledge learners have in these domains can be accessed via an
ongoing, learner-based form of needs analysis.

4 Subjective needs

4.1 The importance of subjective needs

The trends reviewed in 1.2 and 1.3 arose out of two sets of concerns. The first relates to the content of instruction and has involved the development of exploratory procedures and course design structures by which learning programmes can be made to reflect the communicative intentions and functional goals of the learners concerned. These developments were reviewed in Chapter 3, together with suggestions as to how content specification can be linked more closely to the communicative agendas learners bring with them to their language study. The second set of concerns relates to the process side of language teaching, and focuses on the interaction between methodology and the subjective needs of language learners. This type of factor was looked at briefly in 2.5 in terms of the three categories of learner 'beliefs' identified by Wenden (1987) and was alluded to in 3.1 in terms of strategy analysis. Learners' beliefs and expectations about language learning do not, however, appear out of nowhere. They are rather the external expression of a complex array of factors which, taken together, shape the way in which learners perceive and then approach their language study. These factors are varied in origin, but may be grouped together under the general heading of subjective needs, to indicate that they reflect *perceptions of a given situation* (in this case language learning) rather than more externally verifiable or objective factors. While Chapter 3 examined objective needs, the present chapter will focus on subjective needs, and the way in which they influence language learning. Widdowson gives the following definition of these two sets of learning needs:

> The expression 'learner needs' is open to two interpretations. On the one hand it can refer to what the learner needs to do with the language once he has learned it. This is the goal-oriented definition of needs and relates to terminal behaviour, the ends of learning. On the other hand, the expression can refer to what the learner needs to do to actually acquire the language. This is

the process-oriented definition of needs and, related to transitional behaviour, the means of learning. (1981: 2)

If insufficient attention is paid to objective needs, learning outcomes are unlikely to correspond with the learners' target uses of the language, so that the effort invested in learning will be less productive than it should be. Equally well, however, if insufficient attention is paid to learners' subjective needs, the quality of their learning and their affective involvement in the learning process are likely to suffer. This can have consequences every bit as negative on the effectiveness of a learning programme as a neglect of learners' objective needs: indeed, if learners simply give up, as may happen in extreme cases, it may be even more negative.

Since the 1960s considerable attention has been paid to the development of procedures capable of generating language learning programmes responsive to learners' objective needs. Thus, even if some of these procedures have tended to be somewhat external and insufficiently open to learners' own knowledge and insights (3.1; 3.3), the language teaching profession has at its disposal a valuable array of analytical tools which it can use to explore learners' objective needs. Furthermore, there is, in theoretical terms at least, a widespread acceptance of the importance of gearing learning programmes around learners' objective needs. The situation with respect to subjective learning needs is not so advanced, neither in terms of our understanding of the phenomena involved, nor with respect to our ability to accommodate these phenomena in course design. Brindley explains the relative neglect of subjective needs in the development of CLT in the following terms:

> In the early stages of the 'communicative' movement in language teaching, 'objective' needs received a great deal of emphasis, since language was seen primarily as a means to an end: effective communication in the learner's current or future domain of language use. ... 'Subjective' needs, on the other hand,... were thought to be unpredictable, therefore undefinable. Language teachers were thus able, in deciding on both content and methodology, to wash their hands of the extremely difficult business of taking affective variables into account ... The importance of methodology in 'communicative' courses therefore tended to be downplayed in relation to content, with the result that methodology often turned out to be fairly traditional .... (1984: 31–2)

A number of trends have contributed to our current awareness of the role played by learners' subjective needs. One of these is humanistic language teaching's concern with the affective component in language learning. A very significant role has also been played by the learning strategy research of the 1970s and the subsequent work on learner training and learner autonomy. Nonetheless, the language teaching profession still has a fair way to go before it will be able to handle learners' subjective needs in anything like as systematic a manner as it can their objective needs.

Research into subjective needs in L2 teaching would seem, at the present time, to be faced with two main sets of priorities. The first is very basic indeed and relates to the establishment of a generally accepted categorisation (and the terminology which goes with it) of the various factors which may be considered as constitutive of learners' 'subjective' needs. The second is more directly pedagogical in nature, and involves the exploration of the ways in which subjective needs can best be accommodated in terms both of methodology and course design. 4.2 and 4.3 will relate to the first priority, and 4.4 and 4.5 to the second. Throughout, however, readers should be aware that they are faced with tentative attempts to formulate a perspective on a complex area of concern, one which raises a significant number of as yet unresolved questions of both a psychological and a pedagogic nature. Brindley's brief definition gives an indication of the difficulties involved in pinning down and dealing systematically with subjective needs. For Brindley, subjective needs are:

> ... the cognitive and affective needs of the learner in the learning situation, [and can be identified] from information about affective and cognitive factors such as personality, confidence, attitudes, learners' wants and expectations with regard to the learning of [the TL] and their individual cognitive style and learning strategies. (1989: 70)

This is quite a handful of variables. Furthermore, many of them, due to their affective or psychological origin, are far from easy to pin down and analyse in an unambiguous manner. And the combination of these factors, while it undeniably does influence language learning, produces an area of concern which is very complex. However, exploring the role of subjective needs in language learning should not be seen as having to produce a neat, flow-chart based set of procedures: It has far more to do with *the recognition and respect of human difference* and the attempt to work with this diversity in a flexible and constructive manner.

Before going further, however, it may be useful for readers to look at their own experience of language teaching from the point of view of subjective needs – even if the concept itself may still be rather vague. In the preparatory stages of a project on learning styles which will be examined in greater depth in 4.3, Willing (1988) investigated the attitudes of 40 teachers to subjective needs in their teaching. Willing identified the three types of response which are given below, though he does point out that it was only the first category of response that was explicitly espoused. The term 'learning style' is used as the main reference point in the three response types. The concept of learning style will be looked at further in 4.3; for the moment, however, it may be taken as referring to the combined effect of the poles of learner variance mentioned by Brindley above (personality, confidence, attitudes, wants and expectations with regard to the learning of the TL, cognitive style and learning strategies) insofar as they shape learners' preferred ways of learning a language.

REF. Think back to your own experience of learning a language in a formal setting and assess which of the three attitudes given below corresponds best to that held by those who taught you.

- Do not think only of the individual attitudes of one teacher or another; try also to assess the general climate with regard to students' subjective needs in the school, department, etc. in question.

Now look at your own attitudes and the approach to subjective needs which you adopt in your own teaching. Which of the three attitudes below corresponds most closely to your own?

---

1 *Learning style differences are important:*
  - Importance should be accorded to the psychosocial aspects of both learning and teaching. This involves sensitivity to factors such as shyness/self-confidence, introversion/extroversion, etc. that can influence learners' affective involvement in the process of language study. It also requires the teacher to consider factors such as the development of group dynamics and the means of catering for individual psychological needs.
  - The teacher should be flexible and responsive to learner preferences, even if this involves the use of teaching methods she may personally consider to be 'old-fashioned', which run counter to what she has learned or finds most appropriate.
  - The cultural element in language learning is very important and can exert an influence on learners' attitudes to the TL and also on their expectations as to the process of learning.
  - Allowance should also, however, be made for the teacher's own preferences, as the teacher, too, is a full participant in the teaching-

learning process. From the teacher's point of view, involvement in the methodology used is a source of energy.

2 *Learning style differences are not important:*
- There are a certain number of human characteristics that are shared by most (if not all) learners, and these are probably more powerful than the differences that may exist between them.
- There exists a given methodology [whichever one it may be for one teacher or another] which, as a result of the psychological model of learning upon which it is based and the activities by which it is realised, offers learners the best available means of learning a language.
- Individual learners may fit in with the method in question more or less closely, but slight mismatches between learner and method are likely to be outweighed by the positive effects of the method concerned. Furthermore, gently guiding learners to an appreciation of the advantages offered to them by a good method is ultimately in the learners' own best interest.

3 *Learning style differences exist (and may be important) but they are already adequately catered for:*
- If the teacher adopts a sufficiently varied and eclectic approach to her teaching (e.g. by using different techniques and teaching approaches) then, at the end of the day, most learners will be able to find something that suits them and 'things will balance out'.
- Teaching is an essentially intuitive activity. Learning style may well be important, and should be borne in mind by the teacher, but it is just *one* variable, and should not be seen as more important than others (such as motivation, for instance). Indeed it may be unrealistic to try to develop specific decision-making schemes with respect to differences in learning style, as there are simply too many variables involved (age; educational background; ability level; material constraints, etc.).
- Most teachers are already doing their best to accommodate learner differences on an intuitive, *ad hoc* basis: systematising this is probably unfeasible, and perhaps unnecessary.
(Adapted from Willing 1988: 21–6)

A brief word may be helpful at this stage to clarify the way in which three related terms (subjective needs, individual differences, and learning style) will be used in this chapter. *Subjective needs* will be taken as the umbrella term for what Widdowson (1981, op. cit.) refers to as 'process-oriented' needs, which are 'related to transitional behaviour, the means of learning'. The term is thus used in opposition to the objective or end-use related definition of needs. *Individual differences* will be taken to be those psychological or cognitive continua along which learners differ from one another, and which may have a bearing on their interaction with their language study. *Learning style* is seen as the combined result of variance on the range of psychological and cognitive factors falling under the heading of individual differences insofar as they influence learners' preferences for different study modes and activity types: learning style will thus be taken to be the tangible manifestation of individual differences. Other analyses of the relationship between individual differences and learning style are, however, possible.

4.2 Individual differences

This section will examine a number of individual differences which are likely to exert an influence on the way in which learners react to aspects of their language study, and which can shape their preferences with respect to the nature and organisation of learning activities. They are:

- introversion–extroversion
- tolerance of ambiguity and risk-taking
- anxiety and self-esteem
- cognitive style

Two main types of factor are at work in these variables, *psychosocial* and *cognitive*. The former relates to learners' psychological and affective reactions to the interpersonal aspects of language study; the latter relates to the way in which learners organise their experience of the world (in the present context, of language and of language learning) and how they prefer to learn. The distinction between these two categories, however, is far from cut-and-dried. The variables of introversion-extroversion, anxiety, and self-esteem would seem, without too many hesitations, to be psychosocial, and so might be risk-taking too. Cognitive style, by definition, is a cognitive factor. The case of tolerance of ambiguity is less clear, and may include both psychosocial and cognitive factors. Furthermore, the dividing line between certain individual differences can be blurred, and the relationship that exists between them is frequently complex.

In addition to definitional and relational problems of this nature, readers should be aware of the still uncertain nature of the profession's understanding of the whole area of individual differences. Our profession is involved in the process of developing the conceptual and terminological tools which will enable it to get to grips with the area of individual differences in a coherent manner. This is a courageous and worthwhile endeavour, and readers are asked to show tolerance for the ambiguities they are likely to encounter both in the literature at large and in the present author's attempts to present one view of this complex area of concern. Indeed, the treatment of individual differences presented in this section was prepared with two goals in mind. The first is to discuss *the main* variables that are likely to play a role in shaping learners' attitudes to and interaction with the process of language study, and thereby help teachers to understand better learners' reactions to what they may do as teachers. The second is to present *one* analysis of individual differences which readers may then refine and develop on the basis of further reading and of their interaction with their students. The analysis which follows will be largely based on Oxford and Ehrman (1993) and Skehan (1989).

4.2.1 Introversion–extroversion

This psychological variable is perhaps the most familiar one to be examined in this section, and readers will easily recognise the two sets of traits sketched by Eysenck:

> The typical extrovert is sociable, likes parties, has many friends, needs to have people to talk to, and does not like studying by himself. He craves excitement, takes chances, often sticks his neck out, acts on the spur of the moment, and is generally an impulsive individual. He ... always has a ready answer, and generally likes change ... The typical introvert, on the other hand, is a quiet, retiring sort of person, introspective, fond of books rather than people; he is reserved and distant, except with intimate friends. He tends to plan ahead ... and distrusts the impulse of the moment. He does not like excitement, takes matters of everyday life with proper seriousness, and likes a well ordered life ... (1965, cited in Skehan, op. cit.: 100)

These thumbnail sketches recall two of the sets of learning preferences identified by Wenden (1987) (2.5). Her 'use the language' type of learners favoured social contacts and the use of communicative situations as a means of learning; they valued practice, ideally by living in the TL community, and they were meaning-focused, with a high tolerance for error providing communication is not impeded. Learners who subscribed to a 'learn about the language' approach, on the other hand, favoured a more systematic form of learning, and gave priority to grammar and vocabulary; they (self-) monitored for accuracy and considered mental alertness and inquisitiveness to be valuable learning tools. This is not to say that Wenden's categories neatly correspond to extroversion and introversion, but parallels clearly exist.

Skehan (op. cit.: 101–6) makes an interesting comparison between the way in which introversion and extroversion tend to be viewed in general education, as opposed to L2 learning. Research in general education has indicated that extroverts 'underperform slightly' in comparison with introverts. In L2 research, however, Skehan observes that it is extroversion which has been taken to be 'the desirable end of the extroversion–introversion continuum', even if the research evidence in support of extroverts having an advantage in terms of language learning is far from conclusive. Skehan speaks of 'a fairly weak relationship which accounts for only a small proportion of the variance on criterion measures'. Skehan relates this favourable orientation towards extrovert traits to the learning-by-using-the-language theory of learning which underpinned the development of CLT. Within this perspective, the trait of sociability which is characteristic of extroverts makes them more inclined to talk, join groups, participate in class, volunteer and engage in practice activities, and maximise language use opportunities outside of the class-room by using language for communication. In other words, extroverts' greater *sociability* predisposes them towards the type of learning activities frequently favoured in CLT, which has been for some time, and still is, the dominant paradigm in language teaching. The relatively more favourable light in which extroversion has been seen in recent writing on language teaching may thus be the result of a methodological preference within our profession rather than an objective advantage in language learning terms. Teachers should be cautious about such method-based judgements on learning, which can interfere with their ability to interact with students in an open-minded manner.

On the basis of both research and everyday experience, introversion–extroversion does seem to be a psychological variable which can exercise an influence on interactional preferences and learning behaviours. However, it is just one variable, and its visible manifestations may be the result either of an inherent psychological trait or of other indirectly causative factors. Consequently, it would probably be unwise to interpret learner behaviour, even those aspects of it which might seem to be typically related to introversion–extroversion, exclusively around this one variable.

4.2.2 Tolerance of ambiguity and risk-taking

These two variables do not constitute a single psychological trait. Both, however, are likely to influence learners' reactions to the uncertainties inherent in language learning, and it is for this reason that they will be looked at together.

Oxford and Ehrman (op. cit.: 195) define tolerance of ambiguity as 'the acceptance of confusing situations', and point out that '[as] L2 learning is fraught with uncertainty about meanings, referents, and pronunciation, ... a degree of ambiguity tolerance is essential for language learners'. Manifestly, a learner who has no tolerance of ambiguity, and who rejects risk-taking, will either give up completely or will at least experience considerable discomfort in studying an L2, especially in the early stages of learning: such a learner would probably feel at ease only within a highly controlled and sequenced approach to learning. At the same time, too great a tolerance for ambiguity is likely to block progress beyond a relatively imprecise mastery of the TL.

Tolerance of ambiguity is closely related to the psychological trait of orientation to closure, which Oxford and Ehrman define as 'the degree to which the person needs to reach decisions or clarity'. These authors provide two profiles of the learning preferences of students more and less oriented towards closure:

> Students *oriented toward closure* are hard-working, organized and planful, and have a strong need for clarity. They want lesson directions and grammar rules to be clearly spelled out. Such students avoid spontaneous conversations and games in the L2 classroom – unless, of course, they have had adequate time to use metacognitive strategies such as preparing their vocabulary lists and reviewing the rules involved in any given interaction. [...]
>
> Students *less oriented to closure* are sometimes known as 'open learners'. They take L2 learning less seriously, treating it like a game to be enjoyed rather than a set of tasks to be completed and judged, and they avoid too much planning and preparation. Because of their relaxed attitude, open learners ... have been shown to be less dependent on the curriculum and the quality of the syllabus than more closure-oriented learners.
>
> (Op. cit.: 197–8) (Original emphasis)

These poles of learning preference share certain common features with the introversion–extroversion continuum. Learners oriented towards closure manifest the concern with analysis and order, and the avoidance of spontaneity which is taken to be characteristic of introverts. Learners less oriented towards closure manifest the more relaxed or even playful attitude to learning which is generally associated with extroverts. At the same time, the variable of orientation to closure would seem to contain a component that relates to self-directiveness in a manner which does not wholly tie in with the introversion–extroversion variable: learners less oriented towards closure show a self-organisational or self-directive trait, something that would normally be associated with introversion, whereas their activity preferences are closer to these of extroverts. This points, in part, to the complexity and interrelatedness of the factors which fall under the general heading of 'individual differences'; it also, perhaps, says something about the developmental nature of our current understanding of the subjective side of language learning. Most teachers, however, will recognise the psychological reality of the learning preferences outlined by Oxford and Ehrman, and the ways in which they can influence learners' interaction with different methodological approaches and learning activities.

The precise relationship between risk-taking and orientation to closure is unclear, though a link would seem to exist, with learners more oriented towards closure probably being less risk-oriented. In recent language learning research, high risk-taking, like extroversion, has tended to be viewed in positive terms, and presumably for very much the same reasons, namely that it fosters language use. There is undeniably something to this: a rejection of risk-taking is likely to limit learners' exploration of the TL and make them avoid potentially productive learning opportunities. This is probably an oversimplification, however. Skehan (op. cit.: 106), for instance, suggests that, other factors being equal, more successful learners are those who view learning tasks as 'medium-risk, and achievable'. The idea here is that if a task is seen as high-risk, discouragement and possibly avoidance may result; if, on the other hand, the task is seen as low-risk there may be an absence of challenge, resulting in inadequate involvement.

Ely (1986) found that risk-taking was positively linked to classroom participation, and therefore served a facilitating role in at least this aspect of language learning. However, Ely observed a negative relationship between risk–taking and what he terms Language Class Discomfort ('the degree of anxiety, self-consciousness, or embarrassment felt when speaking the L2 in the classroom'). Ely concludes from this that:

> ... simply exhorting students to take more risks and participate more may not be effective. Apparently, before students can be expected to take linguistic risks, they must be made to feel psychologically comfortable and safe in their learning environment. (Op. cit.: 3)

These are very sensible observations, as they place one specific behavioural trait, risk-taking, within the broader context of learners' affective involvement in their language study. Furthermore, they suggest that a given behaviour (e.g. 'excessive' risk avoidance) should not be evaluated in isolation, but as an indication of other, and possibly more significant affective factors.

4.2.3   Anxiety and self-esteem

There is no necessary link between an individual's feelings of self-esteem and the presence of anxiety, neither in life in general nor within the context of language study. Nonetheless, it is generally accepted that certain aspects of language learning can generate anxiety. Furthermore, for certain individuals at least, language learning (particularly in the early stages) may be perceived as threatening to their self-esteem, and may therefore give rise to negative feelings, of which a debilitating form of anxiety can be one. For this reason, it may be helpful to look first at self-esteem.

Oxford and Ehrman (op. cit.: 194–5) define self-esteem as 'a self-judgement of worth or value based on feelings of "efficacy", a sense of interacting effectively with one's own environment'. They then distinguish between *global* and *situational* self-esteem. The former is based on 'self-perceptions of competence in various broad areas, such as academics, athletics, social interaction, physical appearance, and conduct … [and] a personal assessment of the importance of each of these areas'. Situational self-esteem, on the other hand, is 'a much more specific state of efficacy relating to a specific situation, event, or activity type. [For example] a person can feel good about himself or herself globally yet at the same time experience low self-esteem in a particular situation or environment.' Situational self-esteem is probably the more relevant of the two concepts in terms of language learning, though global self-esteem may also play a role: for example, a learner with low global self-esteem may enter his language study with apprehensions or negative expectations based on previous perceptions of failure, or may deliberately set low achievement targets (2.4).

The process of learning a language can negatively affect learners' self-esteem in at least two main ways. One derives from a perceived loss in 'efficacy' resulting from a sudden inability to express oneself with the clarity, confidence or authority to which one is accustomed. Spolsky (1989: 114) expresses this as 'the threat to a person's self-concept in being forced to communicate with less proficiency in the second language than he or she has in the first'. The other relates to what may be perceived as a loss in social prestige, or at least a shift in social role, as the result of finding oneself in the position of a (not yet 'successful') language learner: this is more likely to be felt by adults accustomed to playing a more or less authoritative social role, or learners whose culture attaches importance to the maintenance of 'face' or to the projection of a social persona based on control and/or authority. Not all learners, of course, perceive language learning in either of these ways. Teachers do, however, need to recognise that learning a language, especially in the early stages, restricts learners' normal expressive abilities and, thereby, their ability to 'be themselves' and project their usual social persona, all of which may, in certain individuals, produce negative affective reactions either towards the L2 or to aspects of the learning situation.

Anxiety is one of the more complex and elusive affective variables in L2 learning, as Scovel indicates:

> The research into the relationship of anxiety to foreign language learning has provided mixed and confusing results, immediately suggesting that anxiety itself is neither a simple nor well-understood psychological construct and that it is perhaps premature to attempt to relate it to the global and comparative task of language acquisition. (1978: 132)

One distinction that is frequently made in the literature is between facilitating and debilitating anxiety, which Scovel describes in terms of the 'fight or flight' syndrome:

> Facilitating anxiety motivates the learner to 'fight' the new learning task; it gears the learner emotionally for approach behaviour. Debilitating anxiety, in contrast, motivates the learner to 'flee' the new learning task; it stimulates the individual emotionally to adopt avoidance behaviour. (Op. cit.: 139)

One cannot help wondering whether 'facilitating anxiety' is an appropriate term. Scovel's outline makes it look very much like motivation or desire for achievement combined with a burst of task-oriented effort: these are undeniably necessary for success, but it is less clear whether the term 'facilitating anxiety' captures the essence of the process in the most insightful manner. Indeed, Horwitz (1990) suggests that facilitating anxiety plays a role only in relatively constrained learning tasks, and thus questions whether it is a concept that has very much relevance within the wider context of language learning. The same, regrettably, cannot be said of debilitating anxiety, i.e. a state of apprehension and fear which can block positive learning behaviours in a variety of ways from a reluctance to participate in classroom activities to an avoidance of language learning altogether.

Another distinction in this area is between trait and state anxiety. *Trait anxiety* is a deeply ingrained and relatively stable aspect of the individual's personality and characterises individuals whose overall approach to life is fearful or apprehensive; *state anxiety* is transitory, and arises out of a specific situation or event, and may be triggered by a variety of factors from speaking in public to examinations. The trait vs. state distinction is well-established in the literature and is perceptible in everyday life: how many readers, even those who are relatively 'relaxed' in general terms, do not experience more or less intense anxiety in one situation or another – climbing a ladder, working on computers, speaking in front of a large audience, etc.? The problem for the teacher, however, is to decide whether anxious behaviour is a result of an underlying personality trait (the learner in question is a 'worrier' and is simply transferring his habitual anxiety into his language learning), or whether it is being triggered by specific aspects of the language learning situation. Anxiety can manifest itself in a variety of ways – absence from class when the learner has to speak or 'perform' in some way, reluctance to contribute to class interaction, excessive concern with detail, overboisterousness, complaints about teaching materials or facilities, blushing, nervous gestures such as coughing prior to turn-taking, etc.

Skehan (op. cit: 116–18) criticises the general drift of research on anxiety in L2 learning for being 'simplistic' and 'rather narrow in focus' and makes two recommendations for future research. These are also of relevance to teachers wishing to get to grips with what they perceive as anxious behaviour in their students. The first recommendation is that anxiety be analysed in a situation-specific manner, in other words, that teachers should evaluate the ways in which specific learning situations or tasks may cause anxiety. Skehan's second recommendation is that 'a more ethnographic perspective' should be adopted, one that might help to produce 'a clear understanding of such issues as the role of "face" in the development of anxiety'. This would involve questions of cultural expectations as to the nature of language study and of the roles of teachers and learners, as well as a variety of both individual and culturally-based questions of self-concept (5.3). It would also need to take account of possible mismatches between learners' cognitive style or learning preferences and the methodology being used, and evaluate the affective reactions which this might give rise to.

4.2.4 Cognitive style

Cognitive style differs from the other variables surveyed in this section in that it relates less to learners' affective and psychosocial involvement in the learning process than to their habitual modes of processing information and, in a general sense, of organising their perceptions of and interaction with their environment. Kachru defines cognitive style as:

... a hypothetical construct that refers to the characteristic ways in which individuals conceptually organise the environment; that is, 'cognitive style' refers to ways in which individuals filter and process stimuli so that the environment takes on psychological meaning. It also refers to consistencies in individual modes of functioning in a variety of behavioral situations. (1988: 152)

This definition shows that the term 'cognitive style' is used to refer to a very complex set of processes. A number of bipolar scales have been put forward in the attempt to capture the main axis along which individuals differ from one another in terms of their cognitive functioning. Willing, for instance, lists the following:

simultaneous/synthetic	– sequential/successive
holist	– serialist
impulsive/global	– analytic/reflective
holistic	– analytical

(1988: 41)

Another axis of variance that has received attention in recent years is the relative dominance of the right versus the left hemisphere of the brain. Neurological research has indicated that the left hemisphere is specialised in 'logical, analytical, linear information-processing', while the right hemisphere is specialised in 'synthetic, holistic, imagistic information-processing' (Hartnett 1981; cited in Willing, op. cit.: 146). In terms of language learning, Kachru (op. cit.: 153) suggests that individuals who rely more on left hemisphere processing are better at tasks such as 'producing separate words, gathering specifics of languages, carrying out sequences of operations, classifying and labelling items, etc., while right hemisphere dominant learners are better at 'dealing with language as a whole and show more sensitivity to emotional reactions, metaphors, artistic experiences, etc.'.

The cognitive variable which has received the most attention over the last two decades is field dependence-field independence (FD–FI). This distinction was originally developed by Witkin and a few colleagues (cf. Witkin 1965; Witkin *et al.* 1977) in relation to visual perception. Witkin and his associates developed the Embedded Figures Test, where subjects are asked to identify geometrical shapes embedded within more complex patterns: the task thus monitors for the ability to separate out a given element from its environment (or 'field'). Individuals who perform well on this task are taken as being analytic and able to distinguish the essential from the non-essential, and are referred to as FI; individuals who perform less well, i.e. those who are less able to 'free themselves' from the environment in which the target shape occurs, are taken as having a more globalistic and undifferentiating way of perceiving reality, and are referred to as FD. Berry (1981, cited in Willing 1988: 41–2) suggests that the key element in the FI–FD variable is 'the extent of autonomous functioning', in other words 'whether an individual characteristically relies on the external environment as a given, in contrast to working on it'. FD individuals tend to 'see the world as an unanalysed whole' (Skehan, op. cit.: 111), whereas FI individuals are more inclined to 'work on' their environment in an analytic and self-directive manner.

Few individuals are wholly FD or wholly FI in their manner of interacting with their environment; nor will a given individual's behaviour be equally 'field dependent' or 'independent' in all situations. Berry suggests that most people are able to shift their mode of functioning along the FI–FD continuum as the situation or task at hand seems to require: an individual who is very FI in one domain of activity may thus be relatively more FD in another. Nonetheless, most people's behaviour would seem to be marked by a reasonably stable general preference along this continuum.

The FI–FD distinction was originally developed to encapsulate a certain dimension of cognitive style as understood in a relatively narrow sense. Over time, however, it has come to be applied to a much wider range of behavioural preferences, many of an interpersonal or psychosocial nature. Willing (op. cit.: 43) observes that field dependence-independence is nowadays viewed as 'a pervasive dimension of individual functioning, [which shows itself] in the perceptual, intellectual, personality and social domains'. Inevitably, then, the implications of the FI–FD distinction came to be studied with respect to language learning preferences. This is illustrated in Figure 8, which lists the behavioural preferences of FI and FD individuals (Willing glosses FI and FD with the more transparent terms 'analytical' and 'concrete' respectively). Differences along this continuum are likely to exert a significant influence on the way in which learners react to the structuring of learning materials and activities, and also on their preferences in terms of teacher-student roles and group dynamics. Readers will also note that Willing's analysis of the preferred mode of functioning of FI and FD learners subsumes a number of the traits characteristic of other individual differences that have been surveyed in this section, in particular introversion–extroversion, tolerance of ambiguity and risk-taking. In other words, Willing sees the FI–FD distinction as having a powerful explanatory role in the analysis of learning behaviours.

Analytical (Field Independent)	Concrete (Field Dependent)
Information Processing	
1 this person finds it relatively easy to detach an experienced (perceived) item from its given background	1 this person experiences an item as fused with its context; what is interesting is the impression of the whole
2 the item is extractable because it is perceived as having a rudimentary meaning on its own; thus it can be moved out of its presented surroundings and into a comprehensive category system – for understanding (and 'filing' in memory)	2 item is experienced and comprehended as part of an overall associational unity with concrete and personal interconnections; (item's storage in, and retrieval from, memory is via these often affectively-charged associations)
3 tendency to show traits of introversion (the person's mental processing can be strongly activated by low-intensity stimulus; hence dislikes excessive input)	3 tendency to show traits of extroversion (person's mental processing is activated by relatively higher-intensity stimulus; therefore likes rich, varied input)
4 tendency to be 'reflective' and cautious in thinking tasks	4 tendency to be 'impulsive' in thinking tasks; 'plays hunches'
5 any creativity or unconventionality would derive from individual's development of criteria on a rational basis	5 any creativity or unconventionality would derive from individual's imaginativeness or 'lateral thinking'
Learning Strengths	
6 performs best on analytical language tasks (e.g. understanding and using correct syntactical structures; semantically ordered comprehension of words, phonetic articulation)	6 performs best on tasks calling for intuitive 'feel' for language (e.g. expression; richness of lexical connotation; discourse; rhythm and intonation)
7 favours material tending toward the abstract and impersonal; factual or analytical; useful; ideas	7 prefers material which has a human, social context; or which has fantasy or humour; personal; musical; artistic
8 has affinity for methods which are focused; systematic; sequential; cumulative	8 has affinity for methods in which various features are managed simultaneously; realistically; in significant context
9 likely to set own learning goals and direct own learning; but may well choose or prefer to use – for own purpose – an authoritative text or passive lecture situation	9 less likely to direct own learning, may function well in quasi-autonomy (e.g. 'guided discovery') (but may well express preference for a formal, teacher-dominated learning arrangement, as a compensation for own perceived deficiency in ability to structure)
10 'left hemisphere strengths'	10 'right hemisphere strengths'

Human Relations

11 greater tendency to experience self as a separate entity; with also a great deal of internal differentiation and complexity

11 tendency to experience and relate not a completely differentiated 'self', but rather as – to a degree – fused with group and with environment

12 personal identity and social role to a large extent self-defined

12 greater tendency to defer to social group for identity and role-definition

13 more tendency to be occupied with own thoughts and responses; relatively unaware of the subtle emotional content in interpersonal interactions

13 more other-oriented (e.g. looking at and scrutinizing others' faces; usually very aware of others' feelings in an interaction; sensitive to 'cues')

14 relatively less need to be with people

14 greater desire to be with people

15 self-esteem not ultimately dependent upon the opinion of others

15 learning performance much improved if group or authority figure give praise

Figure 8 Contrasts of the two poles of field independence and field dependence (taken from Willing 1988: 50–1)

REF. Select two or three learning tasks that you have undertaken (or in which you are currently involved) as a learner. Do not think only of language study: the more varied the target activities are (computer programming, horse-riding, carpentry, etc.), the more insights you are likely to obtain. Then, analyse your subjective interaction with each of these learning tasks in terms of the four sets of individual differences surveyed above, i.e.

– introversion–extroversion
– tolerance of ambiguity and risk-taking
– anxiety and self-esteem
– cognitive style, in particular the FI–FD distinction

• Which insights does this give you into the ways in which these differences can influence language learning?
• In which way(s) could you incorporate these insights into your teaching, and in which way(s) might this help you to enhance the learning experience of your students?

4.3 Learning style

The individual differences surveyed in the last section are all likely to influence the way in which learners interact with the process of language study. However, it would be unproductive to construct a pedagogical approach wholly around any one of these differences, even if each may play its role and needs therefore be borne in mind. It is essentially for this reason that researchers have endeavoured to find a single tool for getting to grips with learners' psychosocial and cognitive involvement in their language study. It is with this goal in mind that the construct of *learning style* has been developed. Oxford and Ehrman cite two useful definitions of this construct:

> Learning style consists of distinct behaviours which serve as indicators of how a person learns from and interacts with his [or her] environment. (Gregoire 1979: 234 cited in Oxford and Ehrman, op. cit.: 196)

> Essentially, learning style can be defined as a consistent pattern of behaviour but with a certain range of individual variability ... Styles then are overall patterns that give general direction to learning behaviour. (Cornett 1983: 9 cited in Oxford and Ehrman, op. cit.: 196)

For Willing, learning style is:

> ... a notion of inherent, pervasive sets of characteristics which group people into types or place an individual at a particular point along a descriptive scale ... Learning style is [more concrete than cognitive style], in that it looks directly at the totality of psychological functioning as this affects learning. (Op. cit.: 52)

Learning style is thus a very powerful concept which incorporates a wide range of both psychosocial and cognitive variables and seeks to encapsulate the way in which these are translated into concrete learning behaviours and preferences. In addition to the psychosocial and cognitive factors already considered, learning style would also seem to include a sensory preference variable. Oxford and Ehrman (op. cit.: 196–7) list three categories of sensory preference – visual, auditory, and hands-on. *Visual* learners prefer to read and, in wider terms, to obtain information by means of visual stimulus provided by film, posters, charts, etc.; such learners may find lectures, discussions or oral directions without any visual back-up to be difficult to follow or anxiety-producing. *Auditory* learners, by contrast, can do without visual support quite easily, and therefore tend to enjoy lectures and conversations; they react well to class activities such as role play or discussion, but may experience difficulties with written work. *Hands-on* learners, as the term implies, enjoy a lot of movement and activity within their learning environment, and they react well to working with tangible objects; perhaps not surprisingly, such learners may react negatively to long periods behind a desk and may seem dependent on a lot of variety and direct stimulus.

The combination of these three sets of variables (i.e. an individual's psychosocial, cognitive and sensory characteristics) goes to produce a set of preferred modes of behaviour which may be described as the individual's learning style. Learning style is therefore a practically-oriented construct: it is based less on a relational or causative analysis of the way in which an individual's psychosocial, cognitive or sensory characteristics produce a given set of behaviours, but rather on the analysis and grouping of *observed behavioural preferences*. The main goal of research into learning style is to help teachers to get to grips with their students' learning behaviours around a finite number of poles of difference, and thereby to be better able to respond to learners' subjective needs in an informed manner. It also, of course, seeks to generalise among both teachers *and* learners a fuller understanding of what language learning is and can be.

One of the most thorough investigations of L2 learning styles to date is that conducted by the Adult Migrant Education Service (AMES) in New South Wales (reported in Willing 1988). The AMES survey is particularly valuable for a number of reasons. The first is the very thorough preparation of the survey in both theoretical and methodological terms. The second is the substantial number of subjects involved – 517 migrant learners of English in Australia on whom an impressive amount of biographical data was gathered. Thirdly, the subjects came from a wide range of ethnic, social and educational backgrounds: this means that the data gathered is far richer than would have been the case had the subjects been drawn from a single population whose learning style preferences might have been pre-constrained by a given ethnic and/or educational culture. The survey was constructed primarily around a questionnaire consisting of 30 questions relating to learning style and 15 questions on learning strategies: the discussion which follows will make reference only to the first part of the questionnaire. The development of the questions was strongly influenced by the FI–FD, or analytical vs. concrete modes of functioning (cf. Figure 8, above). The learning style questionnaire itself (Willing, op. cit.: 106–7) was made up of statements of learning preference with four graded response types. The 30 questions relate to six aspects of language study. Questions 1–7 deal with preferred classroom activities; 8–12 with teacher behaviour, 13–17 with the interpersonal aspects of learning, 18–20 with those aspects of language subjects most enjoyed working on, 21–23 relate to sensory preferences, and 24–30 to self-initiated learning activities outside the classroom.

Analysis of the subjects' responses (cf. Willing, op. cit.: 152–62) yielded four categories of learning style, which are given in Figure 9 together with the six questions which clustered most closely around each of the poles of response. The results confirm the presence of the 'analytical' and 'concrete' categories predicted on the basis of FI–FD distinction which had underpinned the preparation of the questionnaire. However, these two categories accounted for only about 10 per cent of the subject population each. The other two categories which emerged, 'communicative' and 'authority-oriented', accounted for about 40 per cent and 30 per cent of the population, respectively.

'Analytical' and 'concrete' learners manifest what Willing describes as FI or FD traits 'in the classic sense' (cf. Figure 8, above). '*Analytical*' learners show a preference for analysis and an interest in working out structure from data, but they are keen on doing this alone, or autonomously. Such learners tend to be (or, at least, behave as if they are) relatively unemotional, with a greater interest in objective tasks or achievement than in other people. '*Concrete*' learners, on the other hand, process data in a more direct, media dependent manner. They also have a stronger people-orientation, though Willing suggests that this expresses itself in a 'spontaneous, unpremeditated' way (e.g. interest in games and excursions) or in close interaction (pair work), rather than around organised class discussion. These learners show imagination and the ability to react creatively to practical situations; they also tend to have a spontaneous, here-and-now approach to their learning.

The '*communicative*' category accounted for the largest number of subjects (40 per cent). 'Communicative' learners see the TL as something living, and seek out learning opportunities in their immediate environment – the media, everyday encounters in shops or on public transport, or simply in verbal interaction with TL speakers. This learning style is reminiscent of Wenden's (1987) 'use the language' type of learner (2.5), and also of the strategies described in the case study 'Beginning Macedonian' at the end of Chapter 6. One might imagine that 'communicative' learners would in the main be FD individuals with a strongly 'concrete' perspective on learning. This would seem not to be the case, however. Willing points out that many 'communicative' learners have a strong FI tendency, but feel that their learning goals can best be achieved by adopting a context-sensitive approach to their learning. In other words, many FI learners seem to have decided that people-orientation and social emphasis in the choice of learning opportunities are the most effective means of attaining their learning goals. The presence of FI individuals in this category is perhaps not as surprising as it might at first seem. Most of their preferred activities involve autonomous processing of data and organisation of learning points, which involves the self-directive approach to learning which is generally taken to be characteristic of FI individuals.

The fourth category of learning style was referred to as '*authority-oriented*', and the reason for this choice of title is relatively transparent from the subjects' preferred activities. Willing suggests that many 'authority-oriented' learners are more FD and, thereby, less disposed to organising information spontaneously, while at the same time perceiving the need for some such structuring. Faced with this dilemma, these learners may look for structuring of information and of learning points 'elsewhere', in the teacher or in an approved textbook. Paradoxically, with the emphasis they place on structure, 'authority-oriented' learners show a typical FI trait, but pursue this in a manner which is more FD. 'Authority-oriented' learners are likely to feel at home in a relatively traditional classroom setting, with the teacher as the authority figure and a clearly structured and sequential approach to language study.

'Analytical'

Q18	I like to study grammar.
Q27	At home, I like to learn by studying English books.
Q13	I like to study English by myself (alone).
Q12	I like the teacher to let me find my mistakes.
Q9	I like the teacher to give us problems to work on.
Q24	At home, I like to learn by reading newspapers, etc.

'Concrete'

Q3	In class, I like to learn by games.
Q5	In class, I like to learn by pictures, films, video.
Q14	I like to learn English by talking in pairs.
Q26	At home, I like to learn by using cassettes.
Q2	In class, I like to listen and use cassettes.
Q17	I like to go out with the class and practise English.

'Communicative'

Q29	I like to learn by watching, listening to Australians.
Q28	I like to learn by talking to friends in English.
Q25	At home, I like to learn by watching TV in English.
Q30	I like to learn English in shops/CES/trains.
Q22	I like to learn English words by *hearing* them.
Q4	In class, I like to learn by conversations.

'Authority-oriented'

Q8	I like the teacher to explain everything to us.
Q6	I want to write everything in my notebook.
Q7	I like to have my own textbook.
Q1	In English class, I like to learn by reading.
Q18	I like to study grammar.
Q21	I like to learn English words by *seeing* them.

Figure 9 Willing's four learning styles and the most popular activities per style (taken from Willing 1988: 156, 158, 160, 162)

Willing interprets these results in terms of an interaction between the FI–FD variable and personality variable of activity ('self-directing autonomy') vs. passivity ('going with the flow'). Thus, while FI individuals generally show less interest in other people, if a FI learner perceives social interaction and/or attention to the social context to be the best way of achieving his learning goals, he will exploit these learning opportunities in a systematic and self-directive manner. The product of this approach is the 'communicative' learning style. Similarly, if FD individuals perceive a need for structure in their language study, they are likely to look for it outside themselves by relying on the teacher's judgements, an authoritative textbook or an approved method. The end-result in this case is the 'authority-oriented' learning style.

The four categories of learning style which emerged from the AMES survey have a ring of intuitive plausibility that many teachers will recognise; they also provide an interpretive framework which casts light on a number of aspects of the learning behaviours teachers are likely to observe in their classrooms. Willing's interpretation of the results in terms of an interaction between the FI–FD and activity-passivity variables also provides an interesting perspective on learning style preferences, though it should not obscure the role that may be played by other factors. For instance, to what extent might a limited tolerance for ambiguity, prior learning experiences and/or culturally-based beliefs about the nature of language learning and the roles of teachers and learners predispose learners towards 'authority-oriented' learning style? There is no general answer to these questions, or to the many others that may arise. They need, however, to be borne in mind if the nature and origin of learners' preferences are to be better understood – by the teacher, of course, but also by the learners themselves.

REF. Analyse your own approach to language learning in the light of Willing's four categories of learning style. Which type of learner are you?

- If you have learned two or more languages, compare your approach to learning in these languages. Did your preferred learning style remain the same, or were there differences? If differences emerge analyse them in terms of the context of learning and the learning opportunities available, your learning goals and attitude to the TL, your age and maturity . . . or whatever else may strike you as relevant.
- Alternatively, interview one or two learners with the same goal in mind.
- Does this leave you feeling satisfied with Willing's four categories? List any reservations you may have and try to explain their cause.

4.4 Methodology and learning style

The recognition of the importance of learners' subjective needs implies a number of changes in the traditional approach to decision-making on the methodological level. The first, of course, is the willingness to re-think the planning and implementation of methodology in response to learners' subjective needs – which can be more complex than might be imagined at first sight. The second is to undertake an analysis of teaching methodology in terms of the learning style assumptions which underlie different approaches, materials or techniques, and also to explore the role played in teaching by the in-built agenda and beliefs (whether these are explicitly stated or not) of the teacher herself.

Richards and Rodgers (1986, cf. in particular pp. 14–30) analyse teaching methods (they use 'method' as a superordinate term, and not, therefore, in the restrictive sense in which it is used by Allwright 1991, cited in 1.4) under the three headings of 'approach', 'design' and 'procedure', as indicated in Figure 10.

The first level, *approach*, deals with the theoretical considerations or premises which underlie the next two levels. This involves a *theory of language*, i.e. the theoretical perspective on language itself and on the nature of language proficiency, and a *theory of language learning*, i.e. the cognitive and psycholinguistic processes that are posited to underpin language learning, and the conditions under which these learning processes can best be activated.

The second level, *design*, deals with the decisions that are required in order to construct a coherent instructional system capable of realising the theoretical perspectives present at the *approach* level. Richards and Rodgers suggest six *design* categories. *Objectives* are the detailed specification of the learning goals which arise out of the basic theoretical premises found at *approach* level. This may involve emphasis being given to communicative, message-based fluency versus structural accuracy, or the gearing of course objectives around a given language skill or the development of a certain learning capacity (cf. Ellis and Sinclair's *Learning to Learn English*, as an instance of the latter). *Syllabus construction* relates to the choice and organisation of content, which is generally apparent if one looks at the contents page of a coursebook: for example, are the component parts of the course expressed in terms of grammatical structures, language functions, different reading skills, or in terms of situationally-constrained tasks such as 'negotiating' or 'business letter writing'? Decisions regarding *objectives* and *syllabus organisation* are then realised by means of specific choices with regard to the *types of learning and teaching activities* selected e.g. structured dialogues + pattern practice; information transfer activities; role simula-

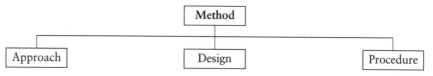

a *A theory of the nature of language*
  – an account of the nature of language proficiency
  – an account of the basic units of language structure
b *A theory of the nature of language learning*
  – an account of the psycho-linguistic and cognitive process involved in language learning
  – an account of the conditions that allow for successful use of these processes

a *The general and specific objectives of the method*
b *A syllabus model*
  – criteria for the selection and organisation of linguistic and/or subject-matter content
c *Types of learning and teaching activities*
  – kinds of tasks and practice activities to be employed in the classroom and in materials
d *Learner roles*
  – types of learning tasks set for learners
  – degree of control learners have over the content of learning
  – patterns of learner groupings that are recommended or implied
  – degree to which learners influence the learning of others
  – the view of the learner as a processor, performer, initiator, problem solver, etc.
e *Teacher roles*
  – types of functions teachers fulfil
  – degree of teacher influence over learning
  – degree to which the teacher determines the content of learning
  – types of interaction between teachers and learners
f *The role of instructional materials*
  – primary function of materials
  – the form materials take (e.g. textbook, audiovisual)
  – relation of materials to other input
  – assumptions made about teachers and learners

a *Classroom techniques, practices, and behaviours observed when the method is used*
  – resources in terms of time, space, and equipment used by the teacher
  – interactional patterns observed in lessons
  – tactics and strategies used by teachers and learners when the method is being used

Figure 10 A framework for the analysis of teaching methodology
(taken from Richards and Rodgers 1986: 28)

tions, etc.), the *roles played by learners and teachers* (e.g. is the teacher an 'expert' guiding 'apprentice' learners towards mastery of the language code, or is she an activity animator with learners acting as 'meaning-discoverers'?), and also the *role of instructional materials* (e.g. clear presentation and controlled practice of target structures, stimulus to fluency practice, input to meaning discovery, strategy-based self-discovery, etc.).

According to Richards and Rodgers, the third level of analysis, *procedure*:

> encompasses the actual moment-to-moment techniques, prac-
> tices, and behaviours that operate in teaching a language
> according to a given approach. It is the level at which we
> describe how a method realises its approach and design in
> classroom behaviour. (Op. cit.: 26)

This level relates to the practical means by which teaching points are presented, practice is organised, and feedback provided. Many basic teacher training courses focus primarily on this level of teaching practice.

Richards and Rodgers acknowledge that methodological development does not always take place in a 'rational' manner, from approach through design to procedure: a teacher or researcher may, for instance, develop a set of teaching procedures and only then systematise them 'upwards'. The key point in Richards and Rodgers' model, however, is that virtually no choice is neutral or without a principled relationship to other levels of decision-making. Consequently, opting for a given activity type, form of teacher-learner relationships or of classroom dynamics has implications at the *approach* level, and is thus based on some underlying belief system about the nature of language and of language learning – whether this is explicitly formulated or not. It also, as a consequence of this, has implications in terms of the approach to learning (or learning style) which will be favoured by the pedagogical choice in question.

The 'method' variable, then, plays a very important role in deter-mining what goes on in the classroom. It would, however, be naive to assume that this is the only factor in operation. As Prabhu points out:

> What a teacher does in the classroom is not solely, or even
> primarily, determined by the teaching method he or she intends
> to follow. There is a complex of other forces at play, in varied
> forms and degrees. (1987: 103)

What actually happens in the classroom (excluding for the moment the contribution of the learners themselves) is thus an interaction of the teaching method which is officially being used and the individual teacher's interpretation of this method. In a very real sense, a method is always realised via the 'processing system' of the individual teacher. It is through this processing system that a given method is, in the first instance, understood and interpreted by the teacher; and only then is it implemented in the classroom. The teacher's processing system thus acts as a filter between the theoretical relationships present in Richards and Rodgers' model and what she actually does in the classroom. Four sets of factors are likely to influence the nature of a teacher's processing system.

The first of these is the degree of (mis)match between the teacher's own beliefs (or 'theory') about language and language learning and those implicit in the method she is dealing with. If divergences exist at the *approach* level, the teacher is likely to feel ill at ease with various *design* and *procedure* level decisions, and may well modify these in the direction of what she feels that language learning 'is really about'. This may, in part, be related to the teacher's professional awareness: the broader her perspective on language teaching the easier it should be for her to recognise the theoretical assumptions which underpin a given method, to agree to differ, but nonetheless to work constructively within the approach to language learning implicit within the method in question.

The second element derives from the teacher's affective reactions to the method, which may be either positive or negative. A given method may, for instance, activate negative feelings linked to the teacher's own language learning experience, or possibly to unpleasant experiences in her training period or early in her career. The opposite is equally possible, and the teacher may feel loyalty and affection towards a mode of learning which she enjoyed and which has served her well and/or has generated good results earlier in her career. Under this heading, it may also be necessary to take account of affective reactions to the decision-making processes by which a method has been selected (or perhaps 'imposed') by institutional or educational authorities. Feelings of resentment or disempowerment with respect to the hierarchical side of method selection are unlikely to predispose the teacher positively to the method in question.

The third element, and that which is perhaps the most complex of all, relates to the interaction between the teacher's own psychosocial and cognitive traits and those which are implicitly favoured by the method. (Mis)matches of this nature can arise on a number of *design* level choices, and also with a variety of *procedure* level practices. Brumfit (1991: 141) points out that teachers, too, are participants in the 'micro-social context' of the classroom, and changes in, for instance, teacher-learner roles affect the teacher as much as the learners. *Design* level choices in this respect can make teachers feel they have forfeited part of their authority and social prestige; they might also, however, seem to force the teacher into a directive or authoritative role she disapproves of or feels ill at ease with (for either ideological or psychosocial reasons). Also, *procedure* level practices that require the teacher to react to learner needs and demands in an unprepared, *ad hoc* manner can place strains on teachers who have a strong orientation to closure or low tolerance of ambiguity as a personality trait. Such teaching procedures can be particularly stressful for non-native teachers who may feel less confident about their ability to provide answers spontaneously, and who may thus fear a loss of face. The teacher, as well as learners, has subjective needs, which are as likely to play as significant a role in shaping *her* teaching preferences as learners' subjective needs play in shaping *their* learning preferences.

What actually happens in a language classroom is thus the result of a very complex interaction between the teaching method used, the teacher's interpretation of this method, and the interaction of the learners with the latter. Responding to learners' subjective needs therefore calls for a critical evaluation of the assumptions which underlie methodological choices. It also requires the teacher to look openly and honestly at her own subjective needs as a teacher and as a participant in the teaching-learning process.

REF. What is your teaching method? Draw up a profile of yourself as a teacher by working through Richards and Rodgers' model and filling in, under each heading, what you believe about language teaching and the sort of teaching practices, at both 'design' and 'procedure' level, which you most favour or find most effective.

- If there are differences between your own preferences and approved practice in an institution where you have taught (or still teach):
  - note where they occur,
  - try to explain the origin of the differences in terms of Richards and Rodgers' model,
  - note how you dealt (or deal) with them.
- Please remember that there are no 'right' answers.

4.5 Recommendations

The conclusion to this chapter might appear relatively obvious, and could be based on Spolsky's Learning Style Preference condition, which states that:

Learners vary (both individually and according to such characteristics as age, level, and cultural origin) in their preference for
learning style (visual, auditory, kinaesthetic, and tactile) and
mode (group or individual); as a result, learning is best when the
learning opportunity matches the learner's preference. (1989:
110)

Teachers might therefore be urged to do everything in their power to
gear their methodological choices to their students' learning style
preferences. This would not be a *bad* conclusion to the chapter. It
would, however, represent a misleading oversimplification of the situation.

To begin with, two models of matching exist, based either on
similarity or on *complementarity*. The former involves the selection of
methodology to fit in with the learning preferences of the target learners.
The latter is compensatory, and is designed to provide a form of teaching
which complements learners' spontaneous preferences, the idea behind
this form of matching being that it enriches the learners' understanding
of language study. Although extreme mismatching of learning and
teaching styles, especially if it is imposed in a dogmatic and uncaring
manner, will almost certainly produce negative results, educational
research is inconclusive as to which matching principle is more effective
(cf. Willing op.cit.: 76–84).

More fundamentally, it should not be forgotten that a learner-centred
approach to teaching has a strong educational component, which aims
to broaden learners' understanding of the options available to them,
with the ultimate goal of learner empowerment (1.4.2). Therefore, it
would be simplistic to assume that sensitivity to learners' subjective
needs involves taking their current awarenesss and preferences as a
given, and exposing them to nothing else. As Oxford and Ehrman
(op.cit.: 198) suggest, learners need to be extended beyond their 'stylistic
comfort zone', even if it is important to do this in a gradual and sensitive
manner.

Learning preferences may well arise out of deeply ingrained cognitive
and/or psychosocial traits. They may also, however, arise out of popular
wisdom, expectations based on prior learning experiences, or the
learner's affective reactions to these experiences. We should not, therefore, deprive our students of the possibility to look at their current
learning preferences objectively in a constructive and non-judgmental
atmosphere, to compare them with other options, and then to come to
their own conclusions in an informed and self-directive manner. Furthermore, it would run counter to the basic principles of learner-centred
teaching to place the ultimate decision about the choice of methodology

on the teacher. The teacher certainly does have an important role to play in terms of the choice of methodology, but this role is primarily *educational* in nature, and is aimed at helping learners to become aware of the options that are available to them so that they are better able to find their own path to learning. Recognising the role and importance of subjective needs in language learning does not offer any neat solutions: on the contrary, it opens up a new and complex area of educational concern.

To conclude this chapter a selection of the recommendations made by Willing (op. cit.) will be presented, as these recommendations provide a valuable set of guidelines to the way in which learners' subjective needs may be accommodated, but without seeking to avoid the complexities inherent in this process, or the demands which it makes on teachers. The headings under which the selected recommendations are grouped have been added by the present author.

DAT/PED. With reference to one or more teaching situations you are familiar with, assess the way(s) in which Willing's recommendations would alter the organisation of teaching and learning.

- How great a change would this call for in the organisation of teaching? In this respect do not think only of changes that directly affect students; include also the changes that would be required from your own point of view and in terms of the organisation of teaching at institutional level.
- Do you see any difficulties in implementing Willing's recommendations? If so,
  - what are they, and which aspects of teaching do they affect?
  - what are the causes of these difficulties (e.g. attitudinal, institutional, material, etc.)?
  - what practical measures could be taken to overcome these difficulties albeit in part?

---

1 **Choice of methodology**
- The cognitive and personality tendencies of the individual should be prime factors in deciding teaching methodology, rather than the teaching method, and choice of materials, being based on a priori commitment of any kind. (Rec. 2)
- Teaching practice should become more flexible. Any teacher should be capable of a wide range of teaching techniques – orderly, systematic, grammatically and functionally based techniques, but also very concrete and holistic 'direct' techniques based on communicative involvement. (Rec. 3)
- Consideration might be given, in appropriate circumstances, to

attempting to 'match' a teacher to a group. This might be done either on the basis of personal and cognitive similarity to the predominant type of learner in the group; or, on the other hand, it might be on the basis of 'complementarity' or 'compensation'. (Rec. 8)

- Different learner types having been tentatively 'identified', any learning arrangement should be structured to permit differential teaching approaches to be carried on in an ongoing way within that arrangement. (Rec. 6)
- Overt indications of learning preference should be accommodated if at all possible, even if such preferences conflict with the teacher's belief about what constitutes effective learning. For example, consideration should be given to meeting the need for materials of a somewhat more 'traditional' type, especially at beginner level, if students express such a desire. (Rec's 7, 25)

2 Teacher preparation

- Teacher flexibility is a key trait, one which should be borne in mind in terms of recruitment, pre-service training and ongoing staff development. (Rec. 3)
- Teachers should develop their ability to identify features of different cognitive and learning styles, so they are able to make at least tentative assessments of the learning styles of their students. (Rec. 4)
- Teachers should be helped to develop their expertise regarding both the theoretical and practical aspects of accommodating learning style differences. This could involve:

  - awareness-raising regarding one's own cognitive biases and their relation to one's own teaching style;
  - in-depth acquaintance with the basic features of various learning styles;
  - investigation of the teaching methodologies which are appropriate to the different learning styles;
  - analysis of materials for their learning style assumptions and biases;
  - awareness of the intercultural aspects of learning style differences;
  - practical techniques for accommodating different learning styles within one classroom or within a single learning project. (Rec. 20)

3 Learner training

- Learners should be helped to understand the concept of learning style itself, and to be aware of different learning modalities such as 'analytical', 'authority-oriented', 'concrete', 'communicative', etc. (Rec. 9)

- Learners should be helped to acquire an understanding, even if only at a rudimentary level, of the methodological ideas lying behind various learning options. (Rec. 10)
- Once learners have acquired a basic grounding in the principles underlying choice of methodology and approach, these should be open for negotiation. Ideally, there should be no area of curriculum planning to which learners may not have access. (Rec. 11)
- Respect for and capitalisation on the strategies learners already make use of is essential. A basic goal of learner training should thus be to discover and build on the learners' existing array of learning strategies. (Rec. 16)
- Classroom practice should be geared to developing appropriate and effective learning strategies. This will involve:
  - exploration of the strategies learners are already making use of;
  - exploration of the relation between individual learning style and the learner's current strategy usage;
  - conscious transfer of known strategies to unfamiliar contexts;
  - exploration of new strategies by means of new activities, discussion of other learners' strategies, etc.;
  - in-class simulations of how particular strategies might be activated in out-of-class contexts. (Rec. 15)

(1988: 167–8. Adapted)

4.6 Summary

a) Our profession has come to recognise the important role played in language learning by subjective needs, i.e. those factors of a psychosocial or cognitive nature which influence the manner in which learners will perceive and interact with the process of language study.

b) Subjective needs can be seen from two perspectives. *Individual differences* are those continua of a psychosocial or cognitive nature (e.g. introversion–extroversion, tolerance of ambiguity and risk-taking, cognitive style) along which learners differ from one another. *Learning style* is a composite concept which englobes a number of poles of individual difference (psychosocial, cognitive, sensory) to produce a profile of learners' behavioural and interactional preferences with respect to language learning. Learning style is thus a composite concept which provides a powerful tool for analysing learning preference.

c) Virtually all teaching methods incorporate a learning style bias, and thus tend to favour one set of learning style preferences over another, and the same is likely to apply to the teaching style of most teachers: both factors therefore need to be taken into account in the attempt to make teaching responsive to students' learning style preferences.

d) Two approaches to the matching of methodology to learning style preference exist. One is based on similarity, and involves the selection of methodological procedures which coincide with learners' spontaneous preferences; the other is based on complementarity and involves exposing learners to modes of study which differ from their spontaneous preferences – this approach is meant to enrich their awareness of learning options and thus has an educational function. Selecting the appropriate form of matching and, in general terms, responding to learners' subjective needs is a complex process which calls for considerable flexibility and educational insight from the teacher.

5 The contextual dimension

5.1 Language teaching in context

5.1.1 Beyond the individual

The last two chapters have highlighted the advantages of incorporating learners' own knowledge and experience into the formulation of learning goals, and of gearing methodology around learners' subjective needs. Learner-centredness has thus been presented as a form of experiential learning, one in which 'immediate personal experience is seen as the focal point of learning' (Kohonen 1992: 14). In the discussion so far, the emphasis has been on individual variability and the importance of accommodating this in course design. Language learners, however, are not disincarnate spirits studying in a social vacuum. Without forfeiting their individuality in personal and affective terms, they are also members of a given sociocultural community, and their membership of this community is an integral part of their identity. Focusing exclusively on the personal aspect of learners' life goals and identity would therefore be divisive in terms of the learners' identity and the full range of their human experience – which would be distinctly unlearner-centred.

Some learners may elect to approach their language study as something apart from the occupational or socially-involved aspects of their life. This is a valid choice and needs to be respected and worked with constructively by the teacher. However, probably the majority of learners undertake language study for reasons which arise directly or indirectly out of the perceived needs of the community to which they belong. Furthermore, their language study will be conducted within an educational framework which is shaped by the socioeconomic conditions of their home community and which will also reflect the attitudes, beliefs and traditions of this community. Contextual factors of this nature play a significant role in creating the learning environment in which language study will occur. Consequently, learner-centred teaching has to be pursued in a socially- and contextually-sensitive manner, in harmony with what Kohonen (op. cit.: 19) refers to as the 'social and moral norms, traditions and expectations' of the community within which teaching takes place. As Hutchinson and Waters (1987: 82) pertinently point out, learning a language is 'not just a mental process' but 'a process of negotiation between individuals and society'.

A variety of contextual factors merit consideration in course design. One category relates to the framework of goals within which learning will be conducted. In particular, do learners' goals arise out of essentially personal factors, or are they shaped more or less directly by the demands of the social context? The latter may take a number of forms, such as the reinforcement of national cohesion in bi- or multilingual states, improved access by the national population to technological and scientific information as a basis for economic development, the establishment of closer political or economic links with other countries, or pressures from the world of commerce for knowledge of a given language as a condition for employment or promotion. Imperatives of this nature may assume a social reality in the form of a national or institutional language curriculum, the use of an approved textbook, or the attachment of socio-economic advantages to success in a given examination (e.g. as an enabling condition for entry to tertiary education or for study overseas). Within such a context, successful completion of the prescribed study programme can have a determining influence on learners' educational or professional careers and, thereby, on their ability to pursue their chosen life goals. A learner-centred approach to teaching simply cannot ignore imperatives of this nature.

Another category of contextual factors relates to the practical conditions under which teaching will be conducted. These most obviously involve considerations such as class size, the range and quality of both teaching and learning facilities that are available, and also a variety of logistical factors. In addition, attention has to be paid to existing levels of teacher training and morale, and the possibilities that exist for teacher development. Consideration also has to be given to the administrative and decision-making structures that are in place, and the manner in which innovation can be initiated in both practical and organisational terms.

Yet another set of contextual factors relates to the learning culture and traditions of learning present both in the educational system concerned and in the community as a whole. Learning style preferences may arise out of a number of individual factors, but they may also derive from the learners' previous language learning experience, and are therefore likely to reflect the traditions of (language) teaching and learning current in their home culture. Furthermore, if language learning is taking place within this culture, learners' expectations are likely to be reinforced by the attitudes, beliefs and behaviour of other participants, such as teachers (including teachers of other subjects), administrators, sponsors or parents. Culturally-based expectations can relate to methodological factors in a more restricted sense of the term, but also to broader considerations such as the role relationships and interactional patterns which are felt to be appropriate within a (language) learning context. In this respect, it is worth bearing in mind Brumfit's (1991: 141) observation that what are considered to be appropriate patterns of interaction in the 'micro-social' context of the classroom are subject to the beliefs and ideologies which are held in the broader 'macro-sociological' context of the community in question.

These factors all go to form the human and organisational context within which teaching and learning will take place. They shape, or at least influence the attitudes and expectations of participants to the process of language study, and in this way constitute as important a set of subjective variables as the individual factors examined in Chapter 4. A genuinely learner-centred approach to teaching needs therefore to work constructively with all of these factors, and therefore to view learners as full human beings – both as individuals and as members of a given social group.

5.1.2   A divided profession?

Holliday (1994b) makes a distinction between two main sectors of the English language teaching (ELT) profession that casts an interesting perspective on the issues raised later in this chapter. One sector is based in Britain, Australasia and North America (the 'BANA' countries), while the other comprises tertiary, secondary, and primary English language education ('TESEP') in the rest of the world. Holliday (ibid.: 4–5) describes the characteristic features of the two systems as follows; in the BANA countries:

- language teaching has developed within a private language school ethos in which there is considerable freedom to develop methodology as a sophisticated instrument capable of responding to the needs of specific markets;
- teaching is instrumentally oriented; students are received on a commercial basis and a specific service is provided;
- teachers can assume favourable classroom conditions and the availability of good teaching and learning facilities;
- teaching procedures assume a 'learning group ideal' which is based on two complementary principles: The first is that group and pair work are effective modes of learning, and the second is that this is best realised in small classes.

In the TESEP sector, on the other hand:

- English is taught as part of a wider curriculum, and is therefore influenced by the imperatives of this curriculum in educational and institutional terms;
- English teaching, as part of students' general education, has to play its role alongside other subjects in socialising students as members of the target community;
- language teaching is simply another subject on the curriculum, and must therefore work within the material and logistical possibilities available to the educational system as a whole;
- restrictions are placed on the choice of methodology by the approach to teaching adopted in other subjects and by the expectations of other participants – the students themselves, teachers of other subjects, administrators, educational authorities and the community at large.

Holliday suggests that most of the intellectual 'technology' of ELT has originated in the BANA countries and has taken as a norm the material conditions, finalities and organisational structures prevailing in private language schools or university language centres in the BANA countries. In other words, insufficient attention has been paid, on the level of theory development at least, to the specificities of TESEP learning contexts. More fundamentally still, Holliday suggests that departures from the BANA ideal have tended to be viewed in deficit terms as 'constraints', i.e. as negative factors impeding the realisation of an ideal that has been developed in different material and organisational conditions and in response to a different set of educational priorities. Holliday's basic message is that each language teaching context merits being analysed constructively in *local* terms and not on the basis of *a priori* judgments of value or efficacy developed in other contexts. Holliday's analysis has relevance beyond the world of ELT, however: much foreign language teaching in BANA countries, for instance, actually has more in common with Holliday's TESEP type of situation than with the instrumentally oriented, language school based BANA type of teaching he describes.

Holliday (op. cit.: 7: 1994a: 174–7) uses the term learner-centred in a much narrower sense than it is understood in this book. There is, nonetheless, a case for seeing learner-centredness as a BANA invention, and the realisation of a learner-centred approach to teaching does tend to be associated with BANA type classroom conditions and organisational structures. This, however, is more a question of manner of realisation than of underlying goals, and there is no reason to believe that the goals of language education and learner empowerment are any less valid or feasible in a TESEP than in a BANA context. Indeed, as the goals of much TESEP type teaching are defined in educational terms, there should be as powerful a rationale for a learner-centred mode of teaching in TESEP settings as in a more instrumentally-oriented BANA type of setting. This, however, calls for a distinction to be made between the *underlying goals* of a learner-centred approach, on the one hand, and the *manner in which they are realised*, on the other. The former may remain similar, while the latter will inevitably vary in response to local conditions – pragmatic, organisational and attitudinal.

This chapter will look at the type of contextual factors which need to be borne in mind in the planning and implementation of a learner-centred approach to teaching. This will be done around the two related concepts of means analysis and classroom culture. Means analysis considers factors of an organisational nature, and the way in which such factors shape the educational context within which teaching and learning will take place. Classroom culture relates to the culturally-based attitudes and expectations with which learners approach their language study. The question as to which set of factors exerts the greater influence on learners' classroom behaviour – their individual psychosocial and cognitive make up, or contextual factors such as the educational system and learning traditions to which they are accustomed – is an intriguing one which it is probably very difficult to answer in general terms. Both sets of factors play a role: the teacher needs to be aware of both and try to assess which appears to be exerting the stronger influence on different learners in different learning tasks.

REF/PED. Draw up a list of the main difficulties which you could imagine arising with respect to the realisation of a learner-centred approach to teaching. Think in particular of:

- practical and material factors;
- the social responsibilities and academic/professional priorities of the students;
- the attitudes and expectations of other participants such as parents, sponsors, educational authorities, fellow colleagues, etc.
- Use this as a point of reference or checklist for your reading of the rest of the chapter.

5.2 Means analysis

As mentioned briefly in 3.1, means analysis is the process by which the target teaching situation is examined to establish contextually appropriate, and thus sustainable parameters for course design. Its goal is to provide insights into the target teaching situation that will allow the development of learning programmes which are responsive to and capable of fitting in harmoniously with local conditions. Holliday and Cooke (1982) argue for an 'ecological approach' to course design, which is in part a reaction against the somewhat technocratic and disincarnate approach exemplified by Munby's model. They examine course design in terms of the growth of a plant, and insist on the importance of an integrative and developmental approach:

> ... whereas in the Munbyan approach, 'constraints' interfere and cause problems during the phase of syllabus implementation (being at the outset totally disregarded), in the ecological version they are taken into account from the very start, in order to try to ensure a course that is acceptable to the ecosystem. For this reason, we no longer think in terms of 'constraints' at all, but simply of 'local features', which may prove to have positive and exploitable features. (Ibid.: 136–7)

Rather than viewing contextual factors as potential 'constraints', Holliday and Cooke suggest a non-judgmental analysis of the target learning situation in terms of 'local features'. These are the features of the situation which will, in one way or another, exert an influence on what can (or cannot) be done in the classroom, on how pedagogical choices will be perceived by the various participants involved, and how these choices will interact with the organisational structures currently in place.

Means analysis focuses on the social, organisational and attitudinal characteristics of the learning situation, and tries to get to grips with that mix of factors which will exert an influence on the realisation of the programme or educational innovation being planned. It is thus complementary to needs and strategy analysis, and seeks to provide guidelines as to what is 'ecologically' appropriate and sustainable in the local context. Holliday and Cooke (op. cit.) look at means analysis with respect to the setting up of ESP projects in TESEP settings. In such cases, means analysis is likely to be particularly important as the project may be (partly) run by specialists and teachers unfamiliar with the local situation, and may be based on views of language education different from those current in the local community. This does not, however, imply that means analysis is of relevance only in such situations. Any change (cf. 8.2.1 for a discussion of learner-centredness and innovation), other than an incremental modification of current practice deriving spontaneously and by mutual consent from the participants themselves, has implications for the host setting, and is thus best preceded by a means analysis. Furthermore, periodic re-evaluations of an innovation should also include a means analysis in order to monitor for changes in one or more situational parameters.

5.2.1 Change is systemic

Writing in the context of ELT project management, Kennedy (1988: 331–2) suggests that educational change is *systemic* in that 'it takes place in an environment which consists of a number of interrelating systems', and that these systems are organised hierarchically, higher-level systems exerting an influence on those systems located below them in the hierarchy. Figure 11 illustrates this diagrammatically. In Kennedy's analysis:

> ... the cultural system is assumed to be the most powerful as it will influence both political and administrative structures and behaviour. These in turn will produce a particular educational system reflecting the values and beliefs of the society in question, a system which must be taken into account when innovating within an institution and ultimately in the classroom. (Op. cit.: loc. cit.)

Kennedy acknowledges that the relative influence of one system on the others will vary from context to context. A political system, for instance, may grow out of a certain culture but then, in time, come to exert a distorting effect on its source culture (this tends to happen with totalitarian regimes); individual educational institutions may develop an organisational culture of their own which differs from the national norm, or conflicts may arise between politico-administrative imperatives and those of teachers and/or students. Kennedy's main point, however, is that patterns of behaviour at classroom level can only be fully understood in the light of the sociocultural forces at work in the community at large. In other words, educational change cannot be effected by viewing the classroom as a reality in its own right, in abstraction of the other social and cultural systems of which it is a part. Kennedy identifies three ways in which innovation can run into difficulty: the first is when the 'outer circle factors' are ignored; the second is when their presence is acknowledged, but they are not worked with constructively; the third is when the objectives of the project are extended to changing these factors. Means analysis is designed to avoid this type of difficulty by facilitating the analysis of those contextual factors which, directly or indirectly, will influence behaviour and expectations at classroom level.

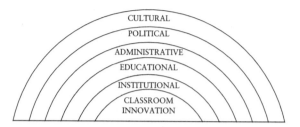

Figure 11 Subsystems influencing classroom innovation
(taken from Kennedy 1988: 332)

One difficulty in means analysis lies in identifying the various factors that need to be examined: this is far from being a trivial point, as the various factors at play merge into a complex attitudinal and behavioural whole. In the rest of the section, this will be attempted under three headings – organisational factors, material factors, and participants. 5.3 will examine the concept of classroom culture.

5.2.2 Organisational factors

These relate to the management and decision-making structures operant in the teaching institution, and the nature of the links that exist between the institution and other educational agents in the host community. Specifically, this involves an analysis of the distribution of roles and responsibilities within the institution, together with the degree and domains of authority accorded to the various participants (teachers, heads of department, administrators, advisors, etc.); attention also needs to be paid to the way in which key pedagogical decisions are made, by whom, and the procedures by which they are communicated and implemented. Another potentially important organisational factor is the degree of autonomy of the teaching institution – is it, for example, one of a large number of State-run schools following a national curriculum, or is it a more or less independent institution such as a private language school or a university language centre? This point will also affect the way in which success or achievement is monitored, and the nature of the relationship between the teaching authorities, the students and other participants.

   White outlines four main types of organisational culture identified by Handy:

> A *club or power culture* is like a spider's web, with a central power source or authority figure, from whom influence radiates. [...]

A *role culture* is one in which the organization is a collection of roles or job boxes. Individuals are 'role occupants', with job descriptions which effectively lay down the requirements of the role. Role cultures are managed rather than led, in contrast to the club or power culture, [...]
Task cultures are job- or project-oriented. A group or team of talents and resources are applied to a project, problem or task, each task getting the treatment it requires, since, unlike a role culture, there is no standardization of procedures across the organization. Similarly, in a *person culture*, there is no standardization, structure is minimal, and individual talents are given priority. (1988: 137, citing Handy [1978]. Emphasis added)

Handy points out that few organisations will manifest one culture exclusively and so it is the relative mix of cultures which characterises one organisation or another. Handy also points out that the various participants in an institution may perceive and interpret their functions in different terms: Handy suggests, for example, that while the staff of British secondary schools tend to see themselves as occupying a task culture, these institutions are predominantly role cultures. The relationship between Kennedy's cultural and political systems (cf. Figure 11) and the organisational culture of any one institution is potentially complex, but societies which have a more democratic or participative approach to social organisation in general are likely to generate educational systems which favour task or person cultures, whereas societies which are organised in a more authoritarian manner are likely to favour power or role cultures. These factors have a direct influence on the way in which key decisions are made; they are also likely to influence, albeit indirectly, the interactional norms that will pertain within the classroom.

The degree of autonomy enjoyed by an institution with respect to the definition of learning goals is a key variable in organisational terms. State-run secondary schools, for instance, are frequently required to follow a national curriculum, prepare their students for a national examination, and may be required to use an approved textbook for all or at least the core element of their teaching in a given subject. This places limits on the scope for negotiation of learning content between teacher and learners, and also has implications for the roles and responsibilities of participants both within the institution itself and within the education system as a whole. The pressures on private language schools or university language centres are of a different nature. They are rarely obliged to follow an externally-designed syllabus, their students are seen as 'clients', courses are frequently tailored to the specific needs (generally of a transactional nature) of the learners concerned, and assessment tends to be diagnostic or informative rather than evaluative. Language education in either context retains a social function, but the macro-social pressures which are brought to bear on the two types of institution are different, which will have consequences for the role culture and management structures which are likely to prevail in each. This in turn affects the scope available for innovation at either classroom or institutional level, as well as the manner in which change will be initiated and implemented.

5.2.3 Material factors

These relate most obviously to the material conditions in which teaching will take place, and class size is a key variable in this respect. Teaching procedures which are perfectly feasible with 10–12 students may need some creative adaptation with a group of 30, but become problematic with groups of 80, 150 or more. This does not necessarily mean that the educational goals which are being pursued with groups of 10–12 need to be dropped or even revised with large classes: the pedagogical procedures by which these goals may realistically be achieved in the two cases, however, will inevitably be rather different. The availability of equipment and of teaching-learning resources is another significant variable. The pedagogical options open to a teacher whose only aid is the blackboard, and whose students can rely only on the notes they make during classtime and possibly a coursebook, are clearly different from those enjoyed by a teacher and students who have access to video and audio equipment in every classroom, good recording facilities, a well-resourced self-access centre or a computer laboratory.

Attention also needs to be given to the learning opportunities available outside the teaching institution itself, and which constitute the broader context of learning. These factors affect the type of tasks learners can be given and also – more fundamentally – the strategic role played by classroom learning within their overall learning programme. In some contexts, the classroom and the materials provided by the teacher represent the only opportunity students have to encounter or use the TL. In others, the teacher can assume that students will have more or less regular contact with the TL (media, interaction with TL speakers, visits to countries in which the TL is spoken for purposes of business, academic or cultural exchanges, or even topping-up language courses), and will be able to incorporate these contacts into her teaching programme.

At least as important as the above are the resources available for teacher salaries, and for teacher training and development (e.g. teacher seminars, staff libraries, support for study leave or participation at conferences). Yeo (1994), for instance, points to the ways in which low teacher salaries and the resulting necessity for teachers to find additional sources of income can constitute an objective factor in course revision: basically, if teachers are poorly paid and have to seek additional income outside their main teaching post, there may be limits on how much extra reading and course development may reasonably be expected of them. A given level of funding for education may result either from the avail- ability, in absolute terms, of resources or from political priorities in the society in question. The practical consequences may be similar in either case, but the psychological effects on teachers (and their students) may be rather different, and these effects, too, have to be taken into account. In a less wealthy country, for instance, the material conditions of teaching may be harsh, teacher salaries low, and only limited funds available for teacher development. However, the society (students, parents, employers, etc.), may accord a high status to education, and teachers may enjoy respect and social prestige both for the inherent value attributed to their profession and in recognition of their efforts to help their students in difficult conditions. On the other hand, in a more affluent society where resources are available in objective terms, but where language education is not seen as a priority, material difficulties may be compounded by poor morale among teachers (and probably students, too).

5.2.4 Participants

The points made above about the attitudinal consequences of funding indicate the role which social forces and imperatives can play in education by shaping the material and psychological climate within which teaching will take place. The planning of any educational innova- tion must therefore take into account the motivations and expectations of the various participants involved in the process, and not just those of the students. This does not undermine the centrality of the learner, but simply acknowledges that language learners are members of a social group and are therefore likely to be sensitive to the beliefs and imperatives proper to this group. Other participants may be parents, sponsors or future employers, administrators, educational authorities or political bodies. (Learner attitudes will be examined in 5.3 in terms of the concept of classroom culture.) The expectations of these social actors influence the status accorded to language education and the level of funding it will receive. They also, however, create the attitudinal climate within which any specific methodological option will be perceived and elevated. As Kennedy observes:

... views held on theories of teaching and learning and views of the educational process and what happens or should happen in classrooms between teacher and student are ultimately context-specific, and derived from the culture and society in which learning takes place. [Thus] a materials project that proposes any change to existing practice will be doing far more than substituting one set of materials for another – it will be attempting to replace one set of behaviours for another. (1987: 166–7)

It is therefore important to evaluate the behavioural implications of a pedagogical innovation, and how they relate to the expectations and value systems of the target community.

Doing this involves, in the first instance, identifying those actors most directly involved in the innovation under consideration. In the secondary sector, they may be parents, educational authorities, or teachers of other subjects; in tertiary education, members of the client faculty are likely to play an influential role, and in a private language school, the employers or sponsors of students. And, of course, there are the beliefs, attitudes to authority and decision-making, and the interactional conventions which underlie the organisation of social life in the community at large. Two main sets of questions need to be addressed in this respect.

1 To what extent do the assumptions upon which the innovation in question is based coincide with or diverge from the (implicit) expectations of the participants concerned and the interpersonal conventions current in the target community? If mismatches do exist between the two, which aspects of the innovation do they affect, and are these aspects of central or of secondary importance?
2 Does the innovation have implications for the organisational structure and/or role culture of the target institution? For example, does it alter the current role relationships between teachers and students or between teachers and heads of department or administrative staff? If so, how 'sustainable' is this change, and how might it best be realised in a consensual manner among those involved?

Analysis of this type of factor does not mean that the status quo should be viewed as something immutable. It is simply a question of being clear about the motivations for change, the assumptions (frequently implicit) upon which a given innovation is based, and the impact the innovation is likely to have on the local environment.

Key players in any form of educational innovation are, of course, the teachers: it is therefore essential to consider their attitudes and expectations, their corporate value system and professional self-image, their level of professional training and morale, and their role expectations

with respect to their students and within society at large. The complex
and multi-faceted nature of the teacher's role is well captured by Prabhu:

> What a teacher does in the classroom is not solely, or even
> primarily, determined by the teaching method he or she intends
> to follow. There is a complex of other forces at play, in varied
> forms and degrees. There is often a desire to conform to
> prevalent patterns of teacher behaviour, if only for the sense of
> security such conformity provides. There is also a sense of
> loyalty to the past – both to the pattern of teaching which the
> teacher experienced when he or she was a student and to the
> pattern of his or her own teaching in the past. (Change in
> behaviour is a form of denial of the validity of past behaviour.)
> There is the teacher's self-image and a need to maintain status in
> relation to colleagues or the authorities. Above all, there is a
> relationship to maintain with a class of learners, involving
> factors such as interpretations of attitudes and feelings, anxieties
> about maintaining status or popularity, and fears about loss of
> face. A teacher's relationship with his or her class is based on
> constant and continuing contact; it therefore needs stability and
> finds change unsettling. Stability is provided by classroom
> routines which support shared expectations of behaviour and
> act as a framework for some balance between conflicting
> motives and self-images. Patterns of classroom activity, there-
> fore, are not just teaching and learning procedures; more
> importantly, they are forms of routine through which teachers
> and learners play their appointed roles and regulate their
> relationship with one another. (1987: 103–4)

For any change, whatever its nature or scale, to be successful, it has to be
accepted by the teachers who will realise it. However, 'acceptance'
involves more than intellectual assent to the goals or academic credentials of the innovation in question. It is also a matter of teachers being
able to live comfortably with the practical consequences in terms of the
professional demands it places on them, and its consequences in terms of
their social and interpersonal relationships both with their students and
with other actors such as colleagues, parents, administrators, and so on.
Without assent for an innovation on this level, its chances of success are
limited.

The factors examined above (organisational and material factors, and
participants) shape the context in which any form of educational
innovation will be implemented. They need, therefore, to be borne in
mind throughout the planning of any new course or approach to
teaching, especially if this involves methodological procedures which are

novel to the target institution or community. In the present context, then, teachers need to evaluate the interaction between a learner-centred and participative approach to teaching and the various contextual factors operant in their current teaching situation or those in which they will find themselves in the future. Ignoring such factors is likely to result in a variety of both practical and human problems. Most fundamentally, perhaps, it risks creating tensions between the learners and other members of the social group to which they belong, which would be difficult to reconcile with a learner-centred view of teaching. Accommodating contextual factors is thus more than simply a matter of avoiding difficulties: it is rather a question of respecting the social as well as the individual identity of learners. Holliday and Cooke suggest that the observations which are made with respect to a given context can be analysed under the following headings:

1 immutable problems, which we can do little to influence and which will, sooner or later, necessitate radical changes in project aims;
2 flexible elements – problematic features which can, however, be worked within and around;
3 exploitable features, which can be used to good advantage.

(Op. cit: 134)

PED. Conduct an analysis (in essence, a means analysis) of a teaching institution you are familiar with in terms of its organisational and material characteristics and the participants involved.

- In the light of this profile, evaluate the potential of the institution involved with respect to the implementation of a learner-centred approach to teaching. Here, you may wish to categorise factors in terms of immutable problems, flexible elements and exploitable features as suggested by Holliday and Cooke.
- What does this say about the 'preparedness' of the institution in question for the adoption of a learner-centred approach to teaching?
- Finally, are there any elements which you consider to be of importance but which have not been covered by this means analysis?

5.3 Classroom culture

Classroom culture is one component of means analysis. However, given the orientation of this book, it appears appropriate to consider it separately. Classroom culture refers to the complex of attitudes and expectations which shape learners' sociocultural personality in the classroom, and thereby their interaction with their language study. The concept certainly incorporates aspects of learners' national or regional cultures, but it is also influenced by the social, economic and ideological climate which prevails in their home culture at any one point in time and by the peer group or sub-culture to which the learners belong. The concept of classroom culture thus encapsulates many of the beliefs and attitudes of the society in question, but as they are perceived and experienced by the specific group of learners concerned. Not surprisingly, therefore, classroom culture is a very complex concept, one that our profession is only starting to get to grips with. Possibly with this in mind, Holliday (1994a) suggests that the concept is best used heuristically, as a tool for exploring the complex social realities of the classroom.

5.3.1 The complexity of the language classroom

Breen (1986) identifies two main orientations in classroom research, which he describes in terms of the metaphors of the classroom as *experimental laboratory* and the classroom as *discourse*. The former approach is represented by Second Language Acquisition research and the latter by studies of the discourse of classroom interaction. Breen sees both orientations as inadequate to account for the complexities of classroom behaviour. The experimental laboratory approach is too narrowly linguistic in focus and ignores the social dimension of class-room learning. Discourse-based studies (the classroom as discourse) do acknowledge the social dimension, but focus on 'the surface text of classroom discourse [rather than] the underlying social psychological forces which generate it (the expectations, beliefs and attitudes of the participants)' (Breen op. cit.: 139). Breen suggests that a more productive metaphor for research into classroom learning is that of classrooms as *coral gardens*, which he derives from Malinowski's studies of Trobriand island cultures:

> Just as gardens of coral were granted magical realities by the Trobriand islanders, a language class – outwardly a gathering of people with an assumed common purpose – is an arena of subjective and intersubjective realities which are worked out, changed and maintained. (Op. cit.: 142)

For Breen, then, the classroom is a complex social and psychological reality which can only be understood if its inherent complexity is acknowledged. The concept of classroom culture, though still relatively unexplored, is part of our profession's attempt to provide teachers and course planners with insights into the ways in which students perceive and interact with classroom learning.

Cortazzi (1990) makes a number of interesting points about the culture of language classrooms. One is that the expectations that students bring with them to the language classroom are formed, in the first instance, by their socialisation in their home culture. This takes place on two levels. The first occurs in the family and with other members of society at a very early stage of the child's development. The second takes place within the framework of formal education. If both family upbringing and formal education occur within the same culture, there is likely to be a strong reinforcement of beliefs, attitudes and expectations between the two environments arising out of the beliefs and value systems shared by different members of the community – parents and family, peers, teachers and so on. This develops in students a set of beliefs about achievement and human values, role models and inter-personal norms, and also about what is seen to be 'good' teaching or education (e.g. the respective roles of teachers and learners, or how a language should best be taught and learned). Another point which Cortazzi makes is that violation of students' implicit assumptions about teaching and learning may lead to a loss of status by the teacher in her students' eyes, which can undermine their willingness to invest confidence in and learn from what she suggests.

Cortazzi illustrates this with reference to the expectations of students who have learned Chinese as their L1:

> Learning to read Chinese is seen as requiring some analysis of character components, but consists mostly of memory, hard work and rote-learning. Arguably this is because of the nature of Chinese writing, but it occurs in an educational setting which may emphasize these qualities in any case. Consequently, Chinese learners are likely to perceive reading skills as involving: the need to know vocabulary; to memorize words; to read slowly and carefully, a word at a time.
>
> Naturally enough, Chinese students and their Chinese teachers would expect other languages to be taught according to these expectations, using a carefully controlled, structured, memory-oriented approach.
>
> This could contrast greatly with an EFL teacher expecting to use recent Western approaches, where prediction, context skills, skimming, scanning, fluency are involved, and the need to memorize words is de-emphasized. Unless there is some adjustment of expectations on either or both sides, the attempt to use Western approaches in China would be perceived by the learners as being inappropriate, or even as bad teaching. (Op. cit.: 60)

In other words, the way in which a learner will perceive and react to a given pedagogical option is closely related to the assumptions which he brings to his language study from his socialisation and prior educational experience. Changes in study techniques therefore represent changes in culturally-based patterns of behaviour. This point was made in 2.3 with respect to 'Mahmoud' and his approach to text comprehension. Teachers and course planners envisaging methodological innovation need therefore to explore the subjective realities via which the innovation will be perceived and interpreted by the learners concerned.

Cortazzi (op. cit.) sketches a comparative profile of Japan and the United States in terms of culture, education and language (Figure 12) and of the expectations which the two national traditions give rise to with respect to the goals and nature of communication. In its own right, neither tradition is 'problematic': there is, in each case, an inner coherence which leads to a consensus with regard to rights and obligations, means and ends. Difficulties may, however, arise when the two traditions meet, as in a language classroom for example, and have to 'negotiate' behaviours (modes of learning or types of teacher-student interaction, for instance) which have evolved out of the value system of one tradition rather than the other. Problems in this area may lie behind the rather painful lesson described by O'Neill (1991) – and O'Neill is fully justified in casting serious doubts on whether this lesson should be seen as an instance of student-centredness or of student-neglect (8.2.2).

Cortazzi concentrates on the national or regional aspects of classroom culture, and these certainly exert a powerful influence on students' attitudes and expectations. Oxford *et al.* for example, trace the following profiles of certain ethnic groups within a language teaching context:

> Arabic-speaking students of ESL/EFL are typically very gregarious, overtly verbal, and interested in a whole-class, extroverted mode of instruction. [...] Likewise, Hispanic students in general are highly social, cooperative (on homework and classwork), desirous of a close relationship with the teacher as a role-model and friend, and responsive to social goals more than to impersonal rewards. [...]
>
> In comparison, ... Japanese and Korean students are often quiet, shy and reticent in ESL/EFL classrooms, indicating a reserve that is the hallmark of introverts. These ethnic groups have a traditional cultural focus on group membership, solidarity and face-saving, and they de-emphasize individualism .... (1992: 444–5)

Culture, education and language

	JAPAN	U.S.A.
CULTURE:	homogenous hierarchical group harmony consensus group dependence avoid confrontation emphasize empathy + non-verbal elements	heterogenous egalitarian individuality independence self-confidence confrontation acceptable stress verbal communication
EDUCATION:	repetition, memory, persistence respect authority exams are crucial fear of failure accept group consensus	understanding develop critical ideas exams less important less fear of failure debate ideas

LANGUAGE:	complex scripts
	strong word orientation
	prefer hints, ambiguity,
	   indirectness
	listener interprets
	use of intuition
	avoid disagreement
	avoid direct questions
	distrust speech
	prefer formal, regulated
	   situations
	reluctance for verbal
	   intimacy
		one simple script
		meaning orientation
		prefer explicitness, being
		   straightforward
		speaker makes clear
		verbal clarity
		disagreement acceptable
		many direct questions
		speech shows confidence
		prefer informal,
		   spontaneous situations
		willingness for verbal
		   intimacy

Goals and nature of communication

	JAPANESE	U.S.A.
CONTENT OF COMMUNICATION	develop interpersonal attitudes	debate ideas
MODE OF COMMUNICATION	use intuition	use logical argument
AIM OF COMMUNICATION	attain social harmony	reach valid conclusions

Figure 12 A comparative profile of Japan and the United States
(taken from Cortazzi 1990: 62)

However, as Holliday (1994c) points out, this level of analysis may not be sufficient to explain the full range of attitudes which students bring with them to the language classroom. Other sources of influence may arise from ideological trends or socio-economic groupings within a given national culture. Fundamentalist as opposed to moderate Islamic student groups in the Muslim world may develop differing attitudes to the learning of foreign languages; equally well, the classroom cultures of State comprehensive and of private schools in the UK are likely to differ in a number of respects. Holliday (ibid.) suggests that the harsh material conditions and large classes found in Egyptian universities have given rise to habits of cooperation and mutual assistance among students which might not exist (because they would not be so necessary) in better-resourced parts of the Egyptian education system. The range of elements that can coincide to produce a given set of student expectations as to what is acceptable or appropriate in the language classroom is thus wide, and the resultant patterns of behaviour can be very complex. The two case studies which follow are designed to stimulate reflection on the type of factors which teachers may need to keep in mind in their attempt to understand, and thereby be able to react appropriately to the attitudes and behaviours they will observe among their students.

5.3.2   CLT in China

Anderson (1993) examines the feasibility of a communicative approach to English teaching in China. The article seems to be based on two assumptions. The first is that CLT is an inherently effective means of language teaching, and is superior to the approach(es) currently used in China; the second is that the Chinese situation presents a number of 'obstacles' that need to be overcome if CLT is to be successfully implemented. One of the 'obstacles' mentioned is student resistance to CLT activity types. Anderson cites the following comments of two American teachers in China:

> The language students tend to be even more conservative than the faculty. Ms Wang said several told her to her face that they consider her 'method' as ridiculous and inappropriate. They refused to sit in a circle and speak English to each other. They don't like to invent conversations or play communication games. They insist on taking conventional exams. Several just don't attend her classes at all, preferring to audit the older professors' lectures on intensive reading and grammar instead. Since the older professors at the center don't care whether they speak English or not, all the students have to do is memorise twenty

new vocabulary words a day and they can pass with flying colours. (Op. cit.: 474)

Oxford *et al.* report similar remarks of an American teacher in China:

> When I began teaching English to Chinese students [in Beijing], I had some vague ideas about what constituted 'good' language learning and teaching strategies. I tried to include visual aids and active games in the curriculum, and I tried to avoid a teacher-centred approach by assigning group- and pairwork, communicative role play, and student presentations. These choices were not due to any awareness on my part of my or my students' learning styles, but rather to my perception of an intrinsic superiority of these strategies – a perception I had acquired through my own experience in language learning and through some superficial reading on the subject of language teaching.
>
> At first, I met with resistance from my students. In teacher-student interaction as well as student-student interaction, it was difficult to elicit more than minimal oral responses. Responses to questions about a text tended to consist of relevant passages quoted from the text, seldom even paraphrased to fit the question. In a role play situation or an informal encounter outside of class, many students were unable to produce a meaningful English utterance.
>
> Discussion of the problem with Chinese and other foreign teachers revealed that my attempts were in opposition to the prevalent teaching style in China. In most classrooms, I was told, students sat in rows facing the blackboard and the teacher, who lectured on the text. Any production of the target language by students was in choral reading or in closely controlled teacher-student interaction. Thus the approach was text- and teacher-centred, and the perceptual channels were strongly visual (text and blackboard), with most auditory input closely tied to the written. Emphasis was on analytic study of grammar and vocabulary. When confronted with my kinesthetic and global styles of teaching, my students therefore reacted with confusion and occasional hostility, perhaps identifying these activities as 'play' not 'real study'. (1992: 448–9)

Both sets of comments manifest a feeling of unease – unease among students with respect to the methodology adopted by the teacher, and unease of the teacher as a result of her students' reactions. In what follows, an attempt will be made to reconsider from the point of view of the learners involved the features of the Chinese situation identified by

Anderson (op. cit.) as problematic (or 'obstacles'). This is purely speculative on the present author's behalf and is meant primarily to stimulate reflection. The analysis of the Chinese situation as presented by Anderson largely coincides with that of Burnaby and Sun (1989), and so it is not the observation of objective phenomena that is at question, but rather the framework of values within which these phenomena are evaluated.

Obstacle 1. Use of traditional, teacher-centred, book-centred, grammar translation methods with emphasis on rote memory. These are approaches to teaching which students have grown used to in their previous language learning experiences (including that of Chinese), and reflect an approach to learning which probably underlies most of their other subjects. It may be asking rather a lot to expect students to alter their mode of study and classroom behaviours simply because they are in an English, as opposed to a history or mathematics class. In any event, China has a long and rich cultural heritage which Chinese students have every right to feel proud of. They may therefore feel entitled to expect foreign views of education to prove their effectiveness before accepting them: just because an idea is considered to be good in the West does not necessarily mean it will be equally good in China.

Obstacle 2. Classes of 50–70 students. This is the case in other subjects, and so it is unlikely that the situation of English would be very different. As teacher-student contact is restricted, it is the teacher's responsibility to provide students with as much learning material as she can: this allows students to work on and assimilate this material at their own pace and in their own way during their private study time. In this way, the teacher shows her respect for the independence and personal responsibility of her students.

Obstacle 3. Students have little or no contact with English speakers, and few have the opportunity to visit an English-speaking country. It may not, therefore, be terribly helpful to focus on a language skill (speaking) that students will have little opportunity to practise in their everyday life. Students do, however, have the opportunity to read written materials in English and to build up their command of the structures and lexis of the language. This will certainly be very helpful to them in the future should they have the chance (or be required) to use the language orally, even if they may not be able to speak very fluently to start with.

Obstacle 4. Existing textbooks emphasise grammar, reading and writing, with little emphasis on speaking. As students are unlikely to have to use the language orally (cf. Obstacle 3), concentrating on the written language and mastery of structures seems a reasonable emphasis in teaching. In any event, exploring the system of a language can be very interesting in itself: detailed study of written texts extends one's vocabulary and provides insights into the culture of the English-speaking world. Learning to speak fluently will come later, as and when it is required. As a Chinese teacher of English cited by Anderson observes:

> The [foreign experts] cannot accept the obvious fact that Chinese students learn better if they can learn in their own way: start with rote memorization, grammar rules, sentence construction and then worry about conversation and shades of meanings, not the other way around .... . Chinese students learn to read, write, speak, and then comprehend aurally in exactly the reverse order stressed by Western pedagogy. The emphasis on grammar means students tend to neglect comprehension, but can easily construct very good sentences. It seems inexcusably formalistic to most foreign language teachers. But in our experience, these students speak English more fluently after four years of study than their counterparts in the US speak Chinese .... . (Op. cit.: 474)

Obstacle 5. Supplementary books or materials are very difficult to find and are extremely expensive. Having access to a wider range of books and materials in English would, of course, be very valuable and would improve students' feeling for the language. China, however, is a very large country which is investing heavily in the effort to provide its population with a good education on the basis of limited financial resources. Most students will acknowledge this and feel a responsibility to make the best possible use of what their country can reasonably afford to provide them with. English may well be important, but so are other subjects, and they too could benefit from extra resources.

Obstacle 6. Teachers' primary responsibility is to prepare their students for a discrete-point, structurally-based national examination which is a requirement for admission to university. One day, the form of the entry examination may be changed, but that is a separate consideration. While the examination is as it is, however, teachers *must* help their students to succeed in it and thereby have access to higher education and/or the sort of work they would like to undertake. A failure to do this would be irresponsible on the behalf of the teachers concerned both as regards the students themselves and the State, which has the task of managing education country-wide. Furthermore, good teachers will always find a way to help their students to learn more than what is strictly necessary for an examination: this depends on the skills and initiative of the individual teacher.

These comments do not imply that ELT in China might not benefit from a more communicative orientation; that is a separate question. Anderson's article however, shows an approach to innovation which is disturbingly method- and culture-centred, and thereby shows little openness either to students' cultural expectations or to the social and educational priorities operant in the wider context of learning. What, from an outsider's point of view, may be seen as 'constraints' or 'obstacles' are generally part of a cohesive whole which constitutes the students' home culture and, as such, part of their cultural identity. Such factors must, inevitably, be taken on board in an educationally responsible approach to course design. To conclude, a brief word is called for with respect to Anderson's use of the term 'communication', which she seems to equate with oral skills and spoken fluency. Meaningful discussion of written material or explicit language study, when this is perceived by students to be of relevance to their educational goals, is probably a richer basis for genuine communication than the simulation of interactive situations which they have never experienced (and may never, in fact, have the opportunity to experience) or the discussion of subjects which their culture does not consider to be appropriate for a public forum such as the classroom.

5.3.3 *The ethnography of autonomy*

Riley (1988) raises two fundamental questions with respect to self-direction in language learning. The first is whether concepts such as 'autonomy' or 'self-direction' are ethnocentric, and the second is whether the cultural background of various ethnic or social groups predisposes them for or against autonomous or self-directive modes of learning. The present author has often had occasion to reflect on these issues with respect to the learning culture of the Université Libre de Bruxelles. The criteria for admission to university study in Belgium are among the most liberal in the European Union: students are admitted to university providing they possess a secondary school diploma which is delivered independently by each school, selection between more and less academically able students taking place at university (generally within the first two years of study). By British criteria, this might be seen as inefficient and unconducive to 'quality' teaching: in Belgium, however, it enshrines the principles of personal freedom and equality of access to university study, which are vehemently defended across the political spectrum. One consequence of the system, however, is that student numbers are high and that most teaching is by means of formal lectures with anything from 50 to 500 students in an auditorium. There is little of the tutorial guidance and close academic support characteristic of, among others, British university education. Lecturers tend to be authority figures; teaching is geared largely round the transmission of knowledge, and most courses are contained in a 'syllabus', or set of lecture notes which are sold by the relevant student associations.

Faced with this system of teaching, students have developed a learning culture which gives them an ambiguous profile in terms of self-direction. On the one hand, faculties pay little attention to the explicit development of students' study skills and learning strategies. On the other hand, however, precisely because of large classes and a rather distant mode of teaching, students *have to* develop their own study techniques – otherwise they will almost certainly fail or at least have to repeat a year or two. On aggregate, it is difficult to assess whether the Belgian or British university systems produce more independent learners. The latter pays far more attention to the explicit development of study strategies and problem-solving techniques, but the close guidance by lecturers and tutors which is more characteristic of the British system is sometimes perceived by Belgian students familiar with the two systems as being intrusive and a restriction on personal liberty. The Belgian system may seem rather indifferent to the learning needs of students, but allows (or obliges) them to assume considerable personal responsibility for their academic careers. The two systems conceive of education differently, and terms such as academic freedom and self-directedness are also understood differently – which underlines the cultural relativity of such terms. Similar points are raised by Holliday (1994a) on a number of occasions.

Riley reports the reactions of four national groups of students (Danes, Americans, Moroccans and Vietnamese) at CRAPEL to a self-directive mode of study in the following terms:

> *The Danes* took to the activity like ducks to water: in fact, they made it quite clear both at the time and in their final reports that my careful explanation and introduction were really quite super-fluous. As for my attempts to justify the activity and its objectives, they obviously thought I was a bit fuddy-duddy, though they were terribly nice about it. They had no problems in sorting themselves out into sub-groups. They were very de-manding in material terms, but asked for almost nothing in the way of methodological help or advice. Nor was any necessary:

they turned up for the final evaluation and pooling with all their tasks satisfactorily completed.

The Americans to my surprise – and I realize that I am revealing my own stereotypes here – though they declared themselves and indeed proved to be in favour of this kind of work, requested far more help and explanation and guidance. They also seemed to have more difficulty getting themselves organized and in understanding the overall purpose of the exercises.

The Moroccans listened politely and agreed with everything I said, in theory. Indeed, during the preliminary discussions, they made it clear that they thought I was the most innovatory pedagogue since Comenius. However, when it came to getting down to brass tacks, all this changed: they dug their heels in over every last detail. Endless time was wasted re-explaining and re-justifying what I thought had been understood and accepted in theory. They protested vociferously, after this had gone on for some time, that the quantity of work was far too great for the time available (which, by then, it was!) and that anyway, since it would be absolutely impossible for them to do similar work back home, it was pointless for them as teachers. Interesting, but pointless. Moreover, their opposition to the project seemed to be about the only thing any of them had in common, as they proved quite incapable of organizing themselves into groups. Time after time individuals came back asking to be put into a group by a teacher.

The Vietnamese said nothing and did nothing. From the start, it was clear that they just didn't want to know, that the work simply was not to their taste. Moreover, they had the greatest difficulty understanding the nature and objectives of the activity. The whole group would go into a huddle at the drop of a hat: afterwards, they would put questions which indicated real unhappiness about the whole business. (Op. cit.: 14)

Riley seeks to interpret these observations with the help of a number of socioattitudinal variables developed by Hofstede (1983). The first of these, *individualism vs. collectivism*, concerns the relation that exists between individuals and the group to which they belong. In some societies these ties are very loose: individuals are expected to assume responsibility for their decisions and their own well-being, and not count on support from the social group as a whole; as a corollary, however, in this type of society individuals tend to enjoy a considerable amount of freedom. At the other extreme are societies in which individuals are defined and act in line with their group membership (extended family, tribe, socioprofessional class, etc.): in this type of society, the tendency is for individuals to be able to count on substantial support from other group members, but in return they are expected to subordinate individual to group interests and to observe a high degree of conformity in both behavioural and ideational terms. Hofstede's second variable relates to *power distance*, or the way in which authority is perceived and/or exercised: in some societies, individuals or roles are invested with a significant degree of authority (which creates a large power distance), whereas in others this authority is diffused among group members (which leads to a more limited power distance between individuals). As Riley points out, this variable is likely to influence the expectations students will have with respect to the role and responsibilities of the teacher and to teacher-student interaction. The third variable, *uncertainty avoidance*, has parallels with the psychological variable of tolerance of ambiguity and risk-taking examined in 4.2. Societies with weak uncertainty avoidance tend to be tolerant of behaviour or opinions which differ from the norm; societies with strong uncertainty avoidance, on the other hand, tend to limit diversity by means of legislation or via political or religious ideologies, and frequently display intolerance or aggressivity. Hofstede's last variable, *masculinity vs. femininity*, relates to whether a society emphasises divisions between the sexes in social and professional life: Hofstede defines as 'masculine' societies which emphasise sex division, and 'feminine' those which minimise them.

Riley's (op. cit.: 23–5) analysis of the socialisation and cultural background of the four national groups yields a number of valuable insights into their reactions to autonomous learning. Riley sees Danish society as being marked by a high degree of social collectivity, widespread early peer-group interaction, low competitiveness and the use of affective rather than institutional sanctions. At the same time, Danes tend to manifest high individualism, very small power distance and extremely weak uncertainty avoidance. Taken together, these traits predispose Danes strongly towards work in small autonomous groups. American society, for Riley, is characterised by two trends. One is the open, debate-oriented tendency which is generally associated with American culture (cf. Figure 12 above). The other is the presence of a complex set of social norms and sanctions which are none the less powerful for being peer-group generated and largely unstated – what Riley refers to as 'the hidden social curriculum'. This may account for the mixed reactions to autonomous learning which Riley observed among his American students – a propensity for openness and debate combined with a closing of ranks within the peer-group in response to the unexpected.

Riley observes a number of phases in the socialisation of Moroccan children, who move from a relatively permissive approach in early childhood towards the imposition of a substantial body of socioreligious rules and sanctions in adult life. This goes together with the granting to the adult (male) Moroccan of a range of rights and privileges, but which are dependent upon conformity to socially defined stereotypes and modes of behaviour. Moroccan society shows large power distance, relatively low individualism and strong uncertainty avoidance, which generates a view of society in which qualities such as initiative and personal ambition may be viewed as egotistic or even anti-social. These traits may go some way to explaining the evident reluctance Riley's Moroccan students felt about engaging in autonomous study. Was it that they were simply unused to this mode of working, did they feel the task set was forcing them to break ranks with their fellow students, or did they feel that their teacher had somehow failed to fulfil his part of the bargain? In any event, there was clearly a sense of unease with autonomous learning, which may not be surprising given Riley's analysis of Moroccan society. Finally, with respect to the Vietnamese, Riley points to the difficulty of distinguishing between underlying national cultural traits and the consequences of the recent history of a country (which has been particularly troubled in the case of Vietnam). Asian cultures related to Vietnam tend to be marked by low individualism, large power distance and strong uncertainty avoidance, none of which predispose students towards autonomous learning. The main trait Riley observed in his Vietnamese students, however, was a strong commitment to the group, with a negative reaction to individual self-direction, which was perceived as anti-social. Group cohesion, mutual support and social relevance were the qualities most valued by the Vietnamese students.

Self-direction is a methodological variable which, like any other, will be perceived in the light of students' cultural background and expectations. In envisaging the adoption of a self-directive or learner-centred mode of learning, the teacher should therefore pay close attention to the sociocultural assumptions which her students bring with them to the classroom. What may be perfectly natural for one group of students may be perceived as being unusual, confusing or even anti-social by another. This does not mean that certain cultural groups are 'unsuited' to self-directive or learner-centred modes of study. It does, however, point to certain tensions that may arise, and underlines the importance of incorporating an analysis of students' cultural expectations into course planning and implementation.

PED. The treatment of classroom culture in this section has been indicative rather than systematic: it has simply tried to show the type and range of factors which may go to form the classroom culture of a given group of learners.

Select a teaching situation you are familiar with and draw up a profile of the classroom culture of the learners concerned.

- What are the main constitutive features of this culture? (In assessing this, you may find it helpful to use Hofstede's four parameters.)
- To what extent can you account for this classroom culture in terms of factors such as national cultural attitudes, the educational traditions of the country or institution in question, economic or ideological forces, or whatever else you may feel to be relevant?

5.4 The importance of adaptability

The contextual factors surveyed in this chapter add an extra dimension to the realisation of a learner-centred approach to teaching. This, however, is inevitable. Language teaching and learning involve more than the interaction between teacher, learners and a given set of learning materials or activities: they are social as well as educational actions which will be conducted in a real-world setting which is characterised by a number of pragmatic and attitudinal factors. Certain basic educational procedures must necessarily be present in any learner-centred mode of teaching – the development of the learners' personal understanding of their learning goals and of the process of language learning, and the gradual development of their ability to play an informed and self-directive role in their learning. The manner in which these procedures are realised, however, is likely to vary considerably depending on the learners themselves, their learning goals, and the characteristics of the context in which they will be studying the language. This section will look very briefly at three topics which may seem somewhat problematic in terms of the realisation of a learner-centred approach to teaching – *class size*, the presence of a *pre-set syllabus*, and the question of *syllabus negotiation*. The goal is not to deal with any of these topics in depth, but rather to talk through the topics briefly to bring out the flexibility and adaptability that is required in order to realise the basic principles of learner-centred teaching in a contextually appropriate manner.

Class size will inevitably have an influence on the form of interaction between teacher and learners upon which learner-centred teaching is based. In a class of 10–12, the teacher can interact directly with each learner to get to know their specific background and learning preferences. This is hardly feasible with a class of 120 or more. To take just one example, learner training with large class groups would probably need to be based on a printed booklet containing explanations, case studies and guided reflection tasks for learners to work through alone or in peer-organised study groups. The teacher could talk through the learner training materials in lecture mode, leaving the exploration of the various topics to the learners themselves. This might seem to be a more didactic approach to learner training than the close teacher guidance and collaboration which is normally associated with learner-centred teaching. This is not necessarily the case, however. A lecture-style presentation of learner training might, in fact, be seen as giving more freedom to learners to think through and explore learning options for themselves. The learners' classroom culture needs to be assessed carefully in this respect. For instance, if the teacher is seen as an authority figure whose main task is to share her knowledge and insights with students, the learners may in fact *expect* to be left to get on with the assimilation and learning of the 'knowledge' which the teacher provides them with. Furthermore, if students are used to large class teaching they are likely to have developed their own self-help and study strategies which can be harnessed and built into the learner training materials. Large classes are not by definition an obstacle to a learner-centred mode of teaching, even if they will call for a pedagogical approach (including accommodation of the positive elements of the local classroom culture and self-help or study strategies) different from that which would be appropriate with small groups.

Some writing seems to imply that the presence of a *pre-set syllabus* is more or less incompatible with the adoption of a participative approach to teaching, which is profoundly misleading with respect to the real nature of learner-centred teaching. In many contexts, particularly in state-run secondary education, there may be a more or less substantial given element in course content – often in the form of a national or regional curriculum. In this type of situation, the challenge is to find means of promoting language education by means of constructive interaction with the existing structures, and in the light of the learners' real-world priorities. Even in a relatively constrained context, a learner-centred approach should seek to enrich the realisation of the syllabus in educational terms, and not to subvert it. Achieving this has a lot to do with openness and clarity as regards the goals and content of the existing syllabus. This need not involve the attempt to convince learners that existing structures are perfect: it is far more a matter of transparency and a realistic evaluation of choices, which is a form of applied learner training. This would resemble what Johnson (1989: 14–15) calls an 'integrated approach' to course design, though in reality it need be no less learner-centred in terms of language education than one in which learners have the opportunity to play a more powerful role in content specification. A teacher would have to do a great deal of soul-searching before allowing her students to orient their learning in a direction which is likely to place them in conflict with the education system they are working in, even if this direction were to be perfectly valid in itself. Few syllabi, however, are so constraining as to allow no scope whatsoever for individual exploration, even if this may be limited to certain sub-parts of the syllabus such as the selection of topics for oral discussion, peer evaluation of written work, or the preparation of grammar exercises by the learners themselves (cf. 7.3–7.5).

Perhaps the most delicate aspect of learner-centred teaching is *syllabus negotiation*, as Clarke (1991) illustrates very clearly. In certain cases, it is feasible to negotiate virtually the whole structure of a course with learners as part of an ongoing process of discovery and decision-making. In others, it is not. This depends on the experiential background and attitudinal disposition of the learners themselves, and also on a number of contextual factors. The cultural background of the learners, as indicated by Riley (op. cit.), will influence their expectations as to the relative roles of teachers and learners, and may predispose certain groups relatively more than others to a collaborative form of learning. The learners' prior language learning experience, in terms of both quantity (how much they have done) and quality (whether it was varied enough to provide them with awareness of a range of learning options), their motivation and their learning goals will also have an effect. Learners with extensive experience of language study, high motivation and commitment to the learning process, and clear, self-generated learning goals are likely to be able to play a stronger role in syllabus negotiation than learners who may be inexperienced in language study and who are 'ticking over' in a course which has limited (perceived) personal relevance for them. Small class size is a help, as it allows more regular feedback and discussion between teacher and learners; good material conditions allow learners to experiment with different modes of study and thus find their own path to learning. And, of course, the presence of an existing syllabus and/or examination may place limits on what can realistically be seen as negotiable.

To give a practical example, Tudor (1991) compared the attitudinal and experiential disposition of second and fifth (final) year Belgian students of business administration (i.e. two sub-groups of the same global population) to a learner-centred mode of teaching. The second year students' limited language learning experience, their degree of personal maturity, their lack of experience of collaborative learning in other subjects, and their overriding concern with examination success as a goal in itself, would have made a negotiative approach to syllabus specification of questionable value. Fifth year students, on the other hand, are older and more mature, have acquired extensive experience of language study (more than 500 hours of instruction in English and in Dutch involving a variety of methodological options, learning materials and teaching styles), and have a keener awareness of the functional relevance of their language study to their professional careers. As a result of these differences, language education would seem to be best realised with second year students in a primarily teacher-led manner by means of learner training, with the goal of helping students develop their under-standing of language, language learning and the study options available to them. With fifth year students, on the other hand, a loose structuring of the course around a few key activity types (persuasively-oriented oral presentations, problem solution tasks, report writing and job interviews) is quite sufficient, further specification in terms of both syllabus content and methodology being conducted negotiatively between teacher and learners. Syllabus negotiation, then, is not a fetish, but rather one manifestation of language education whose effectiveness and feasibility are linked to the strategic awareness and classroom culture of the learners concerned.

Finding the right balance amid these variables requires considerable sensitivity and flexibility from the teacher. In an authority-based culture, for example, an openly negotiative stance from the teacher may violate learners' role expectations and lead to confusion or even a loss of respect for the teacher. This is more than simply an affective problem for the teacher, as it can undermine learners' willingness to participate in activities (or even attend classes) and thus have negative effects on their learning. In this type of context, the teacher may find it necessary to encourage critical reflection (learner training) and channel learner in-volvement in a more 'authoritative' manner than would be appropriate in other contexts. This may call for a skilled use of devices such as mode of address, seating arrangements, task definition or the tone in which suggestions are made. The learners' orientation in terms of the variable of individualism vs. collectivism may also influence the manner in which negotiation is most appropriately realised. With students whose home cultures favour strong group solidarity, such as those of the Moroccan and Vietnamese students profiled by Riley (op. cit.), individual learner training and involvement may take second place to shared or group development. Students from a culture which has a strong collectivist orientation may resent being 'singled out' or feeling obliged to function as individuals – which they may perceive as a lack of solidarity with their fellow students. In such cases, the teacher may find it most effective to interact with learners primarily as members of the learning group, and give individual learners the personal space to work out their own path to learning in a non-public manner. Considerations of this nature relate to the sociocultural aspects of learners' personality and, thereby, of their identity. Respect for these aspects of learners' identity is as much a part of learner-centred teaching as respect for differences of a more personal or psychological nature. Constructive accommodation of cultural variability is thus as much a part of learner-centred teaching as the accommodation of individual variability.

REF. Refer back to the potential difficulties you identified in the task at the end of 5.1.

- How many of these difficulties have been addressed in this chapter?
- How satisfactory have you found the way in which contextual factors have been discussed?
- Which other factors do you feel to be of relevance in assessing the 'contextual dimension' of learner-centred teaching and the manner in which it can be realised in differing contexts?

5.5 Summary

a) Writing on learner-centredness frequently pays insufficient attention to the contextual dimension of language teaching. While language learners are certainly individuals in affective, cognitive and experiential terms, they are also members of a given sociocultural group and will be studying in a context which is shaped by a variety of social, economic, cultural and ideological factors. A coherently learner-centred approach to teaching cannot afford to ignore these factors.

b) Means analysis is the process which involves the study of those factors (the material and organisational features of the setting, and the participants involved) which shape the material and attitudinal context within which language teaching will take place.

c) Classroom culture is a key component of means analysis and refers to the attitudes and expectations which constitute students' sociocultural personality in the classroom, and which will therefore influence their interaction with various aspects of language study. Students' classroom culture derives in part from their national or regional culture, but also reflects the value system of the peer group to which they belong, the ideological trends present in their home society at a given point in time, and the socioeconomic climate of the moment.

d) Sensitivity to the learning context and to classroom culture are crucial in a learner-centred approach to teaching. The teacher therefore needs to show adaptability in realising the basic principles of learner-centredness in a contextually appropriate manner.

e) Acknowledgement of the role of classroom culture and of contextual factors should alert teachers to the cultural relativity of concepts such as 'autonomy' or 'self-direction', as well as to the differing perceptions learners can have of aspects of classroom methodology such as the roles of teachers and learners.

6 Self-assessment

6.1 Self-assessment and language education

Assessment is a term which tends to have a rather bad press among both learners and teachers. It conjures up images of tests, marks, stress, and the words 'pass' or, worse still, 'fail'. For those who have studied a language in a formal context, with a more or less intimidating examination at the end of the course, such reactions are not difficult to understand. This having been said, assessment is simply one stage in the teaching-learning process: goals are set and attainment of these goals is monitored, which then leads to feedback and a renewed cycle of goal-setting and learning. Assessment is therefore an integral part of teaching, as much in a learner-centred mode of teaching as in any other. A major impetus to the investigation of the self-assessment abilities of language learners arose out of the Council of Europe's Modern Languages Project (1.2.2) with its emphasis on a learner-centred and motivation-based form of learning. Trim, in the preface to Oskarsson's *Approaches to Self-Assessment in Foreign Language Learning*, makes the following comments about the role of evaluation in the Modern Languages Project:

> Evaluation was to be seen, not as a means of imposing the objectives of an authoritarian technocracy upon the population of learners, but as a means of enabling learners to achieve more effectively more *objectives* corresponding to their *needs*.
> (1980: ix) Original emphasis

Trim goes on to point out that this calls for 'a close interaction between learners, teachers, planners and experts at all levels and stages in the educational process'. Trim thus links evaluation with needs analysis and the setting of learning objectives; he also sees it as a pedagogical undertaking in which learners should play an active role, albeit as part of a broadly-based pooling of knowledge with other participants. For Trim, then, learner involvement in assessment is an essential component of a learner-centred approach to teaching.

In 1.4.2 it was suggested that the ultimate goal of a learner-centred approach is learner empowerment, or enabling learners to pursue their language–related life goals in an informed and self-directive manner, this goal being achieved by means of language education. The last three chapters have examined a range of factors specific either to the learners themselves or to the context of learning which the teacher needs to bear in mind in the practical realisation of language education and, thereby, in the pursuit of learner empowerment. This chapter and the next look at a number of means by which language education can be integrated into ongoing learning activities. Self-assessment, which is the subject of the present chapter, plays a crucial role both in language education and in terms of learner empowerment. The reasons for this are relatively clear: if learners are to be in a position to operate self-directively, they *must* have the ability to assess:

- the communicative and linguistic demands of their target situations of use;
- their current abilities with respect to these demands;
- the practical learning options that are available to them as means of attaining their goals and their subjective interaction with these options.

In what follows, self-assessment will be presented as an activity which encompasses these three elements – target situation analysis (what learners will need to do in the language), present situation analysis (what they can currently do), and strategic analysis (how they can best attain their desired learning goals in the light of the learning options available to them, their subjective needs and individual learning preferences). Self-assessment will thus be seen as an activity which is central to the active and reflective involvement of learners in their language study, and thus as an integral component of language education.

Oskarsson suggests six main reasons for developing learners' self-assessment abilities which bring out very clearly the powerful educational function of self-assessment:

1 *Promotion of learning.* Encouraging students to think critically about their competence in the TL is beneficial to language education, and can foster a more informed and intelligent attitude among students.
2 *Raised level of awareness.* Training students in self-assessment procedures, rather than expecting them to rely solely on the judgements of others, generates a more independent and discerning attitude not only to assessment *per se*, but also to course content and learning options.
3 *Improved goal-orientation.* Self-assessment leads students to

reflect on the variety of goals that can exist and thereby broadens their vision of what learning a language is or can be. 'Other directed' assessment tends to have a limiting effect and generates passivity. Self-assessment can foster students' creativity in various aspects of their learning, including their participation in classroom activities.

4   *Expansion of range of assessment.* The individual student's understanding of his competence in a language is closer and more deeply and personally felt than that of an outside agent, especially in terms of his affective learning needs. Student involvement can thus produce a richer and fuller profile of learning needs.

5   *Shared assessment burden.* Sharing the responsibility for assessment between both teacher and students, rather than leaving it with the teacher alone as is the case in traditional approaches, can lighten the teacher's load in both practical and psychological terms.

6   *Beneficial postcourse effects.* Training students in self-assessment provides them with a skill crucial to subsequent learning, possibly in contexts where they will not have access to the evaluative advice of a teacher. Self-assessment therefore fosters independent learning. (1989: 3–5 adapted)

Oskarsson sees training in self-assessment as having a positive influence on the general quality of learners' involvement in their language study, and as a means of fostering their ability to assume an active and self-directive role in their learning – both during and subsequent to their formal course of study. He thus accords to self-assessment a pivotal role in terms of both language education and, in his sixth point, learner empowerment.

PED. Analyse the role which assessment plays in your teaching, considering all types of assessment from formal examinations to periodic achievement tests and informal feed-back on learners' classroom performance.

- What are the specific goals pursued by these different forms of assessment?
- In which way do they relate to the learners' personal goals and/or to course objectives?
- How far are the results of these assessment procedures used to inform subsequent teaching, and in which ways?
- Does your use of assessment relate more to the product or to the process side of learning?
- Do you see any scope for expanding the latter?

6.2 Can language learners self-assess?

Oskarsson (op. cit.) suggests that self-assessment can play a positive role in terms of language education. He also suggests, however, that learners can provide objectively useful information on their current abilities and learning needs. The two need not, of course, go together. Learners' motivation and their general awareness of language learning could well be improved by self-assessment activities, without the learners being able to make objectively valid or reliable statements about their language abilities. If, however, learner self-assessment is to be integrated into course design, the teacher needs to have an insight into the objective value of the sort of judgements her students are likely to make of their language abilities.

Assessment is the area of language learning where teachers may feel the most reticence about transferring responsibility to their students, a feeling which is probably shared by a not inconsiderable number of students, especially those who come from a learning culture which has an authority- or knowledge-based orientation (5.3). These are understandable reactions, as assessment calls for the simultaneous use of three types of knowledge. These are knowledge of learning goals, of the linguistic and pragmatic realisation of these goals, and of the methods and criteria of evaluation. Learners may well, on the basis of their knowledge of their target situations of use, have powerful insights into both their communicative goals and the performance criteria that are crucial in these situations. Inevitably, however, their ability to assess how well they can realise their communicative intentions will be dependent upon their current level of competence in the TL. Furthermore, evaluation is a complex process, and it would be unreasonable to expect language learners to possess the expertise and knowledge of evaluation procedures which teachers have acquired as a result of their professional training and experience. There is, therefore, an understandable tension between the desirability in educational and motivational terms of involving learners in assessment, and questions about the objective reliability of their self-assessments.

This tension has given rise to a respectable body of studies investigating the self-assessment abilities of L2 learners. The general trend of results emerging from studies conducted in a variety of settings (e.g. Bachman and Palmer 1989; Blanche 1986; Fok 1981; Lee 1981; Oskarsson 1981; Von Elek 1982; Wangsotorn 1981) is that learners are, in fact, able to make valid and reliable statements about their L2 abilities. Blanche and Merino, in a survey of 21 self-assessment studies, observe that:

The emerging pattern is one of consistent overall agreement between self-assessments and ratings based on a variety of external criteria. The accuracy of most students' self-estimates often varies depending on the language skills and materials involved in the evaluation ... but these estimates are generally *good* or *very good*. (1989: 315. Original emphasis)

These results would seem to indicate that self-assessment merits consideration alongside more traditional forms of assessment such as teacher evaluation or the use of standardised tests, and that it can complement these modes of assessment to provide a more balanced picture of a learner's linguistic and communicative skills.

LeBlanc and Painchaud (1985) describe a study which shows the practical usefulness of self-assessment as a placement technique as well as providing a number of practically relevant guidelines with respect to the development of self-assessment instruments. The study was conducted at the University of Ottawa which, as a bilingual university (English and French), required all new students to take an initial placement test in their second language. The results obtained from this test were used firstly to determine whether students needed additional work on the language, and then, if necessary, to allocate them to one of six levels of language improvement course. On the basis of a study conducted with over 3,000 students, in which the subjects completed both the standardised placement test and a self-assessment questionnaire, the authors found correlations of around .80 (p. < .0001) between student self-assessments and the results obtained on the standardised test. The authors concluded that the self-assessment questionnaire placed students 'at least as well' as the standardised test. In fact the results of the study were so convincing that from September of 1984 language placement was conducted solely on the basis of student self-assessment, instead of the standardised test. Moreover, LeBlanc and Painchaud found that the number of transfers of students from one level of language group to another fell the year that placement was based on student self-assessment. Transfers between groups over four sessions in the academic year 1983–4, when students were allocated to groups on the basis of the standardised placement test, averaged 15.7 per cent, whereas transfers in the year 1984–5, when placement was based on student self-assessment, averaged 12.8 per cent. The authors describe this as an unexpected but nonetheless welcome 'bonus' of placement via self-assessment. The authors also point to a number of practical advantages that arose out of the use of self-assessment as a placement instrument. These included a reduction in the time required for testing (20 minutes for the self-assessment questionnaire against 100 minutes for the standardised test), elimination of the time-consuming administrative organisation of testing with large numbers of students (the self-assessment questionnaire was given to students to complete in their own time), and the removal of the necessity to guard against cheating (an inevitable precaution when standardised tests are used, if only to ensure that students do not make copies of the test to 'help' friends).

LeBlanc and Painchaud do, however, point out that self-assessment needs to be linked in a direct and transparent manner to students' experience of the TL. In an initial phase of the study outlined above, the authors experimented with two different self-assessment questionnaires. The first contained 40 statements such as:

> I understand short and simple written communications (posters, schedules, announcements).
> I understand a text on a known topic (even though I have to use a dictionary).
> I read specialised articles concerning my fields of study fluently.
> (Cited in LeBlanc and Painchaud: Op. cit.)

The students rated their ability to perform the task on a scale from 1 ('I cannot do this at all') to 5 ('I can do this all the time'), the scores 2, 3 and 4 having no performance specification. Comparison of student self-assessments with the results of a standardised placement test produced an overall correlation of .53, which the authors consider to be 'acceptable', but not 'of the highest level'. The second questionnaire contained questions that were linked closely to the students' likely situations of use. For example:

> If I found myself in conversation with a French-speaking student, I would be able to *understand*
> 1 conventional greetings and farewells
> 2 personal information given to me (name, address, phone number, etc.)
> 3 informal exchanges on subjects such as weather, health, current events, courses, etc.
> 4 any compliments or invitations expressed to me
> 5 expressions of personal opinions, personal preferences, etc. addressed to me.
> (Cited in LeBlanc and Painchaud: Op. cit.)

The results derived from this type of question correlated more closely with the placement tests, at .80 or more. The authors conclude that the form of questions used can have a substantial influence on the effectiveness of a self-assessment instrument: the main point seems to be that learners can self-assess more effectively if they are asked to do so on the basis of situations close to their personal experience. This is coherent with the underlying principles of learner-centred teaching in that it indicates that learning (in this specific case, self-assessment) is more effective if it links in meaningfully with learners' ongoing experience of life in general and of language use in particular.

Learners' self-assessment abilities should not, however, be taken for granted. Blue (1988), for example, found that cultural background influences learners' ability to self-assess accurately, some groups tending to overestimate and others to underestimate their abilities: Blue points out that this can raise a number of difficulties for a teacher working with multicultural groups of students. Training in self-assessment techniques, and students' attitudes to learning and to teacher-learner roles also need to be considered. Janssen-van Dieten (1989), in a study involving immigrant learners of Dutch, found virtually no correlation between subjects' self-assessments and objective test scores. The author explains these results, in part at least, by pointing out that the subjects 'were unexpectedly confronted with a kind of evaluation they were not used to, let alone trained in' (ibid.: 44) and insists on the importance of training. Furthermore, LeBlanc and Painchaud (op. cit.: 685–6) found that the assumption of responsibility for one's learning which is implicit in self-assessment can 'create problems with some students who feel that any type of evaluation should be the responsibility of someone in authority, of someone "who knows"'. In other words, some learners can react negatively to the role and responsibilities implicit in self-assessment if these run counter to their attitudes to the learning process (these reactions may result from factors of an individual nature such as those discussed in 4.2, or they may arise out of culturally-based attitudes along the lines discussed in 5.3). Self-assessment, then, like other aspects of learner involvement, is an activity which learners need guidance and time to grow into.

PED. With respect to a teaching situation you are familiar with, analyse the ways in which self-assessment could be used to complement the assessment procedures currently in use.

- Can you foresee any difficulties that might arise in the implementation of self-assessment in the teaching context in question?
- What are they, and what is their origin?

6.3 Self-assessment in context

The main thrust of the self-assessment studies reviewed in the last section relates to learners' ability to provide a meaningful level of input to present situation analysis, which is an integral part of objective needs analysis (3.1). Most self-assessment studies involve learners evaluating their linguistic or communicative abilities against a set of performance descriptors developed by the researcher. This is fine – as far as it goes, at least. If self-assessment involves no more than this, however, it will fail to achieve its full potential for two reasons. Firstly, transferring into the pedagogical field an expert-based approach to the establishment of performance criteria fails to exploit learners' *own* insights into their communicative agendas, as discussed in Chapter 3. Often, initial guidance with respect to performance criteria within the framework of learner training will be necessary, but this is best seen as a transitional phase, one stage along the road to learner involvement and, ultimately, to learner empowerment. Secondly, if self-assessment leads simply to a stock-taking of deficiencies and inadequacies, it is likely to be a somewhat discouraging experience. It should therefore be linked closely with the setting of attainable learning objectives and, in parallel with this, the planning of learning activities by which the learner can progress towards his desired competence in the TL. This will entail consideration of the individual learning needs and preferences discussed in Chapter 4, and also of the pragmatic factors and culturally-based expectations about language learning discussed in Chapter 5.

With this perspective on self-assessment in mind, it may be helpful to consider a study (Tudor and Nivelles 1991) of the strategic awareness of a group of L2 learners at the Université Libre de Bruxelles. The subjects (N = 168) were second year students of Economics and Business Administration following a 90-hour course in English as part of their degree programme. The study had two parts. The first related to the subjects' self-assessment abilities and involved comparison of the subjects' self-assessments of selected aspects of their English proficiency with parallel assessments made by their class teachers and with performance on their end-of-course examinations. The second examined aspects of the subjects' strategic learning awareness.

In the self-assessment component, subjects were asked to rate their overall proficiency in English and four aspects of their oral competence (pronunciation, fluency, range and accuracy of expression) on an annotated scale from 1 to 20. Subjects' self-assessments were compared with parallel subjective evaluations made by their class teacher and with the subjects' performance in their end-of-course examination, which consisted of an oral interview conducted by two teachers other than the subjects' class teacher and a battery of proficiency tests. The results showed significant levels of correlation (p. < .01) between the subjects' self-assessments and both teacher evaluations and examination marks as regards the subjects' oral skills (self-teacher .70; self-examination .55) and their general proficiency (self-teacher .67; self-examination .68). The results of this part of the study thus reflect the general trend of results arising from the self-assessment studies reviewed by Blanche and Merino (op. cit.), namely that learners have insights into their language abilities which merit consideration alongside both teacher evaluations and formal test results.

The second part of the study was designed to yield information on what the subjects perceived to be their *learning priorities* and on the *study techniques* they used. Subjects were therefore asked to list the aspects of English they felt they most needed to improve (up to a maximum of three), and then to give the study techniques they used in each area.

The results revealed that the subjects defined their learning priorities primarily in linguistic terms or with respect to their examinations, 57 per cent of the responses falling into the categories of 'vocabulary', 'grammar' and 'listening comprehension/dictation' (the last category apparently relating to one of the end-of-course examinations, a dictation drawn from a BBC news broadcast). A few subjects did define their goals in communicative terms such as:

- 'to be able to have a conversation and "think in English"';
- 'understanding a TV programme in English';
- 'precise comprehension of texts (I understand the subject and the main points, but not all the words)';
- 'getting used to the English accent (it's different from American)'.

The above selection of responses, however, represented only a tiny minority of those provided. The subjects would seem to have defined their learning goals around their interpretation of the demands of their end-of-course examination, this perspective presumably being shaped by their experience of language learning at secondary school (the subjects were following their first language course since they had entered university a year before) and their overwhelming desire to succeed in their year as a whole. This is despite the fact that their course of study approached language development within a communicative framework and via an activity-based mode of learning. The subjects seemed to be perceiving their course of study differently from their teachers. They thus seemed to have 'interpreted' the course in terms of their immediate experience and life goals, in which success in their end-of-course examination played a significant role, and had only a very vague perspective on the role of English in their future professional life: they did not even seem to perceive their course of study as a means of facilitating social contacts with speakers of English (native speakers or others) or access to English language media. This came as a surprise to both authors, even though we had taught members of the same population for a number of years, which indicates that we had misjudged this aspect of the learners' classroom culture and attitudes to learning.

In terms of the subjects' study techniques the results were even more striking. A first point which deserves mention in this respect is the number of non-responses. Out of a possible total of 504 responses (168 S's × 3 responses), 463 responses were provided for learning priorities, but only 404 for study techniques used, which might in itself point to a weakness in the subjects' strategic learning capabilities. Subsequent to an initial survey of the results, subjects' study techniques were analysed into two categories. The first (strategy +) relates to strategies where mention was made of an activity (e.g. reading texts) together with a specific learning technique (e.g. highlighting useful vocabulary; drawing up a word list). The 'strategy +' category was thus taken to indicate a personalised form of learning involving individual choice and self-direction. The other category of response simply involved the mention of an activity (e.g. reading newspapers; listening to the radio) without any specification of study technique. Of the 262 responses mentioning grammar, vocabulary and listening comprehension/dictation as a learning priority, only 63 (24 per cent) fell into the 'strategy +' category, the rest simply giving an activity (67 per cent) or leaving the study technique element blank (9 per cent).

The results of the study as a whole are rather ambiguous. The self-assessment section indicated that the subjects had insights into their abilities in English which compared well with those of their class teacher and with results obtainable from a battery of proficiency tests. The results of the strategic awareness section paint a rather different picture, showing only limited evidence of the type of learning strategies which Rubin (2.2) found to be characteristic of 'good' language learners. Although the subject population was composed of academically able students with high motivation for success and what seemed to be a positive attitude to the learning of English, one cannot help feeling that many of them were working somewhat in the dark, with very short-term learning goals and an inadequately developed set of study techniques. Thus, had the study been restricted to the self-assessment section alone, it might have painted a deceptively rosy picture of the subjects' overall strategic awareness.

The implications of this study are that learners' self-assessment skills should be developed integratively, within the wider context of their involvement in their language study. In this light, self-assessment is just one part of a wider process of reflection and planning that will recur at regular intervals throughout a learner's course of study. This process has three stages. The *projective* stage involves the identification of the learners' communicative goals based on an analysis of their target situations of use and the communicative intentions they will wish to fulfil in these situations. The *evaluative* stage, in which self-assessment plays a role together with more traditional diagnostic techniques such as teacher evaluation and the use of formal tests, involves a stocktaking of the learners' abilities *vis-à-vis* their communicative goals, and an evaluation of their strengths and weaknesses in the TL. The *strategic* phase calls for the setting of concrete learning objectives and the planning of learning activities, which involves the development of learners' awareness of the learning opportunities potentially available to them and of how these can promote attainment of their learning goals. 6.4 will concentrate on the projective and evaluative stages of self-assessment, while 6.5 will consider the strategic stage. In practice, of course, the three should work in parallel: the topic division adopted here is thus a matter of practical convenience.

PED. With respect to a group of learners you have taught in the past or that you are teaching currently, develop a sequence of self-assessment activities which would allow you to evaluate the learners' overall strategic awareness. Include components relating to:

- the learners' goals (in objective terms) and their perceptions of these goals;
- the learners' current abilities with respect to these goals;
- the learners' awareness of the learning opportunities potentially available to them.

In which way(s) could this information help you to plan subsequent learner training and involvement?

6.4 Self-assessment and goal-setting

In Chapter 3 it was suggested that the networks of conceptual and pragmatic knowledge (3.4) which learners bring with them to their language study, and which are realised in the occupational, interactive and cultural/affective domains (3.5), underpin the communicative agendas they will wish to fulfil in the TL and thereby shape the contribution which learners can make to goal-setting. This is expressed by LeBlanc and Painchaud in the following terms:

> ... adult students, before being learners of a second language, have thoroughly mastered a means of communication, their native language, and they know in a more or less implicit way why and how they use it. Chances are their intended use of the second language will not differ significantly from that of their first language. This is why it is important that adult students are the ones to evaluate their situation, ... for they are the ones who know, albeit intuitively, the relationship between the objectives of the task at hand and their knowledge at any given point in time. (Op. cit.: 675)

A difference exists, however, between the nature of the input learners can provide on the basis of their conceptual and pragmatic knowledge. Conceptual knowledge is largely language-independent and can therefore provide a very direct form of input into goal-setting in terms of the facts, opinions and judgements learners will wish to communicate. Learners' pragmatic knowledge, on the other hand, is linked both to the linguistic system of their L1 and also to the communicative conventions of the speech community to which they belong – conventions which may differ more or less significantly from those which are operant in the TL community. Input to goal-setting on the basis of learners' pragmatic knowledge is thus likely to be *indicative* (in the sense that it provides guidelines as to the interactive skills the learners will wish to develop), and *exploratory* (in the sense that it provides a starting point for the exploration of the communicative resources and conventions of the TL). The objective reliability of learners' self-assessments in the pragmatic field will thus be dependent on their familiarity with the pragmatic conventions of the TL community in their intended situations of use, and also on their awareness of the linguistic and communicative resources of the TL. For instance, learners preparing for academic study at a British university will bring with them their stock of conceptual knowledge (for example, expertise in tropical veterinary medicine, familiarity with the specific problems of their home country, and a research subject), but they may have limited knowledge of the pragmatic conventions operant at British universities. In such a case, the learners' self-assessment skills in the pragmatic field are likely to be less reliable than in the conceptual field, and they will be dependent on their teacher's guidance in evaluating what their learning objectives should be and how close they are to the required performance levels. Other difficulties may arise with respect to distinctions which are explicitly encoded in the language itself, such as that between *Du* and *Sie* in German. Furthermore, pragmatic differences between high and low context cultures (cf. Moran 1990; Platt 1989) and the consequences these have in terms of interactive conventions are subtle, but extremely important in terms of communicative effectiveness. This level of appropriacy can be very difficult for learners to perceive, and guidance from the teacher is likely to be necessary: in these areas, learners' self-assessment will need to operate in conjunction with the gradual development of their understanding of the linguistic and communicative resources of the TL itself and of the pragmatic conventions of the TL community.

In addition to this, it needs to be borne in mind that self-assessment is one part of learners' overall participation in their language study and is therefore likely to reflect the trend from teacher- to learner-direction that marks the move from learner training to learner involvement (2.7) within learner-centred teaching as a whole. With this in mind, it is probably advisable, as a general rule at least, to approach self-assessment in global terms in the first instance. This allows learners to reflect on their language abilities with respect to the relatively familiar and accessible skill concepts of speaking, listening, reading and writing; thus they may build up a shared vocabulary and also develop their ability to reflect on linguistic and communicative concepts that they may not have had to handle actively in the past. In addition, this allows the teacher (2.3) to get a feel for her students' perceptions of language study in general and to deepen her understanding of where they stand with respect to the type of factor discussed in 2.4 (learning goals and motivation) and 2.5 (beliefs about language learning). In this way, self-assessment plays an important role, not only as part of learner training but also in terms of needs analysis and goal-setting. Learner self-assessments which, in objective terms, are systematically too high or too low may simply point to a lack of experience in self-assessment or of functional contact with the TL. They may also, however, be indicative of certain attitudinal dispositions to the learning process: if language study has little perceived relevance to the learners concerned, they may feel that 'getting by' minimalistically is quite satisfactory, while too harsh an assessment may indicate that a learner perceives language learning as a daunting task in which he has little chance of success. And of course, a general reluctance to engage in self-assessment (the 'Why are you asking *me*? Isn't this *your* job?' attitude) may be evidence of a learner's unwillingness to assume an active role in his language study. The activities discussed below therefore move from global (6.4.1) to more specific, task-oriented (6.4.2) forms of self-assessment. Some learners may, of course, positively wish to move directly into the analysis of specific difficulties they have experienced or functional tasks they wish to perform, which indicates a practical, experientially-driven approach to learning, and in this case the teacher may therefore find it most appropriate to get down to specific self-assessment activities immediately.

Oskarsson makes the very sensible recommendation that:

> At every stage of the development of self-management techni-
> ques it is of fundamental importance to keep the target-group
> learner in mind. Materials and instructions must be easy to
> understand and easy to handle, otherwise they may not function
> in the hands of those who have little academic training. (1980:
> 19–20)

This affects the structure and transparency of the self-assessment instruments themselves, the intellectual demands they make of learners, and
also the knowledge of language and of language learning they assume. In
planning self-assessment activities the teacher also needs to take account
of the subjective needs of the learners involved. Learners with a low
tolerance for ambiguity (4.2), or with an 'authority-oriented' learning
style preference (4.3), for example, may react with unease to the whole
idea of self-assessment as a result of a psychological need to feel
'directed' and provided with something 'solid' to hold onto. Similar
considerations apply to the culturally-based expectations learners bring
with them to their language study. Learners' classroom culture (5.3) may
thus lead them to expect that 'serious' matters such as assessment are the
teacher's responsibility, and the attempt to involve learners in assessment
may violate these role expectations and therefore be greeted with
confusion. Also, if the learners' culture incorporates a strong tendency
towards group solidarity (5.3.3) the goals of peer evaluation may need
careful explanation to avoid learners feeling that they are being asked to
'judge' or to 'criticise' their fellow students. The teacher needs to keep
this type of factor constantly in mind in the practical organisation of
self-assessment activities.

6.4.1   Global self-assessment

The four self-assessment formats discussed below, taken from Oskarsson
(op. cit.: 37–45), are meant to provide a few practical ideas about how
global self-assessment might be approached:

1)   *Partial skill description + self-rating scale*
In this, the simplest format suggested by Oskarsson, learners are
provided with skill descriptions only for the two extremes of the target
performance scale: the intermediate levels have no skill description so
that learners place themselves where they feel appropriate between the
two ends of the scale. Figure 13 illustrates this with regard to speaking
skills. The information this format can yield is limited by the lack of
specification of the stages between full fluency and inability to speak: it

is, however, very easy to construct and, if applied to all four skills, can provide a rough initial estimate of how a learner perceives his relative strengths and weaknesses across the four skills and also within each. The weakness of this format is the lack of intermediate skill description – what does a self-rating of five actually mean to any one learner as opposed to another? However, if learners are asked to discuss their self-ratings with each other in functional terms, it can stimulate useful reflection on the learners' perceptions both of their current abilities and of their learning goals.

2) *Situation outline + partial skill description + self-rating scale*
This format (Figure 14) differs from the last in that a situation or activity is added: In this way, learners are asked to self-assess within a more constrained and contextualised frame of reference, which should make the task easier and more focused. For this to be the case, however, the situation provided needs to be relevant to the learners' goals and at least not too distant from their practical experience of using the TL: otherwise, the activity is likely to become a test of learners' projective imagination as much as of their self-assessment skills as such. Indeed, it is very helpful if the teacher can elicit the relevant situations of use or activities from the learners themselves. This constitutes a direct form of learner input to goal-setting, which can then be used as a basis for (self-)assessment.

3) *Expanded skill description + self-rating scale*
Figure 15 may be seen as an expansion of the instrument given in Figure 13. The performance descriptors at the two ends of the scale are, for the skill in question, much the same, but four of the intermediate stages have been filled in, which provides learners with a more detailed set of descriptors against which to assess their abilities. In Figure 15, five stages are left open for learners who feel they do not fit precisely either of the neighbouring descriptors, though these intermediate stages could of course be replaced by further descriptors. The use of detailed performance descriptors can yield a valuable functional profile of learners' abilities. However, developing performance descriptors can be less straightforward than one might at first imagine, if only because learners frequently manifest clusters of sub-skills (e.g. high fluency and range of expression, low accuracy and poor pronunciation) which do not fit neatly into any one descriptor. The use of self-assessment instruments such as that presented in Figure 15 may be most useful with large classes, where the teacher has less chance to discuss matters directly with the learners concerned. Furthermore, if an assessment instrument is to be used by language learners as opposed to teachers, it should not make

Put a cross in the box
which corresponds to
your estimated level.

I am completely fluent
in English. ⟶ ☐ 10

☐ 9

☐ 8

☐ 7

☐ 6

SPEAKING ☐ 5

☐ 4

☐ 3

☐ 2

I cannot speak English ☐ 1
at all. ⟶ ☐ 0

Figure 13 Partial skill description + self-rating scale
(taken from Oskarsson 1980: 37)

READING

Imagine that someone with
no knowledge of English
comes to you with an
English daily paper (e.g.
The Times, the *Guardian*)
and asks you to give as
detailed an account as
possible of what is on
the front page. You have
plenty of time, but must
not use a dictionary.

I would be able
to give a detailed
account of
everything on
the page. ⟶ ☐ 10

☐ 9

☐ 8

☐ 7

☐ 6

☐ 5

☐ 4

☐ 3

☐ 2

How well would you manage
the task?

I would not be
able to say anything. ⟶ ☐ 1

☐ 0

Figure 14 Situation outline + partial skill description + self-rating scale
(taken from Oskarsson 1980: 40)

LISTENING	
☐ I understand the language as well as a well-educated native.	5
☐	4.5
☐ I understand most of what is said in the language, even when said by native speakers, but have difficulty in understanding extreme dialect and slang. It is also difficult for me to understand speech in unfavourable conditions, for example through bad loudspeakers outdoors.	4
☐	3.5
☐ I can follow and understand the essential points concerning everyday and general things when spoken normally and clearly, but do not understand native speakers if they speak very quickly or use some slang or dialect.	3
☐	2.5
☐ I can follow and understand the essential points concerning everyday and general things when spoken slowly and clearly, but in the course of conversation I often have to ask for things to be repeated or made clearer. I only understand occasional words and phrases of statements made in unfavourable conditions, for example through loudspeakers outdoors.	2
☐	1.5
☐ I understand the meaning of simple requests, statements and questions if they are spoken slowly and clearly and if I have a chance of asking for them to be repeated. I only understand common words and phrases.	1
☐	0.5
☐ I do not understand the language at all.	0

Figure 15 Expanded skill description + self-rating scale
(taken from Oskarsson 1980: 41)

Instruction: Imagine that you meet an English-speaking person from another country. He does not know anything about you and your country. Indicate your estimated command of the language by putting a cross in the appropriate box (*Yes* or *No*) for each statement.

1. I can tell him when and where I was born. ☐ Yes ☐ No
2. I can spell my name in English. ☐ Yes ☐ No
3. I can describe my home to him. ☐ Yes ☐ No
4. I can tell him what kinds of food and drink I like and don't like. ☐ Yes ☐ No
5. I can tell him about my interests (hobbies, interests in general, etc.). ☐ Yes ☐ No
6. I can tell him what I usually read (kinds of books, newspapers, magazines, textbooks, etc.). ☐ Yes ☐ No
7. I can ask him what newspapers there are in his own country. ☐ Yes ☐ No
8. I can tell him what I do in my free time. ☐ Yes ☐ No
9. I can ask him how to get to a certain place by public transport. ☐ Yes ☐ No
10. I can tell him what I think of art galleries. ☐ Yes ☐ No
11. I can ask him about the price of a ticket for a certain football match. ☐ Yes ☐ No
12. I can tell him about things that might interest a tourist in my home region. ☐ Yes ☐ No
13. I can ask him questions about traffic-rules in his own country. ☐ Yes ☐ No
14. I can say something about social security in my country (old-age pensions, medical care, etc.). ☐ Yes ☐ No
15. I can tell him what sort of government we have in my country. ☐ Yes ☐ No
16. I can say something about my political views and tell him whether I support a political party. ☐ Yes ☐ No
17. I can tell him how I feel at the moment (if I am hungry, tired, ill, etc.). ☐ Yes ☐ No
18. I can ask him to help me arrange an appointment with a doctor. ☐ Yes ☐ No
19. I can tell him that I take medicine regularly. ☐ Yes ☐ No
20. I can tell him that I am tired and need some rest. ☐ Yes ☐ No
21. I can ask him to repeat slowly what he just said. ☐ Yes ☐ No
22. I can ask him about the pronunciation of a certain word. ☐ Yes ☐ No
23. I can ask him to characterize the climate in his country. ☐ Yes ☐ No
24. I can ask him if he knows the approximate price of a certain piece of clothing in his own country. ☐ Yes ☐ No
25. I can inform him about where he can have his car serviced. ☐ Yes ☐ No
26. I can ask him to ring me up some time. ☐ Yes ☐ No
27. I can ask for his telephone number and give my own number. ☐ Yes ☐ No
28. I can tell him where he can change foreign money. ☐ Yes ☐ No
29. I can describe weather-conditions in the four seasons in my own country. ☐ Yes ☐ No
30. I can tell him where he can eat and drink. ☐ Yes ☐ No

Figure 16 Situation outline + task specification
(taken from Oskarsson 1980: 45)

unreasonable demands on their metalinguistic knowledge, especially if the instrument has to be prepared in the TL itself.

4)   *Situation outline + task specification*
The instrument given in Figure 16 was intended for self-assessment on the Threshold Level (Van Ek 1975), the learner who ticks 25 tasks with 'Yes' being considered to have attained the Threshold Level in the language. It clearly differs from the instruments discussed above by the number of tasks it provides, and might be seen as a specific, rather than a global self-assessment instrument. This would be mistaken, however, as the outcome of the questionnaire is a general performance profile within a given domain of usage, and does not in itself generate a detailed specification of learning objectives. Responding 'No' to question 12, for instance, does not specify *why* the learner cannot tell his interlocutor about 'what might interest a tourist in [his] home country' or what he needs to learn in order to do so. It does, however, point to the need for further diagnostic work with respect to this activity and thus sets an agenda for more detailed forms of self-assessment such as those which are discussed in 6.4.2 below. Working through this or a similarly constructed questionnaire early in a course of study would thus provide a comprehensive set of learning goals which could then be explored in more detail as the course progresses.

6.4.2   Task-based self-assessment

In 3.3 it was suggested that needs analysis operates in two stages. The first will be largely expert-driven and involves the gathering of information from all available sources on the learners' target situations of use and on the communicative demands of these situations. This stage of needs analysis occurs prior to or in the very early part of a course. The information gathered in this way sets the general framework of goals for the course in question. There are, however, limits on how far this approach to information collection can go in identifying the specific communicative needs and intentions of the learners involved. It therefore has to be complemented by a more detailed and learner-based form of needs analysis, which constitutes the second stage of needs analysis. This stage involves the collaborative exploration of learners' communicative agendas by both teacher and learners as an integral part of ongoing learning activities. The second stage of needs analysis is thus *developmental* and *experiential* in nature, and arises out of the growth of learners' ability to channel into their language study their understanding of their target situations of use and of their own communicative goals and intentions. Self-assessment is an integral part of this process, learners' identification of their performance goals going hand-in-hand with the evaluation of their current abilities with respect to these goals. The type of self-assessment activities discussed above would thus generally be used early in a course to involve learners in reflection on their overall linguistic and communicative abilities as a means of setting global learning goals. A more specific and task-related form of self-assessment will, however, be a necessary component of the second stage of needs analysis: learners' exploration of their communicative agendas will thus be complemented by an exploration of their ability to fulfil these agendas in the TL. Both processes will be underpinned by the learners' knowledge in the occupational, interactive, and cultural/affective domains (3.5), albeit with the reservations expressed at the start of this section with respect to the TL-specific aspects of pragmatic knowledge. The activities outlined below provide a few suggestions as to how this process might be realised.

a) Exploring expressive intentions and resources

This activity could be used as a follow-up to 'Why are we here?' (3.6.1) or as input to a learner diary (3.6.3). The activity has two stages. In the first, learners are asked to identify one or more situations in which they have to use the TL and to draw up for each situation a list of the communicative functions they will need to perform and the language resources that this involves. Learners should be encouraged to select clearly definable situations and to be as concrete as possible in specifying their communicative agenda for the situation in question (it may be helpful for learners to do this in their L1). This task involves learners generating a pragmatic map of the target situation, and is therefore a form of awareness development which contributes to the development of the learners' self-directive abilities. This is the projective stage of the activity (cf. 6.3). The evaluative stage involves rehearsal and evaluation of how well the learners are able to realise the communicative goals they have identified. Real-world practice is, of course, preferable as it involves that invaluable pragmatic criteria of accomplishing (or not) an objective with an ascertainable degree of ease (or difficulty). If learners do not have the opportunity to try out their communicative skills in a real-world context, however, they can rehearse by means of simulation or individual practice with a tape-recorder or dictaphone. The usefulness of the latter should not be underestimated, as it can allow the learner to spot areas where he is struggling to express his ideas and which therefore need further preparatory work. The prior preparation of a pragmatic map is a form of learner training as it helps learners plan and monitor their learning in a coherent manner, rather than having them stumble through a situation blindly. Figure 17 contains a formalised version of a pragmatic map which the author prepared in advance of a visit to a university library in Holland. In productive terms, the map proved to be very helpful, but difficulties arose receptively: I could ask most of the questions I needed to, but had difficulties understanding the responses. This pointed to the need to improve my listening skills and to acquire linguistic devices for negotiating my way around difficulties in comprehension.

b) Analysing difficulties

This task could be used to support 'Discussing difficulties: using the telephone' (3.6.1), and would therefore link the analysis of learners' communicative goals with self-assessment to produce a set of learning objectives. In the activity as described in Chapter 3, learners pool their practical experience of using the telephone in the TL, with specific reference to the difficulties they have encountered. This calls for a fair amount of insight into language use and learners might, therefore, need some support to help them analyse their experience in a pedagogically useful manner. Figure 18 provides a framework of reference which could help learners to analyse their language use and their difficulties more easily. In this respect it should be noted that providing learners with categories within which to analyse their experience of the TL can function as a form of learner training, while the practical outcome of such an activity is a genuinely learner-based form of input into goal-setting, and thereby of learner involvement: this activity sequence thus manifests the complex relationship between learner training and learner involvement discussed in 2.7. While the details of Figure 18 relate to the use of the telephone, similar formats can easily be developed for other tasks.

c) Simulation-based self-assessment

Simulations are an integral part of CLT's philosophy of 'learning by doing', and are most often used as a means of generating a situationally-relevant form of language practice. This is certainly a major aspect of the pedagogical role of simulations, especially if learners are given the opportunity to contribute to simulation development on the basis of their knowledge and experience of language use (3.5; 3.6.2). Viewing simulations exclusively in terms of language *practice*, however, over-looks a part of their full learning potential. Simulation work which incorporates learner self-assessment in parallel with the usual teacher-based form of feedback offers a richer and more reflective form of learning. Figure 19 contains an adapted version of a self-assessment instrument used by the author to support the self-assessment of interviewing skills. The instrument was developed as part of a course which involved C.V. preparation and interview/self-presentation skills, the questions being chosen by the learners themselves subsequent to analysis of two job interviews on video. The learners knew prior to their interview simulation that the various topics on the self-assessment sheet would be covered, but they did not know in advance in which order they would occur or from which angle the topics would be approached. As the course was taught in the learners' final year of university study, when they were actively involved in looking for employment and attending interviews, their motivation for the task was very high. The self-assessment sheet was filled in by each learner subsequent to their interview simulation, and their self-assessment was compared with the evaluation made by the interviewing panel composed of other class members. The teacher's role mainly involved discussion of the 'Comments' section, where learners had to note the main difficulties they had experienced in dealing with the topic in question: these varied quite widely, from more linguistic points such as lack of relevant vocabulary or difficulty in structuring longer utterances to pragmatic considerations such as 'not being dynamic enough'. The outcome of the activity was thus a set of individual performance objectives for the activity in question which learners could work on ahead of real-world job interviews.

d) Peer evaluation

The activity sequence described above involved both self- and peer assessment, though the instrument given in Figure 19 clearly relates to the self-assessment component. In an indirect manner, though, peer evaluation may also be seen as a form of self-assessment. The rationale for peer evaluation is that by reflecting critically on the abilities of other learners with respect to a shared goal, learners are involved in the assessment of those linguistic or communicative parameters which are relevant to their own performance. Peer evaluation is thus a practical form of learner training which develops learners' understanding of language usage and of the type of difficulties which they are likely to experience in their own language production, which can then be used to inform their self-assessment skills. Furthermore, it can be easier (and less stressful) to spot certain problems in others than in oneself. Lynch (1988) provides an example of a peer evaluation instrument prepared for use with students of English for Academic Purposes requiring presentation and seminar skills (Figure 20). Such an instrument serves to focus learners' attention on the performance parameters operant in the target learning situation, which is a form of learner training, and provides the basis for peer discussion and correction at the feedback stage. Depending on the learners' maturity and commitment, and the experience they have of their target situations of use, learners can be asked to develop their own self- or peer assessment instrument (as was the case with the instrument given in Figure 19), which can be a very valuable exercise in terms of learner training and the development of learners' self-directive abilities.

e) Negotiative assessment

If factors such as the learners' maturity, their attitudes to language learning, and their understanding of their learning goals seem to be favourable, the teacher may adopt a negotiative approach to assessment. This would involve the discussion and negotiation between teacher and learners of achievement targets and of the performance criteria that are judged to be crucial in the learners' target situations of use, and the degree to which learners have attained or wish/need to attain these goals. Negotiative assessment applied to the learning goals of a whole course, however, is an advanced form of learner involvement, and can raise a number of difficulties relating to learners' perceptions of their learning goals, their awareness of the relevant performance criteria, and (especially when assessment is related to a mark which has a bearing on the learners' academic or professional advancement) their good-will and objectivity. This having been said, all of the self-assessment activities discussed in this section involve an element of 'negotiation', and their ultimate goal is, precisely, to help learners to develop their ability to approach their language use and learning in an informed and self-directive manner.

DAT/PED. Refer back to the four learner profiles in 3.5. Select at least one of the learners profiled and, on the basis of the information given, make an initial evaluation of the way in which you would approach self-assessment with the learner in question.

- Which skill areas would you focus on first, and would you opt for a global or a task-based approach?
- How would you sequence the self-assessment tasks, and in which terms would you formulate them?

Alternatively, do the same with respect to a (group of) learner(s) with whom you are personally familiar.

---

1 LOCATING THE LIBRARY AND THE RELEVANT SECTION
Main structures
- Excuse me. Could you tell me [...]?
- Sorry. I didn't understand [...].
- Where is the [...]?
- So, I go [...] and then I [...]?
- Thank you very much. That is very helpful of you.

Vocabulary
- library, street, floor, steps, corner, shelves, etc.
- right, left, straight on, further, on the other side of, etc.
- humanities, social sciences, language teaching, applied linguistics, book, journal, etc.

2 • EXPLAINING MY AFFILIATION AND SPECIFIC INTERESTS
Main structures
- I am [nationality] and have worked at [place] for [period of time].
- I work at [place] and am [post description].
- What I am looking for is [topic].
- I am currently involved in [topic].
- Do you have a section that deals with [topic]?
VOCABULARY
- lecturer, teaching, learning, students, study programme, ESP, methodology, course design, etc.

3 INQUIRING ABOUT BORROWING ARRANGEMENTS AND PHOTOCOPYING FACILITIES
Main structures
- Is it possible to [...]?
- Where can I [...]?
- Does one need to have [...]?
- When does the library open/close?
- How does the photocopier work?
- Do you have a lot of copies to make?

Vocabulary
- borrow, copy, photocopying key, coins (and numbers), staff member, identity card, library card, etc.

Figure 17 Pragmatic mapping: using a university library

This document is designed to help you to analyse your use of the telephone in [English] and the type of difficulties you may be experiencing.

PART A. WHY AND TO DO WHAT?
For which reason(s) do you generally have to use the telephone in [English]?
- to answer inquiries about your company/organisation
- to provide information about products or services
- to ask for information on products or services
- to deal with complaints or difficulties
- to make appointments and to take messages
- to organise events or meetings
- to discuss projects or to make plans
- OTHER:

If you use the telephone for several of these reasons, indicate which you find the most difficult. Why is this the case?

PART B. MY MAIN DIFFICULTIES
What do you feel to be the main causes of difficulty that you experience in using the telephone for the purpose(s) you have identified above?
Rate these causes of difficulty from 1 (This is rarely a problem) to 5 (I frequently have difficulties with this).

understanding numbers	1	2	3	4	5
understanding names and addresses	1	2	3	4	5
understanding speakers with different accents	1	2	3	4	5
speed of speech	1	2	3	4	5
understanding whether people are being polite or not	1	2	3	4	5
describing aspects of your employer's activities	1	2	3	4	5
finding the right way to be polite	1	2	3	4	5
insisting politely if people aren't being helpful	1	2	3	4	5
thanking people who have been helpful	1	2	3	4	5
OTHER:	1	2	3	4	5
	1	2	3	4	5

Figure 18 Using the telephone: goals and difficulties

* How well do you feel you performed in your interview? Did you manage to say what you wanted to say, and do you feel you created the sort of impression that you would have wished to?

* Rate your own performance on each of the topics raised by the panel from 1 (I dealt with this really well) to 5 (Oh dear!).

* Then try to identify the causes of any dissatisfactions you may feel.

1. My motivation for the post   1 2 3 4 5
   Comments:

2. My studies: what I've learned and what I can do   1 2 3 4 5
   Comments:

3. My outside experience
   - student jobs   1 2 3 4 5
   - participation in university life   1 2 3 4 5
   - accomplishments   1 2 3 4 5
   Comments:

4. My strengths and weaknesses   1 2 3 4 5
   Comments:

5. My personal interests and hobbies   1 2 3 4 5
   Comments:

6. My travel experience and experience of other countries   1 2 3 4 5
   Comments:

General evaluation

- *How happy are you with your overall performance?*
- *What do you most need to work on before your next interview?*

Figure 19 Self-assessment on an interview simulation

Seminar Evaluation Sheet

(Please complete this sheet by *filling in* the spaces or by *circling* the items.)

1. What do you think were the strengths of the presentation?

2. Were you able to follow the main points?
   YES   WITH DIFFICULTY   NO

3. Would you be able to summarise the talk for someone else?
   YES   WITH DIFFICULTY   NO

4. Was the presentation well organized?
   YES   GENERALLY   NO

5. Did the speakers show clearly when they were moving to a new point?
   YES   GENERALLY   NO

6. Did they make good use of visual support (e.g. hand-outs, black-board, overhead projector) to make their points clearer?
   YES   NOT ALWAYS   NO

7. Was their speed of speaking appropriate?
   YES   TOO FAST   TOO SLOW

8. Was the loudness appropriate?
   YES   NOT LOUD ENOUGH   TOO LOUD

9. Did they give sufficient explanation of technical vocabulary?
   YES   NOT ALWAYS   NO

10. Was the amount of information appropriate?
    YES   TOO LITTLE   TOO MUCH

11. How would you judge the speakers' eye-contact with the listeners?
    GOOD   UNEQUAL   INSUFFICIENT

12. If you had serious difficulties in following the talk, were they any of the following?
    speed of speaking   poor organization
    accent   grammar
    loudness   poor signalling of new points
    Mention any other problems here:

13. What advice would you give the speaker for future seminar presentations?

Figure 20 A peer evaluation instrument for seminar presentations
(taken from Lynch 1988: 125)

6.5 Developing strategic learning awareness

In an article entitled 'The learner as manager: managing learning or managing to learn', Holec (1987: 147) suggests that good language learners are those who 'are capable of assuming the role of manager of their own learning. They know how to make all the decisions involved. In other words, they know how to learn.' Self-assessment plays a central role in the development of learners' self-directive abilities as it involves learners:

- looking forward to their ultimate learning goals,
- evaluating their current ability to fulfil these goals,
- setting attainable learning objectives,
- planning learning activities designed to help them achieve these objectives.

It is essential, therefore, that learners' self-assessment skills should be developed integratively, in conjunction with both goal-setting and the selection of learning activities. 6.4 considered the first three points, and this section will look at the last, a few suggestions being made for activity types by which this integration of self-assessment with other aspects of language learning may be achieved.

6.5.1 Recognising learning opportunities

In its most simple terms, planning a learning programme involves two main questions: 'What is to be learned?' and 'How can this be learned?' Answering the second question is clearly dependent upon the learning opportunities that are available and upon the way in which these opportunities relate to the learners' goals. The context in which the language is being studied obviously has a major influence on the range of learning opportunities that are available. In a SLA context the possibilities learners have for contact with the TL are extremely varied – interaction with native speakers at work, in the street or in shops; free access to the media; availability of social, sporting or cultural activities, and so on. In a FLL context, there will generally be fewer opportunities, and they may need to be sought out actively. Indeed, in a FLL context the classroom may be the main or even the sole learning opportunity: in this case, it is a priority for learners to develop strategies for maximising the learning potential of classroom activities. The nature of learners' goals also influences what may be considered to be a useful learning opportunity. For example, watching films in the TL will be a more valuable learning resource for a learner wishing to develop his oral interactive skills than for a learner concerned with the comprehension of specialised written material.

AMEP (op. cit.) suggests an activity designed to develop learners' ability to recognise learning opportunities which is based on brief learner profiles. Each profile outlines a learning opportunity available or a learning need perceived by a given individual, learners being asked to offer advice on how the individual in question could exploit the opportunity or meet the need in question. The profiles provided by AMEP relate to the Australian context of learning, and clearly need to be adapted to the relevant learning context. It could be very demotivating (and hardly very productive) for learners to draw up exciting learning plans which they will never be able to implement: indeed, this would risk creating a culture of deprivation in learning terms. The goal of this activity should thus be to help learners evaluate the options which are practically available to them (whether these are more or less extensive) in a creative and constructive manner:

- Phuong has a TV, but she almost never watches it. Her friends tell her it can help to make her English better, but she does not know how to use it to learn. Should she just watch TV? What kind of programmes should she choose? What can she do while she is watching?
- Demetrios has just made an Australian friend. How can he take advantage of this situation to improve his English?
- Gloria says she likes reading stories, but she is not sure how it can help her to improve her English. Tell her what she can do.
- Ngoc wants to learn to sew. If she took a dressmaking course, what could she do to use this experience also to help her English?
- Mehmet has a long train trip to and from work everyday. He wants to use the time to improve his English. What could he do?
- Maria enjoys listening to songs and music. She would like to improve her English. Can she use the music in some way to help her English?
- Joe is having problems with his pronunciation, but he has no English course and no special teacher. What could he do to help his pronunciation? (AMEP, op. cit.: 45–6)

This activity can be exploited in a number of ways. One is to split the class into groups, each group suggesting and justifying at least one learning activity per profile. If this is approached in a reasonably light-hearted manner, it can yield a variety of learning options and generate an interesting discussion of what language learning is or can be. Furthermore, as learners are being asked to offer advice to others, they may find it easier to think innovatively than if they are asked to plan their own learning. In essence, the activity is a form of guided brainstorming of the relationship between learning needs and learning options.

This type of activity is designed to help learners explore their own learning needs and the learning opportunities that are realistically available to them. To help learners break out of or, at least, to evaluate critically their existing preconceptions about language learning, a follow-up stage, too, might usefully be approached by means of a group activity. For example, each learner might be asked to identify (possibly in consultation with the teacher) what he considers to be his main learning objective, a list of these points then being drawn up for the class as a whole. The class could then split up into groups which would make concrete suggestions as to how each learning objective might be approached within their own context. Each person could then discuss and evaluate the suggestions made by their colleagues with respect to their specific case, and select one or more for experimentation.

6.5.2 Building bridges

In the type of activity discussed above, learners should be encouraged to make active use of their existing knowledge. As we saw in 3.4 and 3.5, language learners are not blank sheets of paper. In the first instance, they possess a given competence in the TL, things they *do* know and functions they *can* perform – no matter how restricted these may be. In addition, they possess a body of knowledge about people, places, events and actions in the world, together with an understanding of the goals and conventions of language use – even if their knowledge of how these goals and conventions are realised in the TL is limited. This knowledge forms the basis upon which learners will wish to use the TL (i.e. their communicative agenda) and should be exploited to guide and facilitate their access to the TL. Learners therefore need to be helped to recognise the value of their existing knowledge and to use it actively in their interaction with the TL: in other words, they should use what they do know to help them understand what they only partially know. This involves the following strategies:

1 identifying patterns in language use as a basis for predicting the message content and interactive goals likely to occur;
2 assessing the likely predictability of the language used in different situations, i.e. grading situations in terms of their contextual predictability.

These strategies serve two main functions. Firstly, and more fundamentally, they can make learners feel that language study is an activity which involves them as full human beings, and which is related to their general knowledge and experience of life. Secondly, they can facilitate learners' access to situations or materials which, in a strictly linguistic sense, may be beyond them. Few things are more disheartening for a learner than to feel that the TL is an impenetrable blur of alien sounds or symbols. This feeling produces discouragement and, quite frequently, an avoidance of learning opportunities. Helping learners see that they can plan their interaction with the TL and play an active role in their learning therefore goes hand-in-hand with encouraging them to experiment with different learning options. The greater a learner's ability to predict the messages being conveyed in a given situation, the greater his confidence will be in approaching this situation for either communicative or learning purposes.

Students' predictive skills can be developed by asking them to make active use of their existing knowledge to build up a pragmatic map (cf. Figure 16, above) or 'script' (Schank and Abelson 1977) of their target learning situations. This involves learners using their knowledge in the occupational, interactive, or cultural/affective domains (3.5) to build a bridge into the linguistic and communicative structure of learning situations or materials. Indeed, the strategy of '*building bridges*', by the fact that it explicitly incorporates learners' existing knowledge and experience into their language learning, is fundamental to a learner-centred approach to teaching and should be brought to learners' attention explicitly from the very start of a course.

6.5.3 Selective focusing

To derive benefit from a given learning opportunity learners need to have at least a relatively clear goal: in other words, they should know why they are engaged in an activity and what they hope to get out of it. Otherwise, they are likely to feel overwhelmed and discouraged and, in the final analysis, will probably learn very little. This is particularly the case with lower-level learners, for whom much of what they hear or read in the TL is unclear or confusing. Selective focusing is a strategy which serves two main purposes. To begin with, it facilitates learning for the reasons given above. Then, it has a motivational function by helping learners feel they can use situations to promote their learning – in other words, that they can get on top of the language rather than being submerged by it. In this way, it is a way of promoting learner empowerment.

Selective focusing is not, however, an easy strategy to acquire. Even for teachers, the temptation to squeeze that last drop out of learning materials (the feeling that 'useful' language can't be left untaught), can sometimes be difficult to resist. All the more so for our students, then! Selective focusing is based on three sub-skills:

1 identifying the learning potential present in a given situation, activity or set of materials;
2 selecting a limited number of learning targets;
3 knowing how to focus in on the target elements.

This assumes that learners have (or can develop) a sufficient under-standing of how language is structured and used communicatively to be able to split up input into meaningful units. Selective focusing as a learning strategy therefore involves an element of language consciousness-raising (cf. Sharwood Smith 1981). On a basic level, this can mean learners being able to distinguish nouns from verbs, to identify tense markers, or to recognise the occurrence of formulaic or context-bound expressions (warnings, polite excuses, greetings, etc.). At a more advanced level it can involve the ability to recognise thematic and collocational patterns in lexis, or register-specific discourse patterns (cf. Swales 1981).

To illustrate the application of this strategy, let us assume that a group of learners have identified a number of shortcomings in their expressive abilities on the basis of a self-assessment questionnaire such as that illustrated in Figure 16. As a first step, the class could prioritise a discrete number of learning goals, such as 'describing my home', 'giving informa-tion about social security', 'saying something about my political views', 'describing weather conditions', and so on. Learners could then split up into groups, each group concentrating on one activity, and explore a pre-selected set of TL materials to find different exponents of 'their' activity. The materials might be coursebooks, written material such as plays or novels containing dialogues (in original or simplified versions depending on the learners' level in the TL), or relevant audio and video sequences. The groups then report back to the class and present the exponents they have found, explaining the context in which they occurred and their attitudinal tone. The target tasks could, of course, be derived from the learners themselves (their learning goals, experience, or interests), which would be preferable.

Less time-consuming ways of generating a list of exponents for a number of language tasks clearly do exist. The explicit product of an activity such as that suggested in the last paragraph, however, is of secondary importance. Its main purpose is to develop the learners' strategic competence by helping them to see how they can make a targeted use of TL material in order to deal with a specific learning objective that they themselves have identified. Selective focusing is thus a form of language education which plays a role in learner empower-ment.

> *DAT/REF.* The case study which follows describes one person's learning experience within a specific setting. Read it carefully with specific reference to the relationship between Christine's learning goals and the learning activities she adopted. Relate these activities back to the strategies of building bridges and of selective focusing discussed in this section.
>
> - In the same situation, which strategies would you have adopted?
> - Analyse any differences between your and Christine's strategic approach to learning with respect to the factors discussed in 4.2 and 4.3.
> - What insights does this give you into language learning in general and the selection of learning activities in particular?

Case study: Beginning Macedonian

The learning experiences described below are those of a native speaker of English in the former Yugoslav Republic of Macedonia. The learner in question, Christine, went to Macedonia for two years to teach English. Prior to her arrival she had learned no Macedonian, and was thus a complete beginner in a country where, outside of her immediate working environment, she could count on meeting very few speakers of English. On her arrival, Christine set out to acquire enough Macedonian to i. *satisfy her immediate transactional needs* and ii. *be able to initiate social contacts with non-English speakers*. The formal teaching of Macedonian that was available was very grammatically-oriented and did not respond to the immediate nature of her learning goals. Christine therefore decided to adopt a self-directed mode of learning. The two activities described below were used by Christine during her first three months in Macedonia.

Activity 1: Listening in on conversations
This involved listening in on as much Macedonian as possible to get a general feel for the sounds and intonation patterns of the language. Christine focused in particular on a number of situations in which the content of interaction was more easily predictable. These were:

- at the bank; at the post office; in shops; at the newsagents;
- in the bus and at the bus-stop;
- in cafés and restaurants, especially when customers arrived, left, or ordered something.

Christine reports that her listening in helped her to learn and reinforce the following points in particular:

1 Intonation patterns, especially question intonation, as this is frequently easy to identify from the context or from gestures.

2 Question forms, and the vocabulary and structures that frequently go with them.
3 High frequency structures and verb forms (e.g. 'I don't know', 'There aren't any ...').
4 Word class distinctions, especially between nouns and verbs.
5 Frequently used set chunks of language (e.g. 'What's the time?', 'You're welcome', 'Is this the number 71?', 'Late again!').
6 Interjections and exclamations.
7 Fillers.

Christine comments that she went through a silent period during which she produced very little Macedonian, but that once she did start to speak, her Macedonian was generally better received by native speakers than that of other foreign residents who had followed a course. She explains this by the fact that it 'sounded more natural', containing more fillers and interjections. Christine points out, however, that Macedonian culture is extrovert and verbal. People speak a lot in public places in quite loud voices, and often use gestures. These aspects of Macedonian culture facilitated Christine's listening in strategy a great deal: she wonders how feasible the same strategy would have been in a more reserved and less verbal culture.

Activity 2: Using the supermarket as a learning resource
Small individually run shops still predominate in Macedonia. During her first few months, however, Christine found it very difficult to use these shops as she had to ask for what she wanted and had neither the structures nor the vocabulary to do so. The supermarket represented a useful learning resource in the following areas:

1 Food/Product vocabulary. A supermarket has a wide range of products on display which can frequently be identified from the packaging or from visuals on the packaging (e.g. a sardine on a tin of sardines). Common product ingredients, such as oil, salt or sugar, are also given.
2 Recurrent constructions. Most product labels contain constructions and vocabulary items such as 'sell by ...', 'imported from ...', 'product of ...', 'bottled in ...', which are highly contextualised and frequently used.
3 Product labels and information. Certain products have highly predictable language and information on their labels – descriptive language on wine bottles or instructions for use on washing powder.
4 Brand names. These can sometimes provide extra vocabulary which is motivated by the nature of the product or supported by a logo (e.g. Blue Seas Salt). Furthermore, familiarity with popular brand names can facilitate comprehension and interaction with native speakers:

'Would you like a Vecchia?', for example, is an invitation to have a brandy popular in Macedonia.

5 Interaction at the check-out desk. This is one instance of the general listening in strategy, and provided basic transactional language frequently used in this context such as 'Thank you', 'Have a nice day', 'That is ... dinars', 'I don't have any change', 'You're welcome'.

As a learning resource, the supermarket had two main advantages. The first was the relatively wide range of products available and the predictability of much of the language present via the use of contextual clues and relevant background knowledge. The second was that a supermarket allows customers to spend as much time as they like walking around and examining products: this allowed Christine ample time to avail herself of the learning potential on offer. After a period of time using the supermarket in this way, Christine has acquired enough vocabulary and basic constructions to use small shops: this opened further learning opportunities as a result of the chance to listen in on more conversations and to try out her Macedonian with shopkeepers and other customers. The supermarket was thus a useful resource at a given stage of Christine's learning of Macedonian, and helped her to move on to more interactive situations.

6.6 Summary

a) Self-assessment plays a pivotal role in a learner-centred approach in two ways. Firstly, by engaging learners in critical reflection on their current abilities with respect to their learning goals, it is a form of learner training which contributes to learner empowerment. Secondly, it provides learners with the opportunity to enrich the setting of learning objectives on the basis of their own insights into their communicative intentions and current abilities, and thus constitutes a form of learner involvement.

b) Research studies have indicated that language learners have meaningful insights into their linguistic and communicative abilities, and that learner self-assessments merit consideration alongside teacher evaluations and standardised tests. This having been said, some learners may not be well prepared for self-assessment in either strategic or attitudinal terms.

c) For this reason, learners may need training and guidance to develop their self-assessment abilities. This may make it preferable to initiate self-assessment in global terms and only then move on to more specific, task-based forms of self-assessment.

d) For self-assessment to realise its full potential it should not be limited to the evaluation of learners' current abilities, but should be linked in to the establishment of learning objectives and the selection of learning activities by which learners can move on towards their target performance.

e) Self-assessment thus plays a central role in learners' involvement in their language study by linking reflection on their learning goals with evaluation of their current abilities, the setting of learning objectives, and the strategic selection of learning activities.

7 Fostering learner involvement

7.1 A strategic perspective on methodology

The discussion of self-assessment in Chapter 6 brought out the interplay between learner training and involvement mentioned in 2.7. Asking learners to reflect on their goals and current abilities with a view to the setting of learning objectives and the selection of appropriate learning activities is a means of increasing their awareness of language learning, and is thereby a form of learner training. It also, moreover, creates a forum within which learners can make a direct contribution to the shaping of their study programme, and is thus a form of learner involvement. This chapter considers learner participation in activity development, and will show the same interplay between training and involvement – learners' participation serving to deepen their under-standing of language study while at the same time channelling their knowledge and insights into programme development.

Two main points emerged in 4.5 with respect to the choice of methodology. The first was that the teacher should show flexibility in her choice of methodology in response to the subjective needs of her students. The second was that teaching should be structured in such a manner as to help learners to broaden their understanding of language learning and, thereby, to be better able to function self-directively in their own language study – language education serving to promote learner empowerment. These priorities call for an approach to course design which is structured not only around the attainment of certain objective learning outcomes but also around the initiation and explora-tion of a range of learning processes.

Hutchinson and Waters contrast three approaches to LSP course design, language-, skills- and learning-centred, in the following terms:

> A language-centred approach says: This is the nature of the target situation performance and that will determine the ESP course.
> A skills-centred approach says: That's not enough. We must look behind the target performance data to discover what

processes enable someone to perform. These processes will determine the ESP course.

A learning-centred approach says: That's not enough either. We must look beyond the competence that enables someone to perform, because what we really want to discover is not the competence itself, but how someone acquires that competence. (1987: 72–3)

The same authors make a similar point elsewhere:

ESP is often seen as the best example of communicative teaching in that it is supposedly closely geared to students' needs. However, we feel that needs analysis has been far too narrowly interpreted, implying, in effect, little more than the analysis of linguistic data from the target situation. But *ESP is first and foremost a learning process*, and it is not possible to have a communicative approach in ESP *unless ESP is seen as primarily an educational matter.* (1984: 112. Emphasis added)

In these two quotations, Hutchinson and Waters make a distinction between two main ways of seeing language teaching which, while not novel, is of perennial relevance. In the first of these, language teaching is primarily a matter of transmitting knowledge (e.g. as in a traditional code-based approach) and/or of training behaviours (as in functionally- or skills-based CLT and LSP). In the other perspective, language teaching involves the creation of a pedagogical framework within which learners engage in activities whose purpose is not simply to teach a given language point or to train a discrete skill, but also to develop the learners' strategic awareness of the process of language learning itself. The latter perspective is clearly educational in orientation. This does not, however, mean that language teaching is simply an open-ended form of learner training: learners have specific goals and, not infrequently, deadlines which must be met. It is rather a matter of *pursuing these objective goals in an educationally-motivated manner*, so that learners acquire not only the relevant language skills, but also a better understanding of the process of learning itself.

Most teachers would agree that fostering their students' strategic learning skills is a desirable goal. The way in which this might be realised other than in an intuitive, *ad hoc* manner, is less evident, however. The development of learning strategies is clearly one way of pursuing this goal, and Willing's perspective on learning strategies provides a valuable pointer in this respect. For Willing:

'Learning strategy' is a means of being specific about *what is intended to be happening, cognitively, for the learner*, that is, how the experience provided is expected to result in actual learning. (Op. cit.: 7. Emphasis added)

Willing thus suggests that the concept of learning strategy may be used as a tool for analysing the type of learning processes that are set in motion by different methodological choices. Viewed in these terms, the learning strategies that a given activity is likely to elicit can be analysed in a manner not dissimilar to the way the objective learning content of activities (practice of a given language skill, consolidation of a structure, etc.) can be analysed. Two categorisations of learning strategies will be examined in the next section. Before that, however, a few points need to be made with respect to learner involvement in language study.

Writing on the subject of learner choice in language study, Littlejohn very sensibly remarks that:

> If we wish to involve learners more in the running of a language course, then we need to devise tasks and materials that specifically develop the learner's ability to choose. Such tasks could involve learners in thinking more deeply about what they need to study and how they need to study. (1985: 260)

In other words, we cannot expect our students to make informed choices if they are not given the opportunity to try out and evaluate different options. In part, this is the task of learner training. However, as has been pointed out previously, learner training gradually merges into ongoing learner involvement in the choice and evaluation of day-to-day learning activities. In essence, then, if learners are to play an active role in their language study, they need to be given the opportunity to develop an informed judgement regarding the learning options which are open to them. For example, a diet of little but gap-fills and discrete-point grammar exercises is unlikely to develop our students' learning repertoire or empower them as learners; the same is true, of course, of a diet of nothing but group discussion and pair work. In either case, the range of learning options to which learners are exposed is restricted in both cognitive and psychosocial terms, which clearly limits their ability to expand their repertoire of strategies. Furthermore, either option will work to the disadvantage of those students whose preferred learning style (4.3) either differs markedly from or coincides closely with that favoured by the activities in question – due to a possible mismatch in the first case, and lack of diversity in the second.

Language education was presented in 1.4.2 and 2.7 as comprising two component parts, learner training and learner involvement. Both are necessary. Learners need, on the one hand, to be initiated into the process of language study in both strategic and attitudinal terms, and this is the goal of learner training. Learners also need, however, to be given opportunities to try out their developing knowledge on the basis of concrete choices relating to the realisation of their course of study: in other words, they need the chance to become actively involved in decision-making. This allows them to deepen their understanding of language learning while at the same time playing an active role in the shaping of their study programme. Learner training thus merges into learner involvement, but without the 'training' element ceasing to be present. Whether, in time, learners opt for an independent mode of study or decide to pursue their language study in a formal classroom context is their personal decision. However, in order for them to exercise their freedom of choice in an informed manner, they need at least to be aware of a reasonable range of study options. Language education is thus a prerequisite for learner empowerment.

Clarke makes five points about the involvement of learners in the adaptation of materials. Although this is just one form of involvement, Clarke's analysis provides a useful indication of the potential advantage of involving learners in the practicalities of methodological choices:

1 *Learner commitment*: External or imposed materials can be made internal to the learners by creative involvement in the adaptation process. By engaging the learner's interest in the nature of the teaching materials through working on them in some way, a greater degree of commitment and sense of purposeful activity will be generated.

2 *Learner as materials writer and collaborator*: Learners can be productively engaged in adaptation tasks which result in the creation of actual teaching materials which can be used in the same or another class. Once again, for learners to undertake tasks which other members of their class have devised is likely to result in a higher degree of commitment. Working on a cooperative basis with other group members and with the teacher develops the role of collaborator rather than 'language receiver'.

3 *Learner as problem solver*: The activity of adapting materials in order to create tasks is a fruitful task in itself and sets learners a meaningful problem to solve. Even when language form might be the content of the task, the learners' principal focus will be on materials creation.

4 *Learner as knower*: By working on the construction of classroom tasks, based on existing materials, learners can change their role yet further, becoming 'knowers' rather than 'assimilators'. By researching certain areas of language in order to produce a piece of material, they become 'expert' in those areas and are then able to transmit their knowledge to others.

5 *Learner as evaluator and assessor*: Through the process of adapting materials and producing tasks for further language work, learners will be better able to assess the relevance and interest of what they are doing and thus take some control over materials content. They will also be better able to assess their own level of achievement, having played a direct part in the creation of certain types of task or activity.   (1989: 135)

Involving learners in constructive reflection on learning activities along the lines suggested by Clarke is not intended to convince the learners in question to adopt any particular set of learning strategies or approach to their learning. Indeed, this would run counter to what has been said a number of times in this book about learners finding their own path to learning. It is more a matter of creating a varied, reflective and strategy-rich learning environment within which learners have the opportunity to explore a variety of learning options and, thereby, be able to make informed choices about their mode of study.

Language education, or the creation of what Hutchinson and Waters refer to as a 'learning-centred' approach to teaching, therefore involves the teacher in making methodological choices not only in terms of objective learning outcomes (as defined in linguistic or functional terms, for instance), but also with a view to creating a strategic learning potential in day-to-day teaching-learning activities.

PED. Assess the degree to which Clarke's suggestions about learner involvement could be realised in a course you are familiar with – either as a teacher or as a student.

- Which aspects of the course would be affected, and how could this be presented to learners in an explicitly educational framework?
- In which way do you feel that this would alter the emphasis of the course from the learners' and also from the teacher's point of view?

7.2   Two analyses of learning strategies

In the last section it was suggested that learning strategies could be used as a means of (to repeat Willing) 'being specific about what is intended to be happening, cognitively, for the learner' in the course of learning activities. In other words, learning strategies could be seen as offering a tool for analysing the learning processes implicit in different pedagogical options, in a manner parallel to that in which activities are currently analysed in terms of their intended linguistic or functional outcomes. For this to be possible, it is of course necessary to have a categorisation of learning strategies which is sufficiently broad to provide a meaningful level of insight into the cognitive and interactional processes that are likely to be set in motion by various pedagogical options. The term 'learning strategy' has been used on a number of occasions so far to refer to the purposeful actions learners engage in (either consciously or unconsciously) with the goal of promoting their understanding of or proficiency in the TL. In the present context, however, a more detailed breakdown of learning strategies is required if teachers are to be in a position to undertake a meaningful analysis of the many and varied learning processes that can be generated by their pedagogical choices. In this respect, however, it is important to recognise the limits of our current understanding of this area of language learning, as Oxford points out:

> It is important to remember that any current understanding of language learning strategies is necessarily in its infancy, and any existing system of strategies is only a proposal to be tested through practical classroom use and through research. At this stage in the short history of language learning strategy research, there is no complete agreement on exactly what strategies are; how many strategies exist; how they should be defined, demarcated, and categorised; and whether it is – or ever will be – possible to create a real, scientifically validated hierarchy of strategies. (1990: 16–17)

Readers should therefore view the two categorisations of learning strategies given below not as received knowledge, but rather as working tools and as stimulus for reflection and practical experimentation.

Oxford (op. cit.) offers an analysis of learning strategies in which there are two main categories of strategy, *direct* and *indirect*, each with three sub-categories and a number of exponents per sub-category. These are shown in Figure 21.

The main distinction Oxford makes is between *direct* strategies, which relate to the ways in which the learner deals with and works on the TL itself, and *indirect* strategies, which relate to the general management of learning. Within the category of *direct* strategies, Oxford recognises *memory* strategies, which help learners to store and retrieve new information, *cognitive* strategies, which learners use to understand and to produce new language, and *compensation* strategies, which are used when learners encounter a gap in their knowledge of the TL and which enable them to deal with this deficiency. Oxford's category of *indirect* strategies includes *metacognitive* strategies, which relate to the organisation of the learning process in strategic terms, *affective* strategies, by

DIRECT STRATEGIES	INDIRECT STRATEGIES
I *Memory strategies* 1 Creating mental linkages (e.g. grouping; associating/elaborating) 2 Applying images and sounds (e.g. using imagery; semantic mapping) 3 Reviewing well (structured reviewing) 4 Employing action (e.g. using physical response or sensation)	I *Metacognitive strategies* 1 Centering one's learning (e.g. overviewing and linking with already known material; delaying speech production to focus on listening) 2 Arranging and planning one's learning (e.g. setting goals and objectives; planning for a language task) 3 Evaluating one's learning (self-monitoring; self-evaluating)
II *Cognitive strategies* 1 Practising (e.g. repeating; recognizing and using formulas and patterns) 2 Receiving and sending messages (e.g. getting the idea quickly) 3 Analyzing and reasoning (e.g. analyzing expressions; translating) 4 Creating structure for input and output (e.g. taking notes; highlighting)	II *Affective strategies* 1 Lowering one's anxiety (e.g. using deep breathing, music or laughter) 2 Encouraging oneself (e.g. taking risks wisely; rewarding oneself) 3 Taking one's emotional temperature (e.g. writing a learning diary; discussing one's feelings with someone else)
III *Compensation strategies* 1 Guessing intelligently (using linguistic or other clues) 2 Overcoming limitations in speaking and writing (e.g. getting help; using mime or gesture; selecting the topic)	III *Social strategies* 1 Asking questions (asking for clarification, verification or correction) 2 Cooperating with others (cooperating with peers or with proficient users of the TL) 3 Empathizing with others (developing cultural understanding; becoming aware of others' thoughts and feelings)

Figure 21 Direct and indirect learning strategies (taken from Oxford 1990: 17–21)

which learners regulate their emotions, motivations and attitudes, and *social* strategies, which direct learners' interaction with other people (teacher, fellow students, proficient TL speakers, etc.) for the purposes of language learning.

Oxford points out that her two main categories of strategy, *direct* and *indirect*, work in tandem, one guiding and being realised by the other. For example the *indirect metacognitive* strategy 'Centering one's learning' can be realised, among others, by the strategy of 'overviewing and linking with already known material'. This strategy, however, is likely to involve the use of a number of *direct* strategies, such as one or more *memory* strategies (e.g. 'semantic mapping') and *cognitive* strategies such as 'Practising' (e.g. 'recognising formulas and patterns'), 'Analyzing and reasoning' (e.g. 'analyzing expressions') or 'Creating structure for input and output' (e.g. 'highlighting'). There is thus a constant interaction among the various categories given in Oxford's analysis. There are, it is true, conflicts between Oxford's view of what constitutes a learning strategy and what other writers maintain. Oxford points out, for example, that her third category of *direct* strategies, *compensation* strategies, are 'unceremoniously thrown out of the learning strategy arena by [some] experts, who think it is merely a communication strategy which is not useful for learning' (Oxford, op. cit.: 22). Both perspectives are valid. In the short term, compensation strategies may serve primarily to ensure communication when the learner does not possess the TL resources that are called for. At the same time, they allow contact with the TL to be maintained, and thus can serve to promote learning. Arguably, then, a further *indirect metacognitive* strategy might be added, along the lines of: 'Use compensation strategies to overcome limitations in order to facilitate interaction with TL speakers and/or to maintain contact with the TL.' We are clearly some way off from a definitive categorisation of learning strategies.

O'Malley and Chamot (1990) put forward a tripartite categorisation of learning strategies, *metacognitive*, *cognitive* and *social/affective*, which is shown in Figure 22.

O'Malley and Chamot's *metacognitive* strategies relate to learners' global planning of their language study, preparation and monitoring of learning tasks, and evaluation of performance and thus cover similar ground to Oxford's *indirect metacognitive* category. *Cognitive* strategies are more detailed, and relate to the ways in which learners interact with TL materials and situations of use, how they analyse or manipulate learning material, and to the choice of learning techniques for a given task. O'Malley and Chamot's *cognitive* strategy category includes a range of what Oxford would classify as *direct* strategies – her *cognitive* strategies, most evidently, but also a number of her *memory* and

I METACOGNITIVE STRATEGIES

1 *Planning*: Previewing the organizing concept or principle of an anticipated learning task (*advance organization*); proposing strategies for handling an upcoming task; generating a plan for the parts, sequence, main ideas, or language functions to be used in handling a task (*organizational planning*).

2 *Directed attention*: Deciding in advance to attend in general to a learning task and to ignore irrelevant distractors; maintaining attention during task execution.

3 *Selective attention*: Deciding in advance to attend to specific aspects of language input or situational details that assist in performance of a task; attending to specific aspects of language input during task execution.

4 *Self-management*: Understanding the conditions that help one successfully accomplish language tasks and arranging for the presence of those conditions; controlling one's language performance to maximize use of what is already known.

5 *Self-monitoring*: Checking, verifying, or correcting one's comprehension or performance in the course of a language task.
   a *Comprehension* monitoring: checking, verifying, or correcting one's understanding.
   b *Production* monitoring: checking, verifying, or correcting one's language production.
   c *Auditory* monitoring: using one's 'ear' for the language (how something sounds) to make decisions.
   d *Visual* monitoring: using one's 'eye' for the language (how something looks) to make decisions.
   e *Style* monitoring: checking, verifying, or correcting based upon an internal stylistic register.
   f *Strategy* monitoring: tracking use of how well a strategy is working.
   g *Plan* monitoring: tracking how well a plan is working.
   h *Double-check* monitoring: tracking, across the task, previously undertaken acts or possibilities considered.

6 *Problem identification*: Explicitly identifying the central point needing resolution in a task or identifying an aspect of the task that hinders its successful completion.

7 *Self-evaluation*: Checking the outcomes of one's own language performance against an internal measure of completeness and accuracy; checking one's language repertoire, strategy use, or ability to perform the task at hand.
   a *Production* evaluation: checking one's work when the task is finished.
   b *Performance* evaluation: judging one's overall execution of the task.
   c *Ability* evaluation: judging one's ability to perform the task.
   d *Strategy* evaluation: judging one's strategy use when the task is completed.
   e *Language repertoire* evaluation: judging how much one knows of the L2, at the word, phrase, sentence, or concept level.

II COGNITIVE STRATEGIES

1 *Repetition*: Repeating a chunk of language (a word or phrase) in the course of performing a language task.

2 *Resourcing*: Using available reference sources of information about the target language, including dictionaries, textbooks, and prior work.

3 *Grouping*: Ordering, classifying, or labelling material used in a language task based on common attributes; recalling information based on grouping previously done.

4 *Note-taking*: Writing down key words and concepts in abbreviated verbal, graphic, or numerical form to assist performance of a language task.

5 *Deduction/Induction*: Consciously applying learned or self-developed rules to produce or understand the target language.

6 *Substitution*: Selecting alternative approaches, revised plans, or different words or phrases to accomplish a language task.

7 *Elaboration*: Relating new information to prior knowledge; relating different parts of new information to each other; making meaningful personal associations to information presented.

   a *Personal* elaboration: making judgements about or reacting personally to the material presented.

   b *World* elaboration: using knowledge gained from experience in the world.

   c *Academic* elaboration: using knowledge gained in academic situations.

   d *Between parts* elaboration: relating parts of the task to each other.

   e *Questioning* elaboration: using a combination of questions and world knowledge to brainstorm logical solutions to a task.

   f *Self-evaluative* elaboration: judging self in relation to materials.

   g *Creative* elaboration: making up a storyline, or adopting a clever perspective.

   h *Imagery*: using mental or actual pictures or visuals to represent information; coded as a separate category, but viewed as a form of elaboration.

8 *Summarization*: Making a mental or written summary of language and information presented in a task.

9 *Translation*: Rendering ideas from one language to another in a relatively verbatim manner.

10 *Transfer*: Using previously acquired linguistic knowledge to facilitate a language task.

11 *Inferencing*: Using available information to guess the meanings or usage of unfamiliar language items associated with a language task, to predict outcomes, or to fill in missing information.

III SOCIAL/AFFECTIVE STRATEGIES

1 *Questioning for clarification*: Asking for explanations, verification, rephrasing, or examples about the material; asking for clarification or verification about the task; posing questions to the self.

2 *Cooperation*: Working together with peers to solve a problem, pool information, check a learning task, model a language activity, or get feedback on oral or written performance.

3 *Self-talk*: Reducing anxiety by using mental techniques that make one feel competent to do the learning task.

4 *Self-reinforcement*: Providing personal motivation by arranging rewards for oneself when a language learning activity has been successfully completed.

Figure 22 Metacognitive, cognitive and social/affective learning strategies (slightly adapted from O'Malley and Chamot 1990: 137–139)

compensation strategies. *Social/affective* strategies relate to the ways in which learners interact with others to support or advance their learning, and to the control of learners' affective involvement in learning tasks and/or situations of use. This category corresponds closely to Oxford's *affective* and *social* categories of *indirect* strategy. O'Malley and Chamot put forward a number of different analyses using the same tripartite analysis (cf. O'Malley and Chamot, op. cit.: 46; 119–20), but that given in Figure 22 is the most complete.

O'Malley and Chamot's categorisation needs to be viewed with the same degree of constructive reserve as Oxford's: further strategies could well be added (particularly under the social/affective heading), and existing ones could be re-arranged. Furthermore, there will be interactions between O'Malley and Chamot's three categories along the same lines as those observed among Oxford's six categories of strategy. Despite the differences between the two analyses, though, the common ground is very evident, and O'Malley and Chamot and Oxford clearly agree to a substantial degree on the type of behaviours that can be classified under the general heading of learning strategies. Both analyses are valid and insightful: Oxford's is perhaps more accessible, while O'Malley and Chamot's is probably simpler to use – three categories being, in general terms, easier to work with than six. Primarily for the latter reason, it is O'Malley and Chamot's analysis that will be used in the rest of the chapter. This choice, however, probably says more about the present author's own cognitive style than about the relative merits of the two analyses. Readers may therefore wish to 'translate' O'Malley and Chamot's categories into their equivalents in Oxford's analysis if they feel more at home with the latter. Or they may wish to mix the two analyses in any way they feel may help them to get to grips with their learners' strategic interaction with their language study.

In what follows, a number of teaching-learning activities will be discussed and analysed from a strategic point of view. This will involve a survey of the means by which the activity in question may be realised, and then an analysis of the learning strategies that are likely to be generated by each of these techniques within the framework provided by O'Malley and Chamot's categorisation of learning strategies. The goal is not to recommend any one set of activities, but rather to cast a strategic perspective on the choice of methodology. This, it is hoped, should provide teachers with guidelines about how to create an activity environment which is varied and strategy-rich, one in which learners are able to try out their learning preferences and to develop their judgement as language learners. In practical terms, let's say that a teacher feels that the activity of 'error correction' has to play a part in her teaching of writing: the question then arises as to how she might go about realising this.

Should she, for example, directly correct errors on learners' completed written work, or should she adopt an approach in which the learners work together in both generating and correcting text, with the teacher as consultant? Or should she possibly combine the two? In the rest of this chapter, different options of this nature will be evaluated in terms of the learning strategies they entail, to help the teacher make her choice not only in terms of learners' objective learning goals, but also in terms of the strategic or process-oriented agenda she is pursuing with her class.

DAT/REF. Compare the two learning strategy inventories of Oxford and of O'Malley and Chamot with Rubin's (1975) inventory of learning strategies given in 2.2 and Wenden's (1986c) metacognitive and cognitive distinction given in 2.6.

- What do the two more complete categorisations reproduced in this chapter add to your understanding of the place of learning strategies in language learning?
- Which of the two categorisations (Oxford's, or O'Malley and Chamot's) do you find the most insightful and the most easily usable? And for which reasons?

In the rest of this chapter, three types of teaching-learning activity (grammar, correction and project work) will be examined in terms of the type of learning strategy usage they can potentially elicit. ('Potentially' is used as it is very difficult to anticipate what will actually take place in learners' minds while they are involved in a given activity, though this should not prevent the teacher from attempting to create a framework which offers the potential for a rich and varied form of learning.) The goal is not to suggest any one approach to, for instance, the teaching of grammar, but simply to stimulate reflection on the possibilities that exist for creating a varied and strategy-rich learning environment and, thereby, of helping learners deepen their understanding of language study. In this respect it may be appropriate to recall certain points made in 2.6.4 regarding the evaluation of learner training. The objective product of a number of the activities suggested below might well be attained in a simpler or more 'cost-effective' manner by adopting a traditional teacher-based approach to the activity type in question. This, however, is not the point at issue. A learner-centred approach to teaching seeks not only to help learners attain a given level of linguistic or functional competence in the TL, but also to do this in an educationally motivated and enriching manner which can aid students to develop their self-directive abilities, and thereby empower them as learners.

The *strategy analysis* which follows each activity outline is designed to indicate the types of strategies which are likely to be used – though this can never be predicted with full confidence. The strategies are thus meant to be indicative and provide guidelines for reflection and exploration by the individual teacher. Practically speaking, readers may find it helpful to refer to O'Malley and Chamot's categorisation of learning strategies given in Figure 22 while they are reading the strategy analysis. This should help them to get a feel for the strategy classification itself and also for the internal operation of the activity in question. As elsewhere in this book, what is suggested should not be viewed prescriptively but as a basis for personal experimentation and reflection.

7.3 Grammar

'Grammar' is a term which means different things to different people. It has often been observed, for instance, that when learners ask for 'more grammar' (which would seem to relate to a certain type of learning content), what they frequently have in mind is a more structured approach to their language study as a whole (which relates more to learning form). 'Grammar' may also, for some learners (and teachers) be a form of shorthand for the goal of accuracy of expression and the elimination of structural errors; for others, it may be a term loaded with negative associations arising out of their prior learning experiences. Furthermore, there are ambiguities with respect to the scope of the term: where, for example, is the dividing line between syntax and vocabulary? And does the term 'grammar' relate just to sentence grammar or does it include the global structuring of discourse? A useful step at the start of a course is thus to discuss what participants understand by 'grammar', their past experiences of grammar instruction and their present expectations. Within this context it is also helpful to discuss the role that grammar should play in learners' study programme as a whole. This type of preliminary discussion is by no means wasted time. To begin with, it can avoid subsequent misunderstandings and tensions, and it is also a form of learner training in that it involves a sharing of perspectives and expectations both between teacher and learners and also among learners themselves.

The activity types considered in this section relate to one grammatical distinction in English – that between the present perfect and simple past. The goal is not to suggest any one approach to the teaching of these constructions, but simply to consider alternative means of approaching a given grammatical point in terms of the learning processes which they engage. The traditional approach to the teaching of grammar has at least two main components – presentation of the rules governing the use of the construction in question, and then controlled (and frequently graded) practice in the use of the construction. This approach is well illustrated by Murphy (1985: cf. Units 20–1, pp. 40–3 for the present perfect – past simple distinction).

7.3.1 *Student preparation of exercises*

One very simple modification to the traditional approach would be to maintain the explanation and illustration stage (i.e. to present learners with an 'expert' analysis of the target constructions), but to ask the learners themselves to write the exercises. Two possibilities exist here. One would be to provide learners with an example of a few exercise formats and ask them to produce a number of exemplars of each format. Alternatively, learners could pool their prior learning experiences and the range of exercise types they have already encountered: in this case, learners could select a few exercise types that seem to be appropriate to the grammatical distinction in question and put together an exercise on each format. If the class is split into groups, each group could then take one exercise format and prepare a number of questions for their fellow students.

For this approach to work effectively, the teacher would obviously need to circulate among the various groups to provide them with advice and guidance in the preparation of their exercises. This function is essentially a tutorial one and allows the teacher to work with learners on a one-to-one or small group basis. Such an approach is undeniably more time-consuming than using existing exercises. Furthermore, not all learners may feel ready to perform a function which they might consider to be that of the teacher, and this is a pedagogical factor which the teacher has to evaluate in advance. Learner-based exercise preparation, however, offers rich scope for an explorative approach to learning in collaboration with the teacher, and also creates a forum for practical learner involvement in programme development.

Table 2 Strategy analysis

Metacognitive strategies

- planning and self-management: in the organisation and execution of the exercise preparation task;
- selective attention and problem identification: focus on the target constructions and the contexts in which they are used;
- self-evaluation (in particular production and language repertoire evaluation):

in learners' evaluation of their understanding of and ability to use the target constructions.

Cognitive strategies

- resourcing, deduction/induction, and transfer: involved in learners gathering information on the use of the target construction from the sources available (e.g. a grammar book, the teacher, or their existing knowledge of the TL) to guide exercise preparation;
- grouping: gathering together instances of use of the target constructions as a basis for exercise preparation;
- translation: possible use of the learners' L1 as an aid or starting point for exercise preparation.

Social/Affective strategies

- questioning for clarification: asking advice from the teacher about the use of the target construction and/or other aspects of the exercises being prepared;
- cooperation: sharing insights and ideas with fellow students in exercise preparation.

7.3.2 Exploring textual material

The traditional approach to grammar teaching relies heavily on deduction from a given rule to instances of usage. A more inductive or discovery-based approach is also possible, though this has cognitive and attitudinal implications which the teacher has to evaluate with respect to the learners involved (there is no one approach which is equally suited to all learners in all situations). A discovery-based approach might involve the collection of a body of textual material in the TL containing instances of the construction or distinction in question. Two options exist with respect to the collection of material. The simplest is for the teacher herself to pre-select the material: in this case, the teacher has the possibility of signposting the target constructions by means of underlining or highlighting. Alternatively, learners can be set the task of monitoring TL sources for occurrences of the target constructions: possibilities are a given news broadcast or television programme (e.g. 'The government has announced new measures to combat tax evasion ...'), one day's edition of a newspaper (e.g. 'At its last meeting, the World Bank announced that it has suspended aid to ...'), or advertising in banks or shops (e.g. 'Have you ever thought of buying your own home? If so why not call our mortgage advisor on ...'). In either case, however, some form of guidance will be required to avoid confusion among learners – though the degree and nature of this guidance will vary from one group of learners to another.

This exploratory form of learning may either precede and lead up to rule formulation, or it may be used as a follow-up activity, in which learners can 'discover' the rule in action in real language use. Neither option is better than the other in absolute terms, though one is likely to be relatively more suitable for any one group of learners: this again, is a matter for the pedagogical judgement of the teacher. Readers may wish to look at Flowerdew (1993) and Okoye (1994) as instances of a guided discovery-based approach to the development of quite complex professional communication skills.

Table 3 Strategy analysis

Metacognitive strategies

- planning and self-management: in the organisation of the text exploration task;
- selective attention and problem identification: in the focusing of learners' attention on instances of the target construction in the text corpus;
- self-evaluation (in particular, language repertoire evaluation): learners' evaluation of their mastery of the target construction during both the text study and feedback stages.

Cognitive strategies

- resourcing, deduction/induction, and transfer: use of available information sources, including the teacher and learners' current knowledge of the TL, to guide text exploration;
- elaboration (in particular, world and academic elaboration) and inferencing: in trying to work out the principles underlying the uses of the target constructions in the text corpus;
- grouping and summarisation (and, possibly, note-taking): gathering together and summing up by learners of their explanation of the constructions occurring in the text corpus.

Social/ Affective strategies

- questioning for clarification and cooperation: asking for assistance/guidance from the teacher and sharing text exploration with fellow students.

7.3.3 *Telling a story*

This activity involves learners telling (orally or in writing) a story which entails both historical events (using the past simple) and the present implications of these events (using the present perfect). Clear task specification which establishes these production parameters would be necessary to ensure that learners think about and use the target constructions in a focused manner. Various possibilities exist with respect to the type of story to be told: it may relate to the learner's own life, to a news event, or to the life of a well-known individual. Story telling would probably be most suitable as a follow-up activity once the main lines of the target grammatical distinction have been dealt with, although it could also be used diagnostically. It might be suggested that constraining the task around the use of a certain construction is 'unauthentic'. However, as Breen (1985, 1986) points out, the classroom has its own dynamics which are shaped by the shared goal of language study and which generate their own authenticity – this is especially likely to be the case in FLL environment where learners have little opportunity to use the TL in interactive situations.

Table 4 Strategy analysis

Metacognitive strategies

- planning and self-management: in the organisation and preparation of the learner's story;
- selective attention and problem identification: focus on the target constructions and their communicative use in story preparation;
- self-monitoring (in particular production monitoring, but also perhaps strategy and plan monitoring): during story preparation and delivery;
- self-evaluation (in particular, production and language repertoire evaluation): the learners' evaluation of their mastery of the target constructions during preparation, delivery and feedback stages.

Cognitive strategies

- repetition: use of the target constructions during story preparation and delivery;
- resourcing, deduction/induction, and transfer: use of available sources of information, including the learner's current knowledge of the TL, to select and structure the story to illustrate the target constructions;
- note-taking, elaboration (in particular, creative elaboration), and (possibly) translation: to guide the detailed realisation of the story.

Social/Affective strategies

- questioning for clarification: asking advice from the teacher and/or fellow students.

> *PED.* Which techniques do you most often use in teaching grammar, and how broad is the range of learning strategies that they are likely to generate among learners?
>
> Does your approach to grammar teaching vary from one group of learners to another? If so:
>
> • If so, what are the differences?
> • In which way do these differences relate to the characteristics of the learners involved, their learning goals, or to other factors?

7.4 Error correction

As in the case of grammar, a first step with respect to error correction is the establishment of certain basic parameters. This would generally involve discussion of learners' goals and of the relevant performance parameters so that a consensus may start to be formulated about what constitutes more and less crucial errors. The definition and prioritisation of errors thus becomes an integral part of goal-setting and the establishment of learning objectives. This process is likely to provide practical insights into learners' beliefs about language learning, since their perceptions of what are more or less crucial errors are likely to reflect their underlying preconceptions about the nature of language and language learning (2.5). In part, this initial discussion of goals and learning priorities may be seen as a form of learner training; it also, however, creates a framework for learner involvement in that learners can provide input from their experience of their target situations of use and their perceptions of their learning needs.

Insofar as learners' goals relate to the linguistic system of the TL or to interactive conventions specific to the TL community, the teacher's role as 'knower' (8.3) will come into play. This may take place in the traditional manner, where the teacher directly assumes the role of correcting errors. Alternatively, the teacher may seek to involve learners in the process of correction. This will, of course, call for guidance from the teacher, but offers a number of the educational advantages identified by Oskarsson (1989) (6.1). The activities described below are meant to provide an indication of the forms this type of involvement might take and the learning processes that it can engage.

7.4.1 Peer correction

Peer correction exploits the dynamics and sense of shared purpose of the learning group to cater for a form of collaborative learning. Edge identifies four advantages of peer correction:

Firstly, when a learner makes a mistake and another learner corrects it, both learners are involved in listening to and thinking about the language.

Secondly, when a teacher encourages learners to correct each other's mistakes, the teacher gets a lot of important information about the students' ability. Can they hear a particular mistake? Can they correct it?

Thirdly, the students become used to the idea that they can learn from each other. So, peer correction helps learners cooperate and helps make them less dependent on teachers.

Fourthly, if students get used to the idea of peer correction without hurting each other's feelings, they will be able to help each other learn when they work in pairs and groups, when the teacher can't hear what is said. (1989: 26)

Edge illustrates the operation of peer correction by means of a brief scene relating to the practice of question formulation in the simple past tense on the basis of the following stimulus:

What time	go to bed last night?
	get up this morning?
	have breakfast today?
	leave home this morning?
	arrive at school?

The teacher asks one student to start by asking any one of the questions above. The student who answers asks another question, and so on:

Student 1:   What time did you have breakfast today, Rosa?
Rosa: Half past seven.
               What time did you go to bed last night, Carmen?
Carmen: Eleven o'clock.
               What time you arrive at school this morning, Luis?
Teacher: (*turns head as if didn't hear properly*)
(*pause*)
Carmen: ... Aah ... What time, ah, you come to school?
(*pause*)
Teacher: Can anyone help? ... Yes, Fernando?
Fernando: What time did you arrive at school?
(*pause*)
Teacher: Yes, Carmen?
Carmen: Ah, yes. What time did you arrive at school, Luis?

(Op. cit.: 25)

Table 5 Strategy analysis

Metacognitive strategies

- planning (in particular, advance organisation): focusing on the goal of the correction task;
- selective attention and problem identification: concentrating on the target construction and the contextual factors which govern its use;
- self-monitoring (in particular, production monitoring) and self-evaluation (in particular, production and language repertoire evaluation): learners' assessment of their performance and ability to use the target construction.

Cognitive strategies

- deduction/induction, elaboration (in particular, academic elaboration), and transfer: learners' use of their existing knowledge of the TL to monitor and correct the language use of their fellow students.

Social/Affective strategies

- cooperation: learners sharing their knowledge and insights about the TL and their learning difficulties as a form of collaborative learning.

Readers may wish to read Lynch (1988, op. cit.) and Mangelsdorf (1992) for two discussions of the practicalities of peer correction and evaluation. Lynch examines peer evaluation of speaking skills with specific reference to the development of a peer evaluation questionnaire for oral presentations (6.4.2). Lynch suggests that peer evaluation is a resource which is most profitably used in conjunction with teacher and self-correction. Mangelsdorf focuses on peer reviewing of written compositions: she emphasises the flexibility required of the teacher in assessing learners' attitudes to and readiness for peer evaluation, and the importance of clearly defining the evaluation tasks that learners are asked to perform. A similar point is made by Makino (1993) with respect to self-correction: Makino suggests that the effectiveness of self-correction is heavily dependent upon the quality of the guidance which learners are given. Thus, while Lynch, Mangelsdorf and Makino all point to the potential advantages of peer and self-correction, they emphasise the crucial role that the teacher has to play in guiding learners' exploration of the TL.

7.4.2 Self-correction – pronunciation and the dictaphone

One activity for the remedial teaching of pronunciation employed by the present author involves guided self-correction using a dictaphone or tape-recorder. The activity is recommended for self-study with learners who manifest an intrusive level of pronunciation or intonation problems in their spoken language during class activities.

The first stage of the activity is teacher-based and involves the teacher diagnosing the main pronunciation problems (certain minimal pairs, L1-based errors, inappropriate intonation patterns at either word or sentence level, swallowing of word endings, etc.) of the learner concerned on the basis of observation of his classroom participation. The next stage involves consultation between teacher and learner and the establishment of two or three main target areas for remediation: this is best done subsequent to an oral presentation (or another relatively sustained oral production activity) undertaken by the learner so that instances of error can be related back to what he will recently have been working on.

The learner then selects a text which is relevant to his general study orientation and records his reading of the chosen passage onto a dictaphone or tape-recorder (the main advantage of the dictaphone is its portability). One reading, however, is rarely enough, and the learner is asked to monitor his own reading and attempt to improve his initial version on the basis of the guidelines given by the teacher and his own judgement of appropriacy: three readings would seem to be what most learners consider the norm in this respect. The learner then gives the text and the recording to the teacher who highlights in the text those areas where there are still problems and goes over these with the learner, producing a model version (which is preferably recorded directly onto the learner's dictaphone) and providing further guidance.

Table 6 Strategy analysis

Metacognitive strategies

- planning and self-management: text selection and organisation of the task of reading aloud and self-correction on the basis of the teacher's guidelines;
- selective attention and problem identification: attending to the specific problems diagnosed by the teacher;
- self-monitoring (in particular, production and auditory monitoring) and self-evaluation (in particular, production and performance evaluation): assessment by the learner of his mastery of the target aspects of pronunciation or intonation.

Cognitive strategies

- repetition: repeating and self-correcting by the learner of those aspects of pronunciation/intonation identified as requiring attention;
- resourcing: use of the teacher's advice and the learner's own insights into the TL to direct task performance.

Social/Affective strategies

- self-talk: the learner providing himself with encouragement to persevere and talking himself through the task.

7.4.3   Peer and self-correction of written work

This activity sequence has been used by the author with students of business administration to deal with report writing. The first stage is for learners to plan and write a report in groups of about three: this is partly related to the fact that learners generally perform the initial situation analysis upon which the report is based in groups, but it also caters for a form of collaborative learning at the writing stage itself. The teacher then corrects the completed reports using a simple coding system to indicate errors or inappropriacies: the coding system is explained to the learners in advance and they are provided with a key and a few examples and guidance questions per error type.

Learners read over their corrected report and try to correct the problems identified; they then exchange their corrected report with another group and try to correct as many of the errors as they can in their colleagues' report. At this stage, the teacher should provide clues and pointers rather than simply providing the correct solution. The teacher then goes over each report in detail on the OHP. By this stage, two groups will already have seen each report, and these groups should thus be best able to suggest appropriate solutions: when all else fails, of course, the teacher provides the solution. The learners note down the corrected version and thus accumulate over the course as a whole a number of well written reports which have been prepared and at least partially corrected by group members themselves.

This activity sequence involves a collaborative form of learning which includes both self- and peer correction. It also caters for an element of peer teaching. Readers may wish to refer to Assinder (1991) for a description of a more extensive form of peer teaching.

Table 7   Strategy analysis

Metacognitive strategies

- selective attention: directing attention to the elements highlighted and coded by the teacher;
- self- (and peer) monitoring (in particular, production, visual and style monitoring): learners checking over their own and fellow students' written production;

- self-evaluation: assessment by the learners of their performance of the writing task in both linguistic/communicative and strategic terms.

Cognitive strategies

- resourcing and transfer: learners' gathering of insights from the teacher, fellow students and their existing knowledge of the TL to find the appropriate TL forms for the highlighted elements;
- translation: possible reference to the learners' L1 as one means of understanding the causes of a given error.

Social/Affective strategies

- questioning for clarification: discussion with fellow students to clarify the intended meaning of problem elements and with each other and the teacher to select appropriate forms;
- cooperation: sharing insights and knowledge of the TL to correct written work.

PED. On which basis do you approach error correction in your teaching? In particular, do you involve learners in the process?

- If you do, then in which way(s)?
- If you do not, what are your reasons, and do they relate more to the learners themselves or to your own teaching preferences?

7.5 Project work

Project work is frequently associated with learner-centred teaching for a number of reasons. One is the transfer of responsibility for the management of learning from teacher to learners, as Maley suggests:

> Project work [...] provides one solution to the problem of learner-autonomy, of making the learner responsible for his own learning. By its very nature, project work places the responsibility on the students, both as individuals and as members of a co-operative learning group. Autonomy becomes a fact of life. (In the foreword to Fried-Booth 1986: 3)

Another reason relates to the type of learning activities which are activated by project work, and this is linked to the concern with the learning process, which has been one of the driving forces behind the move towards more learner-centred approaches to teaching (1.2; 1.3). Fried-Booth lists the following stages in project work:

1 *Stimulus.* Initial discussion of the idea – comment and suggestion. The main language skills involved: speaking and listening, with possible reference to prior reading.
2 *Definition of the project objective.* Discussion, negotiation, suggestion, and argument. The longer the total time available for the project, the more detailed this phase will be. Main language skills: speaking and listening, probably with some note-taking.
3 *Practice of language skills.* This includes the language the students feel is needed for the initial stage of the project, e.g. for data collection. It also introduces a variety of language functions, e.g. introductions, suggestions, asking for information, etc., and may involve any or all of the four skills (particularly writing, in the form of note-taking).
4 *Design of written materials.* Questionnaires, maps, grids, etc., required for data collection. Reading and writing skills will be prominent here.
5 *Group activities.* Designed to gather information. Students may work individually, in pairs or in small groups, inside or outside the classroom. Their tasks will include conducting interviews or surveys, and gathering facts. All four skills are likely to be needed.
6 *Collating information.* Probably in groups, in the classroom. Reading of notes, explanation of visual material, e.g. graphs. Emphasis on discussion.
7 *Organization of material.* Developing the end-product of the project. Discussion, negotiation, reading for cross-reference and verification. The main skill practised, however, will be writing.
8 *Final presentation.* The manner of presentation will depend largely on the form of the end product – chart, booklet, video display or oral presentation – and on the manner of demonstration. The main skill required is likely to be speaking, but could be backed up by other skills.

(Op. cit.: 9–10)

Fried-Booth's list brings out the rich strategic and linguistic potential of a collaborative project, a point made by Tudor (1988) with respect to learner video production. The two project types outlined below are simply two instances of the potentially open-ended range of project options available (cf. Fried-Booth, op. cit. for a survey of possibilities).

7.5.1 Identifying the group's learning problems

This activity is based on Campbell and Kryszewska's (op. cit.: 26–8) 'My learning problem' and involves a collaborative project within the learning group relating to the language learning priorities of group members. The first stage is for the teacher to introduce the idea of the learners themselves providing input to the setting of learning objectives on the basis of their own perceptions of their learning problems. This may be done in terms of their mastery of different grammatical constructions, their ability to perform certain functions, or in terms of specific language skills. Doing this is in itself a form of learner training in that it involves teacher and learners discussing the terms in which they will formulate learning objectives. At the same time, the discussion and shared exploration of learning difficulties constitutes a form of learner involvement. There are two reasons for this: one is that the survey can yield valuable input into the establishment of learning objectives, and the other is that it creates a collaborative form of learning, in which learners as well as the teacher provide advice and guidance for their colleagues.

Once a common vocabulary has been worked out and a list of learning problems drawn up for the group as a whole, the class is split up into groups, each of which has to investigate in greater detail one of the learning problems identified. This may involve the learners who expressed certain problems analysing them further or the analysis may be carried out by other learners on the basis of interviews, the latter probably being preferable in view of the follow-up stage. Each group then reports back to the class. The goal here is for the speakers to explore what their fellow students find difficult, why this seems to be the case, and then to suggest the means by which they can overcome or work on the problem in question. These suggestions can then be discussed and evaluated both by the class as a whole and, of course, by those learners whose problem is being looked at. The teacher's role is that of learning counsellor and guide (8.3).

Table 8 Strategy analysis

Metacognitive strategies

- planning: present in the organisation of the class survey by each group;
- directed attention and problem identification: organising the survey to focus on learners' *main* learning problems;
- self-evaluation (in particular, language repertoire evaluation): the diagnosis by each learner of his specific learning problems.

Cognitive strategies

- grouping: gathering together the main problem areas identified by fellow students;
- note-taking and summarisation: collation by each group of the problems identified during their survey of their fellow students' difficulties.

Social/Affective strategies

- cooperation: using information from and discussion with fellow students to establish learning objectives for the group as a whole.

As in the self- and peer correction of written work described at the end of 6.4, this activity involves an element of peer teaching.

7.5.2   A content-based project leading to an oral presentation

This is a relatively standard type of project which is used with fourth year business students at the Institut de Langues Vivantes et de Phonétique, Université Libre de Bruxelles. At the start of a 90-hour course in English, students are informed that they have to prepare a project on a subject related to their own area of specialisation. They are required to produce a written report and also make a formal oral presentation to the group at the end of their course. The oral presentation has to be clearly structured and of a standard suitable for a professional context of use, which entails the use of visual support, handouts and various audience involvement techniques. Students are encouraged to work in groups of two or three to allow them to experiment with the use of transitional and linking functions of language (e.g. 'Jean-Claude will now talk to you about ...'; 'As I mentioned in the introduction, ...') and also to encourage a collaborative approach to learning. Students choose their own topic, providing this conforms to certain criteria. One is professional relevance, students having to choose a subject linked to their study orientation; the other is specificity of topic: 'The economy of Zaire', for example, would be rejected as being too general and descriptive, whereas 'Opportunities and threats for the Zairean economy into the 21st century' would be accepted since it is likely to necessitate the use of language functions such as comparison and contrast, prediction, and evaluation, which form part of the goals of the course as a whole. This level of content specification is thus teacher-based; the students are, however, free to organise the topic treatment and structuring of the presentation itself as they feel most appropriate. Students work on their project over one semester with a few guidance/consultancy sessions with their class teacher. The project also counts for part of the students' examination mark, which is a powerful motivation. The strategy analysis below is based on a survey by the author of the strategies reported by two class groups (38 students in all).

Table 9 Strategy analysis

Metacognitive strategies

- planning and self-management: initial and ongoing organisation of the project in content terms;
- directed attention: concentration, during the earlier stages of the project, on the main ideas and overall structure of the project;
- selective attention: focusing on key aspects of the language to be used during the preparation of the written project report and of the oral presentation;
- self-monitoring (in particular, production, style, plan, and double-check monitoring): ongoing checking of the content structure and language used in the project, particularly during its final stages.

Cognitive strategies

- repetition: in the main, this involves rehearsal of the oral presentation;
- resourcing: using available sources of information both for the content of the project and for the TL forms required for its expression;
- note-taking and summarisation: keeping track on the content and language required both for the written report and the oral presentation; preparation of support notes for use during the oral presentation;
- elaboration (in particular, personal, world, academic, and between-parts elaboration): use of specialised knowledge and creativity to structure the content of the written report and oral presentation;
- translation: incorporation of reference material in the students' L1 (French) as input into the content of the project and explicit avoidance of inappropriate lexical transfer from French into English.

Social/Affective strategies

- questioning for clarification: gathering information about the content of the project from various individuals (generally done in the learners' L1); discussion among project group members about the content of the project, the language used in both the written report and the oral presentation, and the presentational techniques employed together with their formulation in English;
- cooperation: sharing of the task of project preparation and delivery among group members.

PED. If your current teaching practice includes project work:

- identify its goals (do they relate more to the product or to the process of learning?);
- assess the type of learning strategies that it generates, e.g. by interviewing learners on the basis of O'Malley and Chamot's strategy categorisation (in this respect it may be interesting to make your own prediction of the strategies that might be used and to compare this with what students will actually report);
- specify the way in which the project work in question fits into learners' study programme as a whole.

If you do not use any form of project work, think how its introduction might aid the development of your students' strategic learning skills.

7.6 A few guidelines for innovation in methodology

Most of the activities considered in the last three sections involve a collaborative approach to learning: the reason for this is that collaborative learning offers the possibility of learners engaging in the use of a broader range of strategies than would be the case in a wholly teacher-centred mode of study. This having been said, collaborative learning is a means to an end and not a fetish. The teacher therefore needs to bear in mind that it is the *learning processes* engaged by a given activity that are the key element, and not the *surface form* of the activity itself. If the teacher already makes use of forms of collaborative learning, she may wish to use the ideas put forward in this chapter as a basis for an investigation of the type of learning strategies actually being used by her students: setting up frameworks which should generate a certain type of strategy usage does not guarantee that they will do so. On the other hand, if teaching is conducted in a 'traditional' manner, the teacher may wish to assess the range of strategies which are currently being used by her students – both within class time and in their private study: she may thus discover a number of valuable strategies which, to begin with, should not be lost, and which can also serve as a basis for further strategy development work. In either case, teachers should beware of assuming a direct relationship between the surface form of learning activities and the learning processes which they give rise to among students. Moreover, any form of pedagogical change should be realised gradually and on the basis of an assessment of the strategic and attitudinal preparedness of the students, as well as the contextual appropriacy of the innovation in question (not to mention its practical feasibility). The following points may merit consideration in this respect.

1 Learners' ability to take advantage of the learning opportunities offered by a given activity is heavily dependent on them having a clear understanding of what they are doing, why they are doing it, and how the activity in question can contribute to their language learning. Learner training thus plays a key role.

2 Active learner involvement can be demanding, and if learners' motivation and commitment to their language study is limited (or constrained by other obligations), they may be unwilling (or unable) to invest the effort that is required to make a collaborative form of learning work effectively. The teacher thus needs to assess realistically the demands a given activity type will make on learners' commitment: setting modest but attainable goals is far more likely to produce positive results than demanding more than learners feel ready to give.

3 Learners' strategic awareness and beliefs about language learning, as well as their culturally-based expectations about language study, including the respective roles of teachers and learners, will exert a significant influence on how they perceive and interact with learning activities. If, for example, students' prior learning experience has predisposed them to believe that the teacher's task is to transmit knowledge and students' is to assimilate this knowledge, they may find a collaborative approach to learning confusing or even disconcerting. In this respect, the teacher should analyse her students' classroom culture to assess whether it contains study habits which can be exploited productively to foster language learning. These might be the spontaneous formation by students of self-help groups outside of class, or the diligent study of a set of lecture notes or study materials produced by the teacher. As has been suggested previously, teachers need to have the confidence to act locally, in response to the realities of their own teaching situation, and not to feel emprisoned by conventional wisdom (of a 'traditional' or an 'innovative' nature) about what is or is not 'good' teaching practice.

4 Contextual factors, of which class size is one, may also exercise an influence on what is feasible in pedagogical terms. If a certain activity type genuinely is not feasible in a given context, the teacher should not feel uneasy about not using it (whatever its theoretical credentials). She should, however, explore the alternative ways in which the same, or at least comparable underlying goals can be achieved.

Oxford *et al.* (1992) and Bassano (1986) provide two useful sets of recommendations with respect to innovation in learning procedures.

Oxford *et al.*'s recommendations relate primarily to the ways in which the teacher can avoid 'style wars', or conflicts arising out of mismatches between the learning style favoured by a given approach to teaching and students' learning style preferences (4.4). Oxford *et al.* consider this primarily with respect to multicultural groups of tertiary level ESL/EFL students, but their recommendations remain pertinent to the expansion of learners' strategic awareness in any context. Oxford *et al.* make the following 10 recommendations:

1 *Assess the learning style of both the teacher and the students.* In addition to the assessment of students' learning style preferences which is part of basic learner training, Oxford *et al.* recommend:

   – discussion of the style assessment results to show the range of styles present in the class as a whole to help individual learners to find others with whom they can identify;
   – a positive and open discussion by the teacher of her own learning style preferences;
   – cross-cultural comparison of learning styles.

   In these ways, Oxford *et al.* seek to favour the creation of a climate of mutual respect for difference and a genuine sharing of perspectives both among students and between students and the teacher.

2 *Alter the teaching style in order to create teacher-student style matching through a range of activities.* Two points are made here. The first is that an effort should be made to match teaching style with students' learning style – in this respect it should be recalled that matching can operate either by similarity or by complementarity (4.5). However, Oxford *et al.* cite Ellis (1989: 260) to suggest that 'Matching is best achieved by the teacher catering for individual needs during the moment-to-moment process of teaching (i.e. by emphasizing group dynamics and offering a range of activity types)' rather than assigning teachers and students to homogeneous groups on the basis of style groupings.

3 *Provide activities with different groupings.* Learning tasks should allow, for instance, both introverts and extroverts to find activity types congenial with their natural learning and interactional preferences. Students should sometimes be grouped on the basis of style similarity (for greater efficiency) and sometimes on the basis of style variance (to encourage greater flexibility).

4 *Include and encode different learning styles in lesson plans.* This would involve the teacher coding activities in terms of the learning strategies they are likely to favour or elicit.

5 *Encourage changes in students' behaviour and foster guided style-stretching.*

6 *Prepare an ESL/EFL learning environment that welcomes and accommodates a variety of styles and cultures.* The environment in which students work should reflect an openness to difference, e.g. by means of displays representing different approaches to learning put together by the teacher or class members during learner training sessions.

7 *Gather exciting displays reflecting different styles and cultures.*

8 *Improve the physical setting.* Make the classroom pleasant and welcoming, possibly with different seating arrangements for specific activities.

9 *Leave the classroom occasionally.* Studying in settings other than the classroom can provide variety and help students feel that language learning is not restricted to the classroom.

10 *Change the way style conflicts are viewed.* Consider differences not as wrinkles to be ironed out but rather as means by which students (and teacher) can learn from one another in a climate of mutual respect.

Bassano's recommendations (op. cit.: 15–19) relate to helping students adapt to unfamiliar methods. Bassano seems to be concerned primarily with ensuring the implementation of 'high participation, effective, oral practice' (op. cit.: 14). This, of course, is simply one mode of learning. Providing, however, the teacher is sufficiently open to learner diversity and is not too attached to any one set of teaching procedures, Bassano's recommendations can be very helpful:

1 *Become aware of students' past classroom experiences and their assumptions about language learning.* This is an aspect of basic learner training which allows the teacher to get an idea of her students' background and expectations and which also initiates the sharing of learning experiences among group members.

2 *Build student confidence in your expertise and qualifications.* Bassano's point is that students are unlikely to have confidence in a novel suggestion made by the teacher if they doubt her professional competence. This is probably of particular importance if the teacher is working with students from a cultural background different from her own.

3 *Begin where the students are and move slowly.* Bringing out what is positive in students' current approach to learning is far more productive than homing in on inadequacies: this helps to create a non-judgemental climate within which alternative approaches can be shared and evaluated constructively.

4 *Show them achievement.* This may be seen in terms of the metaphor of the glass which is, depending on one's perspective, half full or half empty. Rote learning of word lists, for instance, is not the only means of acquiring vocabulary and it may not be the most effective: it is,

however, one means of doing so which can patently produce positive results for many learners.

5 *Allow for free choice as much as possible.* Students are far more likely to experiment with new learning options if these are presented to them in a constructive manner but without any constraint.

6 *Become aware of students' interests and concerns, their goals and objectives.* The success of change is likely to be linked with the degree to which students can relate the change in question to their past experience and aspirations.

The recommendations made by Oxford *et al.* and by Bassano might be summed up in terms of two main principles:

– *Be flexible*: i.e. don't get stuck in seeing any one approach to language teaching or any one set of teaching procedures as a goal in itself.
– *Be responsive*: gear teaching decisions around the specific needs, expectations and characteristics of the respective learners at that point in time.

These two recommendations might be perceived as being vague and possibly unhelpful. And, in a sense, they are, if one is looking for neat, pre-defined solutions. On the other hand, they do point language teaching in a fairly clear direction, namely one which is geared around the needs, experience and expectations of each separate group of learners, and also the characteristics of the broader context within which language teaching is taking place. 'It depends' may well be an irritating response, but it is frequently the only realistic one in both human and educational terms.

PED. Evaluate the ways in which the recommendations made by Oxford *et al.* and by Bassano could help you to create a more varied and strategy-rich approach to your teaching.

- Do you feel that these authors have missed any important point(s)?
- If so, what are they, and which aspects of teaching do they relate to?

7.7 Summary

a) A learner-centred approach, as any other, has to ensure that learners attain their objective learning goals, whether these are defined in terms of mastery of a given range of structures and lexis or with respect to number of situationally defined functional skills.

What is specific to a learner-centred approach, however, is that this goal should be pursued in an educationally-motivated manner which will help learners to develop their strategic awareness of language study.

b) This involves learners being given the opportunity to try out and evaluate a variety of activity types and modes of learning so that they can broaden their vision of what language learning can mean, and also get a feeling for their individual learning needs and preferences. Learner-centred teaching should thus cater for the creation of a strategic learning potential in everyday teaching-learning activities. This is a practical form of language education which is integrated into learners' ongoing study programme, which develops learners' self-directive potential and thereby contributes to learner empowerment.

c) With this goal in mind, a number of pedagogical options were discussed under the headings of grammar, error correction, and project work, and were analysed in terms of the type of learning strategies which they can potentially activate.

d) These options call for an active involvement of learners, something for which not all learners may be prepared. Flexibility and responsiveness are therefore required of the teacher in evaluating the nature of the demands which are made of learners. This involves consideration of their experience of language learning and of their target situations of use, the culturally-based expectations of the learning group, as well as the learning style preferences of individual learners.

8   The teacher's perspective

8.1   Learner-centredness and the teacher

The adoption of a learner-centred approach to teaching has a number of implications for the learners involved. The most evident of these is the more active and participatory role allocated to learners in the development of their study programme and the importance given to their subjective needs and learning preferences. A learner-centred approach to teaching also has implications for the role and responsibilities of the teacher (Tudor 1993). This may be seen in two ways. To begin with, studying a language is an interactive process between the teacher and her students: if a change takes place in the role of learners then a parallel change in the role of the teacher is virtually inevitable. Furthermore, a number of the pedagogical procedures which are proper to a learner-centred mode of teaching involve a range of educational skills not explicitly developed in all teacher training programmes. Opting for a learner-centred mode of teaching can therefore represent a challenge to the teacher's professional skills and adaptability. For this reason the present chapter will focus on the teacher's role in a learner-centred approach.

8.1.1   Learner-centredness and innovation

As was indicated in 1.2 and 1.3, a number of influential trends in language teaching over the last three decades may justifiably be seen as 'learner-centred' in one way or another. CLT, for instance, developed a variety of procedures for gearing learning content to learners' real-world communicative needs, while humanistic language teaching has yielded a number of insights into the process side of learning, with particular emphasis on learners' affective involvement in their language study. Work on learner training and learner autonomy, and the development of the concept of the learner-centred curriculum have taken place within the general framework of goals established by CLT, but have incorporated insights into the subjective aspects of language study arising out of the learning strategy research of the 1970s. In a very real sense, then,

230

'learner-centredness' may be seen as the *leitmotif* for many recent developments in language teaching. One might therefore question whether it is necessary to regard a learner-centred approach to teaching as 'innovative'.

There are, however, certain reasons why the linking of 'learner-centredness' and 'innovation' is justified. One relates to the degree to which the individual teacher's training and prior professional experience have prepared her for a learner-centred mode of teaching: in this sense, the degree of innovation involved will vary from teacher to teacher. More fundamentally, however, there is something inherently innovative about a learner-centred approach to teaching for the very simple reason that no one group of learners will ever be quite like another, and no teaching situation will have precisely the same configuration of participants and imperatives as another. The teacher who is committed to a learner-centred mode of teaching needs therefore to be open to change, and be able to react flexibly to the needs of her students and of the educational context within which she is working.

Gaies and Bowers (1990: 170) mention a number of causes of difficulty for teachers, which include:

- the adoption of new textbooks,
- the introduction of methodological or pedagogical reforms that teachers have not been trained to implement,
- the establishment of new goals for a language teaching programme,
- the prescription of new teacher-learner role relationships in the classroom.

A move in the direction of a more learner-centred approach to teaching may result in changes in any of these four points. For instance, learner-centred teaching by no means excludes the use of existing *textbooks*, but it will encourage the use of a variety of other materials deriving from the learners' occupational concerns or from their affective/cultural interests. The teacher may thus find herself dealing with a range of textual materials that is considerably broader than she is used to, and which may be derived from sources that she is unfamiliar with in either conceptual or linguistic terms. In terms of *programme goals*, few teachers would question the desirability of language education and learner empowerment. These, however, are far broader and less easily definable goals than, for instance, the mastery of a given range of structures and lexis, or the attainment of proficiency within a discrete number of interactive situations. Teachers who have been trained within a specific approach to teaching (whether 'traditional' or 'innovative'), or whose experience has been within a framework defined by adherence to a pre-established curriculum, the use of recommended textbooks or of a given method, may find that the essentially open-ended and exploratory nature of learner-centred teaching places new demands on their pedagogical skills. One particular instance of this are *teacher-learner role relationships*. While the teacher will never forfeit her role as 'knower', in a learner-centred approach this will be subsumed within the roles of learning counsellor and educator. And a shift in role relationships can be trying, as Prabhu points out:

> A new perception in pedagogy, implying a different pattern of classroom activity, is an intruder into teachers' mental frames – an unsettling one, because there is a conflict or mismatch between old and new perceptions and, more seriously, a threat to prevailing routines and to the sense of security dependent upon them. (1987: 105)

Depending on her training, prior experience and personal approach to teaching, a learner-centred approach may thus represent a more or less marked innovation with respect to the skills and classroom behaviour of the individual teacher.

The potential innovativeness of learner-centred teaching does not, however, stop with the teacher. The attitudes of other participants (students, colleagues, educational authorities, the community at large) have to be taken into consideration, too, and it is the teacher who, in the first instance, must 'negotiate' acceptance of the innovation with these agents. Figure 23 schematises the network of questions that the teacher may wish to consider in this respect. For instance:

- Does the innovation fit in or conflict with (certain aspects of) an existing curriculum, prescribed textbooks, or the content of an examination students must take?
- Does the innovation imply behavioural changes for students and/or for teacher-student relationships, and how far does the students' classroom culture predispose them for these changes?
- Does the innovation have implications in terms of the manner in which goals are decided upon? Specifically, does the collaborative approach to decision-making implicit in a learner-centred approach conflict with the organisational structures of the institution in question?
- Are the attitudes of other participants likely to support the innovation or not? In the latter case, for which reasons and which aspects of the innovation are most 'problematic'?

Interactions between the various agents are also possible. For instance:

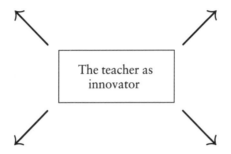

Students – motivations for learning – expectations/classroom culture – likely attitudes to the innovation	Administrative and decision-making structures – current structures – compatibility of the innovation with these structures

The teacher as innovator

Curriculum, prescribed course and related examinations – official status – role in students' life goals – content and methodology – compatibility with the innovation	Attitudes and expectations of other participants – fellow teachers – teachers of other subjects – institutional authorities, etc. – parents, sponsors

Figure 23 The teacher's perspective on the context of innovation

- To what extent does the curriculum influence student attitudes, and in which way?
- Who, in the first instance, does the teacher most need to convince of the value of the innovation: students, parents or sponsors, the administration or management of the institution? In which way will their assent facilitate the implementation of the innovation?

These questions clearly relate to the contextual factors considered in 5.2 and 5.3, and may be seen as being part of means analysis. From the point of view of the individual teacher, however, they relate to the pedagogical choices she will make and thus play a strategic role in the planning of innovation. Or, to put things more directly, they are points the teacher needs to think about carefully if she wishes to avoid unnecessary and potentially unproductive tensions.

8.1.2   Knots

The adoption of a learner-centred mode of teaching need not necessarily be a source of tensions – neither for the teacher, nor her students, nor for the educational system within which they are working. Nevertheless, tensions may arise, and it is preferable to be prepared for them so that they can be evaluated objectively. Tensions can have two main sources. One is a mismatch between the teacher's training and previous experience and the demands of a learner-centred mode of teaching; the other is a conflict between the latter and the expectations of other participants and/or priorities proper to the target learning situation. This can lead to what Wagner (1988) refers to as 'knots'.

Wagner underlines the importance of psychological factors in methodological innovation and uses Laing's (1970) idea of psychological 'knots' to analyse the tensions which teachers may experience in implementing new approaches to teaching:

> Knots emerge when an individual holds imperatives which are incompatible with reality or with other imperatives. Knots are contradictory obligations which cannot be solved ad hoc and trap the individual. If a situation activates contradictory norms, a psychological conflict results. If a situation activates a knot, the individual gets into a psychological dilemma. (1988: 113)

Wagner (op. cit.: 113–15) distinguishes between three types of knots, which he refers to as R-, I- and E-knots.

R-knots arise out of a contradiction between an imperative generated by an innovation and the perceived reality in a teaching institution:

> R-knots have to do with more or less implicit assumptions of methods about the context of teaching: often methods are not designed for certain institutions, but are supposed to work 'in general'. Consequently methods idealize the context of teaching with regard to a number of factors, including the learners' motivation, number of learners, size of classroom, language ability of learners and teachers, and so forth. (Op. cit.: 113–14)

Wagner gives a classic example of this type of knot with respect to the imperative of CLT to encourage language use as experienced in larger classes:

> I should get every learner to talk much more,
> but that is impossible with 30 learners in my class.

Similar knots arise out of the imperatives of a given method and either the demands of examinations or students' objective learning requirements, for example:

> I should get my learners to talk much more,
> but for my learners it is essential to write letters.

Holliday (1994a) refers on a number of occasions to 'knots' of this nature experienced by teachers in TESEP contexts with the imperatives of CLT which, Holliday suggests, generally assume BANA type teaching conditions – hence Holliday's plea for the study of what constitutes 'appropriate' methodology in the light of local conditions.

I-knots result from conflicting or contradictory imperatives. The familiar conflict between accuracy and fluency is an example of this type of knot:

> I should get every learner to talk much more,
> but then I cannot correct all errors.

A further instance of this type of knot cited by Wagner is the tension between the teaching of grammar and the teaching of communication skills.

E-knots relate to a mismatch between the imperatives of a given method and the teacher's own learning-biography. The example given by Wagner of an E-knot is:

> I should get the learners to talk much more,
> but I learned English perfectly well by translation exercises,
> so why shouldn't they?

E-knots can be particularly tricky in that they relate to the teacher's (possibly implicit) beliefs about language and language learning (4.4). They may also have an affective component – affection for a mode of learning which the teacher enjoyed personally or attachment to a manner of teaching which the teacher has used confidently (and with apparent success) for a number of years.

As Wagner points out, knots can paralyse change and make teachers feel confused and disempowered. Knots can rarely be resolved in a neat, rule-based manner. Two strategies are needed to untie knots. One involves the willingness to trace imperatives back to their underlying assumptions in an honest and clear-sighted manner; the other involves a realistic and non-judgemental analysis of the target learning situation. Two recommendations made by Wagner with respect to innovation are of particular relevance in this respect.

• Innovation must be based on an analysis of teaching conditions in an institution, i.e. of official and less official goals connected to teaching and learning as social activity.

- Teacher training has to start from the complex reality of institutions and teachers' perceptions of them. Teacher training has to elaborate and develop the complex schema of teaching foreign languages.

(Op. cit.: 115–16)

DAT/REF. The knots given below are just a few of those which teachers might encounter in adopting a learner-centred approach to their teaching.

- In each case, what advice would you give to help the teacher untangle the knot in question?

Which knots have you experienced (or, do you feel you might experience) with a learner-centred mode of teaching?

- Identify the type of knots (R-, I- or E-knots) involved and their causes.

If you have not or do not expect to experience any knots, assess why.

- Which factors, either in you as a teacher or in your teaching situation are responsible for this lack of tensions?

R-knots: (i.e. contradiction between a methodological imperative and the perceived reality of the teaching situation)

1 I should involve my students more actively in course development but in their other classes they are expected simply to take notes and learn what the teacher tells them.
  They are not used to being consulted.
2 I know from experience what my students need to learn.
  They, however, have no direct experience of their target uses of the language.
  If I attempt to negotiate learning content, students will ask for 'fun' type activities which will not be very helpful to them in the future.
3 I would like to discuss goal-setting and methodology with my students.
  But they expect me to tell them what they need to learn and how to go about it.
  By asking for students' point of view, I may give them the impression I don't know what is best, which may undermine my authority and status.

I-knots: (i.e. conflicting or contradictory imperatives)

1 Language education and learner empowerment are unquestionably worthwhile goals.
However, course time is limited and students have to assimilate a given body of structures and lexis in order to follow their next course profitably.
How much time can I legitimately take from the language programme *per se* to devote to wider, educational goals?

2 The course is built around the demands of an externally set examination: the examination is rather traditional in goals and format, but it plays an important role in students' careers.
If I open up discussion of learning content and goal-setting, students might lose confidence in the value of what they are doing, and become confused or demotivated.

3 I am not opposed to the principle of learner involvement, but my timetable is already full.
If I have to 'negotiate' with students, how am I going to plan my courses in advance?

4 My students and I would like to adopt an exploratory approach to language learning and to aim at self-direction.
My colleagues, however, have more traditional ideas about language teaching.
They feel that staff members should stick together and all follow the same course and approach to teaching.
I hesitate to break ranks with my colleagues, who are all experienced and committed teachers.

E-knots: (i.e. tensions between the imperatives of a given approach and the teacher's own learning experience)

1 I have considerable experience of language learning and teaching, and my students have in the main attained good levels of success in the TL.
My students do not have anything like as much experience as myself: asking for their point of view might motivate them, but how useful is their contribution likely to be?

2 Trends (or fashions) in language teaching come and go so frequently it is difficult to keep up with the latest.
The approach I adopt to teaching may not be the most recent and is probably very 'teacher-centred', but it has always produced good results in the past.
Why should I change until I am convinced that the new approach is really more effective?

8.2 Routine and response

8.2.1 Teachers have subjective needs, too

From the 50s through to the 80s, writing on language teaching was characterised by a strong concern with 'method' and with teaching procedures – the latter including activity types, modes of classroom management and the use of technological aids such as the video or, more recently, computers. This probably reflected a need felt by the language teaching profession to forge new tools to deal with the increased demand for language learning which arose out of various social and economic phenomena during this period. In recent years, however, more attention has been paid to the subjective realities of language teaching and learning. From the learner's point of view, this has led to more importance being accorded to subjective needs and to developing a more educationally-sensitive approach to language teaching in general, as witnessed by work on learner training and autonomy. In parallel with this increased awareness of the subjective realities of language learning from the learner's point of view, there has also been a recognition of the subject realities and thus the complexities of language teaching from the teacher's point of view (e.g. Freeman and Richards 1996).

In particular, it has been observed (Larsen-Freeman 1991) that what teachers actually do in the classroom is at least as strongly influenced by their personal agenda and set of beliefs about language teaching as by the method or approach which they are, in theory, following. In other words, teachers as much as learners have their own private agenda which they bring with them to the process of teaching. The teacher therefore needs to be aware of the subjective factors which influence her own attitudes and behaviours in the classroom. Indeed, Larsen-Freeman (op. cit.) suggests that one of the causes of the generally inconclusive results obtained by method-comparison studies such as Levin (1972) and Scherer and Wertheimer (1964) was that the difference in classroom behaviours between teachers using theoretically different methods was not controlled for and, in fact, may not have corresponded to what teachers were supposedly doing in terms of the methods concerned. In other words, teachers may have been following their own individual teaching agendas, and were interpreting methods in the light of what was referred to in 4.4 as their own 'processing system'. Teachers too, then, have subjective needs and perceptions of the classroom, and these influence their behaviour in a way similar to that in which learners' subjective needs and perceptions influence their behaviour.

Richards (1994) makes two main points about teachers' instructional decisions. One is that they are based on the teachers' own belief systems or 'the information, attitudes, values, theories and assumptions about teaching and learning which teachers build up over time and bring with them to the classroom' (op. cit.: 3). These beliefs form a structured set of principles through which teachers analyse and interpret methodological options and filter their own instructional decisions. The second is that teachers' classroom behaviours tend to be consistent with their underlying belief system. This may be seen in the way in which they prepare lessons and evaluate outcomes, and also in the 'routines' by which they manage their classes and interact with learners. Teaching would thus seem to be coherent and principled behaviour. The source of this coherence, however, should probably be sought in the personal belief system and operational principles of the individual teacher rather than in the precepts of any externally defined method.

A learner-centred mode of teaching is by definition exploratory by virtue of its openness to learners' motivations, knowledge and experience, and to their subjective perceptions of language study. Some teachers may find this stimulating or challenging. Others, depending on their belief system and habitual modes of behaviour in the classroom, may find it unsettling. In either case, however, it is useful for the teacher to take a close look at her own subjective attitudes to teaching prior to or while initiating a learner-centred approach to her teaching.

Richards identifies three main perspectives on teaching:

> A *teacher-centred perspective* sees the main features of a lesson primarily in terms of teacher factors, such as classroom management, teacher's explanations, teacher's questioning skills, teacher's presence, voice quality, manner, and so on. This view of a lesson sees it as a performance by the teacher. A different view of a lesson, which can be termed the *curriculum-centred perspective* sees a lesson in terms of a segment of instruction. Relevant foci include lesson goals, structuring, transitions, materials, task types and content flow and development. A third perspective on a lesson can be called the *learner-centred perspective*. This views the lesson in terms of its effect on learners and refers to such factors as student participation, interest and learning outcomes. (Op. cit.: 9. Original emphasis)

The three perspectives will co-occur in the decision-making of all teachers, but different teachers will favour one relatively more than the others as the primary focus of their actions.

REF. Analyse yourself as a teacher using Richards' three perspectives given above. Which of the three corresponds the closest to your dominant set of concerns when you are preparing, giving and evaluating the success of your own classes?

- Do you feel that there is something missing from these three perspectives?
- Add any additional elements you feel necessary to fill out your own profile of yourself as a teacher.
- In which ways does this predispose you towards a learner-centred mode of teaching and why? Where might you experience difficulties and why?

8.2.2   The challenge of responsive teaching

Richards (op. cit.) picks up on Shavelson and Stern's (1981) use of the term 'routines' to describe the mental scripts and the use of trusted behavioural patterns which characterise the practice of experienced teachers. Richards thus uses the term in a positive sense, to refer to the habitual modes of response to situations which teachers develop over time. Such routines simplify interaction by allowing the teacher to deal with questions, difficulties or various other aspects of classroom management in a fluid, confident manner. In this sense, routines play a facilitative role in teaching – as in most aspects of human interaction. There is always the danger, however, that routines can become frozen into norms of behaviour or even goals in their own right. In this case, they can stultify growth and distort the way in which reality is perceived – a class of round or triangular pegs being made to function as if they were square. Thus, while routines are a positive element in teaching, ROUTINE is negative.

Learner-centred teaching has far more to do with openness to learner variability and to learner input than with any one set of teaching procedures. This means that the ability to listen to learners and respond to their needs in a flexible manner is crucial. In other words, while 'routines' will inevitably play a role in learner-centred teaching, responsiveness is the key quality. In this respect Brumfit's cautionary remarks about humanistic language teaching are equally pertinent with respect to learner-centred teaching:

> ... descriptions of what to do in humanistic teaching may easily be converted into sets of separate instructions and thus lose their wholeness and integrity. [...] Learning to teach is not to pick up formulae but to act on internalised principles – to borrow

terminology from religious instructions, we are concerned not with outward and visible signs, but with inward and spiritual graces. The signs are the conventions of particular times and places, but the internal motivation and sensitivity of the good teacher will transcend the limitations of particular local conventions through the process of relating to people – the class. Each teacher recreates the principles of teaching in relation to each new class and each new student. (1982: 16–17)

With Brumfit's remarks in mind, it may be useful to look more closely at the lesson described by O'Neill and mentioned in 5.3.2.

A lesson observed

Six Japanese businessmen are having a lesson with an experienced English teacher in an evening class in Tokyo. The teacher, a young woman, is highly-qualified. She has agreed to allow me to observe the lesson. The Director of Studies (DoS) is also a guest. He and I are introduced to the class and then sit down at the side. The teacher begins by giving each member of the class a sheet of paper with ten statements about women, such as:

1 In Japanese society it is better for women to stay at home than to work.
2 Women do not get the same educational qualifications as men because they are not as intelligent as men.

At the top of the page, there are the following instructions:
Discuss these statements with others in your group. Find out if they agree or disagree.

The teacher does not speak while handing these statements out to the group, and after doing so, she sits down silently at a slight distance behind the group. There is a period of complete silence while the six businessmen study the statements and look up words in their Japanese-English dictionaries.

What we must do now?

Afterwards, the teacher gives the class no indication of what to do but just sits there, impassively and silently. Only after one of them actually says – in barely comprehensible English – 'Please, what we must do now?', does she point wordlessly to the instructions at the top of the page.

There is another and shorter period of awkward silence, but finally one of the men takes the role of group-leader and asks the man nearest to him on his right.

'Mr Yamaha. Sentence one. You agree or disagree?'

Mr Yamaha-san still has difficulty in interpreting the question, but after a while nods and mutters 'Agree'.

It takes another ten or fifteen minutes for the group-leader to get the same stereotyped answer, either 'Agree' or 'Disagree' from the other members. There are no follow-up questions. There is no discussion. There is only the same knitting and furrowing of eyebrows, the same repeated interrogation 'Agree or disagree', the same one-word affirmation or negation.

Almost half the lesson has now passed and suddenly, in a dramatic gesture (dramatic only because it is such a contrast to her previous behaviour), the teacher gets to her feet. She distributes another sheet of paper to each student, and then strides to the cassette-player at the front of the class, inserts a cassette, hands the machine to another student and sits down again. The student looks helplessly at her. She gestures silently to the 'play' button on the machine and then to the 'stop' button.

A listening phase

The student guesses that he is supposed to play the cassette to the class, which he does. We hear about three minutes of a recorded discussion between two Americans, a man and a woman. They are talking about an incident in the woman's career when she felt she did not gain a promotion because she was a woman, even though she had all the necessary qualifications. The discussion seems to be spontaneous and authentic. The problem, for me at least (I cannot speak for the six businessmen), is that parts of it are very difficult to understand. One of the speakers, the man, is further away from the microphone than the woman and tends to mumble. The female speaker is reasonably audible most of the time but speaks quickly and at times uses quite difficult vocabulary and rather long, even rambling sentences. Although, as a native speaker, I can usually understand her, I wonder if the businessmen do, as well. I suspect from the blank, but polite, expressions on their faces that they do not.

Now the teacher gets up and gives the students another sheet of paper.

There are questions on it about what the two speakers in the recording have said.

Above these questions there are the following instructions:

Work in groups of two. See if you can answer these questions. If you cannot because you don't remember or didn't understand what the speakers said, ask someone in your group to play that part of the recording again.

Confusion and pair work

This again causes a lot of confusion but finally, after about three minutes of near silence and grunting, the class divides into three pairs. I listen carefully to the pair nearest me.

S1 This question here. You understand?
S2 This question?
S1 *(pointing)* This ... no, that question ...
S2 Oh ... yes ... what?
S1 Answer, please.
S2 Answer?
S1 Yes, you answer the question. You understand?
S2 Your answer?
S1 No, please. You, please. Please.
S2 I ... I understand the question.
S1 Yes. You can answer?
S2 Yes. I can answer. I understand.

(The two students sit silently for a minute, looking thoughtful. Then the first student points to another question.)
S1 The question here. Your answer?
S2 Yes *(long pause)* I can answer. I think ... very difficult to understand.
S1 Yes, agree.   (1991: 293–5)

In conversation with O'Neill after the lesson, the teacher's Director of Studies (who patently did not share O'Neill's negative evaluation of the lesson) pointed out that the lesson manifested three key pedagogical principles:

1 Minimal teacher intervention: the teacher intervened only when strictly necessary; the students took autonomous control of the running of the class. The lesson was thus learner-centred and communicative.
2 There was a lot of peer-talk: the students negotiated the question and answer work among themselves.
3 Exposure to authentic English.

These might seem to be typical manifestations of a learner-centred mode of learning, but were they realised in this manner in the class in question? Certain quite basic pedagogical questions arise in this respect, for example:

- Had the learners in question been prepared for the type of role the teacher wished them to play? In other words, had there been appropriate learner training and negotiation of methodology?
- Had the learners been prepared for the specific roles the teacher assumed they would play in the activities in question?
- To what extent did the teacher-learner roles implicitly present in the teacher's choice of methodology coincide with the learners' cultural expectations and classroom culture?
- Was the learners' English sufficient to allow them to function in the way the teacher wanted?
- In connection with the last point, what was the learners' attitude to making errors or 'losing face'? In other words, did the activity type plus the learners' current level of English create a situation with possibly negative psychosocial implications for them?
- To what extent did the teacher monitor learners' performance of the tasks set, and what ongoing support and pedagogical guidance did she provide?
- What was the goal of the lesson, and what were the learners expected to learn – either in linguistic terms or with respect to their understanding of language learning?

O'Neill questions whether the lesson was an instance of student-centredness or of student neglect. In fact, the lesson seems to reflect what Richards (op. cit.) describes as a teacher-centred perspective on teaching. The teacher applied a variety of 'approved' teaching procedures ('learner-centred' ones in this case), but without much apparent feeling for the needs or reactions of the learners concerned (not terribly learner-centred). Indeed, this lesson can be seen as a good example of how a 'highly qualified' teacher, not to mention her DoS, has confused possible *surface manifestations* with the reality of learner-centred teaching. This is a permanent danger, viz. that certain typical manifestations of a given mode of teaching come to be seen as synonymous with the approach itself. A genuinely learner-centred approach to teaching will, almost inevitably, vary considerably in response to the specific needs of the learners involved and the characteristics of the teaching context. Learner-centredness, then, cannot be reduced to a set of techniques. It has far more to do with the willingness to work with learners as they are in a realistic and non-doctrinaire manner. This, however, demands a great deal of flexibility and responsiveness from the teacher. In this respect, Strevens' (1979) idea of the teacher as chameleon is well worth bearing in mind.

Nunan (1988: 91–5) reports on a study in Australia comparing teachers' and learners' assessments of the usefulness of a range of learning activities. The results showed that the two groups differed in their ratings of all but one of the activities in question (conversation practice), and that the divergence between teacher and learner ratings were particularly marked with respect to pronunciation practice, error correction, learner self-discovery of errors and pair work.

In an attempt to explain these differences, Nunan contrasts the 'belief systems' of the two groups of respondents. As far as the learners are concerned:

> Learning consists of acquiring a body of knowledge.
> The teacher has this knowledge and the learner has not.
> The knowledge is available for revision and practice in a text-book or some other written form.
> It is the role of the teacher to impart this knowledge to the learner through such activities as explanation, writing and example. The learner will be given a programme in advance.
> Learning a language consists of learning the structural rules of the language and the vocabulary through such activities as memorisation, reading and writing.
>
> (1988: 94, citing Brindley 1984: 97)

The teachers' beliefs, on the other hand, seemed to be that:

> Learning consists of acquiring organising principles through encountering experience.
> The teacher is a resource person who provides language input for the learner to work on.
> Language data is to be found everywhere – in the community and media as well as in textbooks.
> It is the role of the teacher to assist learners to become self-directing by providing access to language data through such activities as active listening, role play and interaction with native speakers.
> For learners, learning a language consists of forming hypotheses about the language input to which they will be exposed, these hypotheses being constantly modified in the direction of the target model.
>
> (Nunan, 1988: 94)

Nunan also provides certain representative comments by both groups of respondents which reflect the tensions generated by these two differing belief systems. For the learners:

> Without the grammar, you can't learn the language.
> I don't want to clap or sing. I want to learn English.

> I want something I can take home and study. We do a lot of
> speaking, but we never see it written down.
>
> (Op. cit.)

While for the teachers:

> All they want is grammar.
> I tried to get them to watch a video, but they didn't like it.
> They didn't want to go on excursions. They wanted to stay in
> the classroom and do grammar exercises.
> They kept asking for a textbook.
>
> (Op. cit.)

Brindley (1984: 97) prefaces his outline of the learners' activity
preferences given above with the comment that 'many learners do
have rather fixed ideas (in some cases culturally determined) about
what it is to be a learner and what it is to learn a language.' Nunan
does not feel the need to make similar comments about the teachers,
even though most AMEP teachers are of Anglo-Celtic origin and have
probably followed similar professional training: in other words, *their*
views of language teaching, too, may justifiably be seen as being
culturally determined. The classroom expectations of the teachers and
learners, both of which presumably arose out of their cultural background and prior experience of language learning or teaching, thus
differed in a number of respects. This, however, is simply an observation, and does not help a great deal to generate an appropriate
pedagogical response.

Three main options would seem to exist in this respect. *Option A*
would be the 'teacher knows best' approach. This would involve the
assumption that, as qualified professionals, the teachers have the best
understanding of what learning a language entails and how it is best
conducted. Learners' current activity preferences would thus be seen as a
transitional competence in strategic terms. Ironically, perhaps, this
approach would correspond to certain learner expectations, at least as
regards the role of the teacher as authority figure. It would hardly,
however, allocate very much place to the learners' subjective needs.
Option B, on the other hand, would involve 'giving them what they
want', i.e. gearing learning activities wholly round the learners' current
preferences. This option would be less than ideal, however. How far, for
example, do the learners' preferences arise out of prior experience or
popular wisdom as opposed to representing a clear and informed choice
among available options? So would simply giving them a further diet of
what they have already experienced help learners expand their repertoire
of learning skills (4.5; 7.1), and thus grow as learners? *Option C* would

involve a compromise between the two sets of preferences which would respect and accommodate the learners' current preferences, while at the same time introducing them to alternative modes of learning within a reflective framework designed to help them to evaluate the relative merits of the different options available to them and thereby develop their self-directive abilities.

Option C is clearly the most desirable in pedagogical terms. This having been said, it has a number of implications for the teacher. To begin with, it complicates advance planning. If methodology (and, hence, the materials and activities used) is chosen in response to learner characteristics, the teacher will need to do a lot of thinking on her feet and be willing to re-evaluate her approach at regular intervals, all of which adds to her overall workload. Furthermore, if the teacher acknowledges the need to modify or diversify her approach to teaching in response to learner preferences, she will have to master a range of materials and pedagogical procedures which may go beyond her habitual (or preferred) mode of teaching. This calls for flexibility and possession of a broad pedagogical repertoire (4.5). To sum up, then, openness to learners' subjective needs and preferences can place extra demands on the teacher with respect to advance planning and the range of pedagogical skills she has to master.

REF. Analyse your professional training and previous teaching experience with respect to the perspective on methodology outlined in this section.

- Which approach to methodology were you trained in, and which have you adopted since? In particular, have you generally worked within a single methodology or have you adopted an 'eclectic' approach? If the latter is the case, look carefully at the criteria that have guided your choices.
- What is your personal reaction to the idea of 'responsive' teaching? Which implications would it have for your day-to-day teaching practice?

8.3 Enabling conditions

A learner-centred approach to teaching can alter a number of very practical aspects of course planning, a fact which needs to be borne in mind and catered for both by the individual teacher and by educational authorities. Nunan makes this point very strongly:

> If teachers are to be the principal agents of curriculum develop-
> ment, they need to develop a range of skills which go beyond
> classroom management and instruction. Curriculum develop-
> ment will therefore be largely a matter of appropriate staff
> development. (1988: 171)

Teacher preparedness is thus a key enabling condition within a learner-
centred approach. This section will therefore consider the skills required
of teachers in a learner-centred mode of teaching with reference to what
has been said in previous chapters, and will also briefly examine the
institutional climate in which a move to learner-centred teaching may
most effectively be made.

8.3.1   The demands of learner-centred teaching

Those who have never stood at the chalkface frequently underestimate
the professional expertise, interpersonal skills, and energy which language teaching calls for. This is true even when a relatively clear-cut
method with its own set of pre-ordained teaching procedures is being
employed. As a result of its essentially open-ended and exploratory
nature, however, a learner-centred mode of teaching can make greater
demands on the teacher's abilities. These demands may be considered in
terms of the following areas of expertise:

Needs analysis skills

These relate, on the one hand, to the identification of learners' objective
needs and to goal-setting. This will involve the use of a variety of needs
analysis (3.6) and self-assessment (6.4) procedures to explore learners'
communicative agendas and their current ability to realise these agendas
in the TL. Learners also have needs relating to the process side of
language study. The teacher therefore has to explore learners' attitudinal
disposition to language learning and their current level of strategic
awareness (2.5; 4.2–4.3) as a basis for formulating the strategic learning
goals which will be pursued in parallel with their objective (or product-
oriented) learning agenda in their course of study. These priorities add a
substantial load to goal-setting in comparison with, for instance, a
course in which learning goals are defined on the basis of a pre-
established body of structures and lexis, or a discrete set of language
functions.

Familiarity with a wide range of teaching methodologies, learning materials and study options

If the teacher wishes to gear her choice of methodology around the cognitive and psychosocial preferences of her students (4.5), she clearly needs to be familiar with a wide range of teaching-learning options, and also to understand the learning style implications of these options (4.4). This is also necessary if the teacher wishes to help learners to expand their understanding of language learning and to extend gradually their learning strategy repertoire (7.1). In other words, familiarity with a wide range of pedagogical alternatives allows the teacher to be responsive to learners' subjective needs as a classroom teacher, and also to fulfil her role as learning counsellor. This, however, places heavier demands on the teacher's pedagogical knowledge than the assimilation of a limited number of teaching procedures arising out of a given 'method' (in the sense used by Allwright 1991 [cited in 1.4]).

Course planning skills

This category of skills is necessary in two main ways. To begin with, they are needed to channel into a coherent and workable programme of study the priorities arising out of the exploration of learners' needs – both objective (or product-oriented) and subjective (or process-oriented) needs. This will also require the teacher to strike a balance between language instruction *per se* (i.e. the development of learners' language skills and communicative abilities) and language education (i.e. the development of learners' understanding of language study and of their strategic learning skills). Depending on the context within which teaching is being conducted, the teacher may also need good planning skills and a solid pedagogical judgement to pursue the goal of language education in harmony with the administrative and curricular imperatives of the institution or educational system in which she is working (5.2). It is hardly necessary to point to the difference between this range of tasks and those involved in the implementation of a pre-set content syllabus supported by an approved textbook or set of learning materials.

The comments made on these three skill areas show clearly that a learner-centred approach to teaching by no means deprives the teacher of her professional expertise or the role of 'knower' – quite the contrary, in fact. The teacher's role as 'knower' with respect to the TL will, of course, manifest itself in the same variety of ways as in any form of language instruction; it will also be present in her guiding of learners' own discovery of the TL along the lines suggested in 7.3 –

7.5. The teacher's professional and pedagogical expertise will also be present in her role as learning counsellor, i.e. the member of the learning group who, by virtue of her professional training and experience, counsels and guides learners along the path leading to self-directiveness and empowerment.

Educational skills

These are most obviously required in terms of learner training (2.3 – 2.6) and in the gradual involvement of learners in the shaping of their study programme (2.7; 3.6; 4.5; 6.4; 7.3–7.5). They also intervene in the teacher's evaluation of learners' cognitive and psychological disposition towards language learning (4.2; 4.3) and of their culturally-based expectations (5.3). In general terms, then, the teacher's educational skills involve her reaching out to learners' existing knowledge and experience of life and helping them relate this meaningfully to the process of language learning. This calls for a variety of human and interpersonal skills, among which empathy, intuition and personal maturity have particular importance. These skills are central to the teacher's role as learning counsellor and are arguably the most important of all. Good teachers have always possessed and made active use of these skills, which is presumably what made them good teachers. The difference is that in a learner-centred approach these skills are crucial to the approach as a whole. In this respect, Underhill's (1989: 260) comment that 'doing the same things with a different awareness seems to make a bigger difference than doing different things with the same awareness', sets a challenge to all teachers, but in particular to those committed to a learner-centred mode of teaching.

Flexibility and adaptability

As was suggested in 8.1, there is something inherently innovative about learner-centred teaching, even if only because no one group of learners will ever be quite like another. Flexibility will be a particularly important quality for teachers working with multicultural groups and those who have learner groups of differing cultural backgrounds (5.3). Adaptability may also be required for another type of reason. A teacher used to playing a 'traditional' or directive role in the classroom may, initially at least, experience unease with a more collaborative mode of interaction with her students. The opposite may also arise, though: a teacher whose professional training or personal value system predisposes her towards a 'liberal' and participative mode of teaching may find that, in certain contexts, language education is most appropriately pursued in a manner which is more 'authoritarian' than she would spontaneously feel at home with (5.4).

8.3.2 *Reconciling classroom and organisational methodologies*

In 5.1 it was pointed out that language teaching is rarely conducted exclusively between a teacher and learners, but is rather a social activity which therefore has to be accountable to society at large. Furthermore, it is an activity which will be undertaken within a context shaped by a variety of pragmatic, attitudinal and organisational/administrative factors (5.2). Most teachers will belong to a given institution which, in turn, will have more or less direct links with related institutions or be part of an educational system operating at regional or national level. The decision to opt for a learner-centred mode of teaching, either by the teacher as an individual or by the relevant educational authorities (language planners, heads of department, etc.) will, therefore, interact with the administrative and decision-making structures of the institution or educational system concerned. These factors were alluded to in Chapter 5 from the point of view of the choices the teacher is confronted with. They will be considered here from the point of view of educational authorities, with specific reference to the decision-making structures within which a learner-centred approach might be implemented. The treatment will be too brief to do justice to this complex area of concern and is intended simply to raise a few issues which readers may then reflect on or investigate further on their own.

A learner-centred approach to teaching may be seen as incorporating two main guiding principles. The first is the respect for the learner's individuality and for the diversity and richness of the human experience which learners bring with them to their language study. The second is a belief in the value of a participative approach to decision-making. These principles underlie the perspective on language teaching which has been adopted in previous chapters in terms of *learner* involvement. It would therefore seem coherent to work with the same principles as regards the interaction between *teachers* and educational authorities. This is a matter of compatibility between the methodology to be implemented at classroom level and the decision-making procedures (or organisational methodology) by which this methodological change is presented to the teachers concerned. Teachers, too, have their own personality, expectations, abilities and subjective needs: in other words, they have their own individuality, just as learners. Furthermore, teachers' contribution to methodological innovation at institutional level should not be seen as less valid than learners' contribution to the realisation of methodology at classroom level. In other words, the methodology of innovation at institutional level should reflect (and thereby reinforce) the principles which underlie the classroom methodology in question. In the present case, then, it should involve respect for the individuality of the teachers concerned and cater for participation and negotiation in decision-making.

It has been pointed out on a number of occasions in previous chapters that if learners have been used to a content-based and teacher-led form of learning, they simply may not have had the opportunity to develop the skills that they need in order to assume a self-directive role in their own learning. Something similar may apply to teachers. Many teacher training programmes focus on the implementation of a discrete set of pedagogical or classroom management procedures with little analysis of the cognitive, psychosocial or cultural implications of the procedures concerned. Furthermore, many teachers' professional experience will have led them to define their task in terms of the transmission of a pre-established body of knowledge enshrined in the form of a grammatical or functional syllabus, a given examination, or series of coursebooks. For either or both of these reasons, teachers may not have had the opportunity to develop the skills they need to manage a participative approach to course development comfortably. This is not the fault of the teachers concerned, but does point to the importance of catering for ongoing teacher development and support as an integral part of the implementation of a learner-centred approach to teaching.

DAT/PED. Analyse the organisational culture (5.2.2) in place in an institution you are familiar with and the strategies used to implement change.

- What profile emerges of the organisational methodology of the institution in question?
- How compatible is this with the classroom methodology of learner-centred teaching?

What scope exists for teacher development and support?

- How is this realised?
- How adequate is it to provide teachers with assistance in the adoption of a participative approach to course development?
- Which practical recommendations would you make to improve this aspect of the system?

8.4 Practical advice

The few pieces of advice given below do not claim to constitute a programme for teacher preparation. They are simply the main points which, in the author's opinion, the teacher may need to bear in mind to help her initiate (or develop further) a learner-centred approach to her teaching in an effective and sustainable manner. The advice which follows is addressed to the individual teacher, but should clearly be thought through by educational decision-makers or heads of department from their own point of view.

1 Share the process of discovery with your students

Language teachers are frequently individuals who have a strong personal interest in language and in language learning. They will often have pursued language studies at university, learned one or more foreign languages to a high level, or worked in foreign countries where they have had to get to grips with a different culture and language. Teachers have also followed more or less extensive professional training programmes, they read about language learning, and are in contact with a variety of language teaching materials on a daily basis. It may therefore be difficult for them to feel 'from the inside' how difficult language study can be for some of their students. Furthermore, while many learner training activities or forms of learner involvement may appear relatively straightforward on paper, they can be very challenging for the students who have to undertake them – especially if they are based on a view of language learning different from that which the students have experienced in the past. While this does not mean that such activities should not be attempted, it does point to the importance for the teacher of gauging her demands closely around her students' capabilities and current level of strategic awareness.

Two practical suggestions could be made in this respect. The first is that the teacher should personally work through all the activities she is going to set her students as if she was a language learner herself. This is particularly important with activities relating to attitudes to language learning and to the subjective needs side of learning (2.5; 4.2–4.3) as the teacher's attitudes and needs will play a significant role (whether consciously or unconsciously) in the creation of classroom dynamics. The second is that the teacher should select a parallel learning activity (preferably an unfamiliar one) for which she has no particular talent and try to transfer to this activity the type of tasks which she is asking her students to perform with respect to their language learning. The teacher may then compare her own development as a learner in this domain with the comments of an expert. This can be a very insight-generating task.

2 Do your homework

Any form of education involves starting from where learners are and helping them to move on to a deeper understanding of the activity domain in question. This, however, implies knowing where learners are, mentally, at the start of a course or learning programme and relates in part to the concept of classroom culture (5.3). Flowerdew (1995), for instance, says that one reason for incorporating CALL (computer-assisted language learning) in the learning programme of students at the Hong Kong University of Science and Technology was the high face validity that the computer had as a learning tool among technologically-oriented students. In another context, where learner attitudes are different, the computer might be perceived as impersonal or as a block to human interaction, and would thus lose some of its pedagogical value, whatever its inherent potential as an aid to learning. A colleague told me that one of her research tasks during her Post-graduate Certificate in Education (French) was to visit newsagents and discover which comics or confectionery were bought by the local secondary school pupils, and to find out their favourite TV programmes and their sporting or media heroes. This information might seem to have little to do with the teaching of French. The goal, however, was to help the trainee teacher to see her pupils not simply as learners of French, but also (or primarily) as individual members of a certain community and peer group and, thereby, to gain an insight into their mental world, expectations and value system. These are considerations which will have an influence on the appropriacy and effectiveness of a variety of pedagogical choices and aspects of classroom management.

Investigating learners' attitudes may call for some ethnographic action research, but this need not be seen as synonymous with formal research or as something intimidating. Action research in this domain revolves around the use of a relatively simple set of small-scale investigative procedures designed to help the teacher get a feel for the mental world, aspirations and expectations of her students as a basis for decision-making. In terms of a learner-centred approach to teaching, particular attention should be paid to learners' (and society's) attitudes to authority, teacher-learner roles, and the concept of self-direction. This is particularly important in the case of teachers working in a culture different from their own for two reasons: the first is that this culture may have a value system different from that of the teacher, and the second is that it can take quite some time for a foreign teacher to be able to empathise with her students as she would with members of her own culture.

3 Take things gradually

Various forms of learner involvement have been suggested in previous chapters. None of these, however, are goals to be pursued in their own right, and it is wisest to try out and explore different forms of learner involvement gradually. To begin with, this allows learners to grow into a participative form of learning at a sustainable pace, which is very important if this approach to learning is novel to them. It also allows the teacher to get a feel for the activities in question, how they are best managed, how learners can best be prepared for them and the type of guidance they will need. As has often been pointed out in previous chapters, it is the quality of learners' involvement in their language study that counts and not the external form that this assumes. In practice, this would probably involve starting with an unrushed learner training programme which caters for a genuine sharing of views and expectations, moves gradually in the direction of more direct learner involvement in response to learners' abilities and willingness. Pushing learners through a form of learning for which they are not fully prepared in either strategic or attitudinal terms can result in confusion, hostility and a withdrawal of cooperation.

4 Keep thorough notes and files

A participative approach to learning can, in the initial stages especially, add to the teacher's work load (cf. the case of 'Sally' described by Nunan, 1987: 61–73; 1988: 163–170). Over time, however, the teacher will build up a bank of materials suited to different learner types and will acquire more experience in reacting to different learner needs. Keeping track of the decisions she has made, her reasons for making them, and the activities or materials she has used with different groups of learners may in the short-term seem to add even more to the teacher's work load. In the long-term, however, it is time well spent. Keeping track of this type of information is likely to be more than simply a question of collecting teaching materials: if done thoughtfully, it may become a form of learning diary for the teacher herself and thus serve as a means of self-initiated professional development. In this way, the teacher's professional development can parallel that of her students as language learners.

5 Share experiences with colleagues

In a form of teaching where there are few solutions which are 'right' in absolute terms, but where there are many appropriate ways of responding to situations, it can be very helpful to share experiences, problems, doubts and discoveries with colleagues. To begin with, this can help the teacher avoid a form of tunnel vision resulting from aspects of her own personality or prior experience of either teaching or learning. Sharing experiences with colleagues can also provide a source of moral support and encouragement as well as creating a forum for the exchange of practical experiences and materials.

6 Be realistic and pace yourself

Good teaching, whatever the approach that is adopted, calls for a considerable investment of time and energy from the teacher, and the extra work involved in a collaborative form of teaching should not be underestimated. The teacher should therefore be realistic and pace herself, especially in the early stages. The teacher, too, is a participant in the negotiation of the learning programme, and she needs her expertise to build up gradually without her becoming overburdened or stressed, which will tend to undermine her ability to interact calmly and (dare I say?) wisely with her students. The teacher's commitment must be sustainable for her as a person and as a professional. This is not simply a piece of advice to the teacher as an individual: it is a key contributory factor to the success of a collaborative form of teaching, where the teacher's ability to provide guidance and advice to her students in a realistic and educationally-motivated manner is central to her role.

REF. What is your reaction to the advice given above?
Do you feel that some key points have been omitted? If so,

– what are they?
– which aspects of the teaching (or organisational) process do they relate to?

Compare your reactions with those of a few colleagues and try to account for any differences which appear.

8.5 Recommended reading

The references included in each chapter provide an overview of the literature relevant to the topic in question. The goal in this section is to provide a manageable number of references which readers may use as a starting point for their own reading. The choice of publications will inevitably have a subjective element, and probably contains many of the publications which the author found most helpful in developing his own understanding of learner-centredness. Readers should also bear in mind the developmental nature of our profession's understanding of what learner-centred teaching may mean, and this will be evident in the range of perspectives that are adopted by the authors referred to. In all the publications surveyed below, however, learner-centredness is seen in educational terms, and with no attempt to avoid the complexities which surround its practical realisation. In recent years there has been a tendency for the term 'learner-centred' to be used in so vague a manner (much as occurred with 'communicative' in the 70s and 80s) that there is a risk of it losing any real value as a tool for discussing language teaching in a meaningful manner. Readers are thus advised to monitor critically the sense in which the term is being used in their exploration of the literature at large.

The recommended reading materials are split into three categories. The first contains a number of key background references pertinent to the general area of learner-centred teaching (with the variety of perspectives mentioned in Chapter 1). The second relates to the practical realisation of learner-centredness in terms of learner training and involvement, and the third to the investigative procedures ('action research') which the teacher will need in order to explore various aspects of classroom interaction, learners' attitudes and expectations, or characteristics of the wider learning environment. (Full details of the publications listed are given in the bibliography.)

Background reading

1 Nunan, D. *The Learner-centred Curriculum*. 1988.
Nunan's seminal work is essential reading, being clear, thoughtful and realistic throughout. Its particular value lies in its thoroughness of treatment of the rationale and guiding principles of a learner-centred approach at course design level. Nunan emphasises the cohesive links between CLT and the learner-centred curriculum – the latter building on and developing the former. In this way, Nunan fits his perspective on learner-centredness firmly into the mainstream of language teaching running from the work of the Council of Europe's Modern Languages Project up to the present time.

2 Brookes, A. and P. Grundy (Eds.) *Individualisation and Autonomy in Language Learning*. 1988.

This collection of papers offers the reader the opportunity to explore a wide range of the themes and issues which fall under the general heading of learner-centredness – autonomy, individualisation, learner training, syllabus negotiation, self-assessment and self-access. The collection includes both theoretically- and practically-oriented papers, and its value derives precisely from this richness of topic and treatment. It may be seen as complementary to Nunan's book in providing a survey of the main trends in the pedagogic exploration of learner-centredness during the 1980s. These two publications are crucial reference points and are strongly recommended as a joint starting point.

3 Brindley, G. *Needs Analysis and Objective Setting in the Adult Migrant Education Program.* 1984.
Brindley's report is a thorough and informative survey of the theoretical principles which underpinned the AMEP learner-centred curriculum project. It also provides valuable insights into the way in which such a project can be planned and prepared: in this sense, it has considerable value in terms of the methodology of innovation within a learner-centred framework of reference. Unfortunately, the report is not easily available outside Australia, and the same applies to other AMEP publications (Ref. 10 below). Inquiries should be addressed to: National Centre for English Language Teaching and Research, Macquarie University, Sydney NSW 2109, Australia.

4 Wenden, A. and J. Rubin (Eds.) *Learner Strategies in Language Learning.* 1987.
Wenden and Rubin's collection of papers traces the development of research into the role of learning strategies in language learning from the pioneering work of the 1970s through to more recent work on learner autonomy. In this way, it provides an overview of research into a key aspect of the process side of language learning. The third part of the book deals with the promotion of learner autonomy and thus brings out the close relationship between learning strategies and self-direction. In addition to this, the collection offers valuable insights into the means by which learners' strategy usage can be investigated, and thereby provides an introduction to more specialised research articles. Taken together with the next reference, Wenden and Rubin's collection provides a thorough survey of research into the process side of language learning upon which subsequent work into this aspect of learner-centredness has been built.

5 Willing, K. *Learning Styles in Adult Migrant Education.* 1988.
Willing's study is the clearest and most thorough discussion of subjective needs and learning style currently available. It therefore provides valu-

able background reading for anyone wishing to get to grips with their students' (and their own) learning style preferences and the way in which these can influence language learning. Furthermore, it is an excellent exemplification of the methodology involved in the investigation of learning style and is well worth reading from this point of view, too. While not explicitly geared to the details of pedagogy, Willing's report provides many valuable and pedagogically relevant insights into the subjective or process side of language learning. Strongly recommended.

6 Stevick, E. W. *Humanism in Language Teaching.* 1990.
The present author has somewhat mixed feelings about the humanistic movement in language teaching. On the one hand, it has undeniably enriched our profession's awareness of the importance of the affective aspects of language learning and has generated a number of very useful pedagogical insights. On the other hand, it has given rise to a lot of vague and sometimes dogmatic thinking about the finalities of language teaching. Stevick's book, however, offers a calm and balanced analysis of the underlying principles of humanistic language teaching which has value for any teacher. He also provides insightful analyses of the work of two well-known humanistic schools of language teaching (Curran's Community Language Learning and Gattegno's Silent Way) which are of interest not only with respect to the two schools in question but also in broader educational terms. Stevick thus offers a clear and committed but non-partisan insight into humanistic language teaching which should help readers perceive the influence it has had on the development of learner-centred thinking in mainstream language teaching.

7 Holliday, A. *Appropriate Methodology and Social Context.* 1994.
Holliday's book considers the role which social and cultural variables play in the planning of language education programmes. It stresses the importance of gearing pedagogical choices around the attitudes and expectations of the participants (students, in the first instance, but also local teachers, administrators and members of the target society in the broad sense), the traditions and interactive norms of the educational system in question, and the practical conditions in which teaching will be conducted. Holliday thus rejects a normative and universalist approach to language teaching, as well as the tendency to equate language education with any one set of teaching procedures. Holliday's book is recommended as a stimulus to reflection on the cultural relativity of language teaching procedures and, in the present context, to warn against too ready an equation of learner-centredness with a given set of surface manifestations rather than its underlying educational rationale and goals. (It should be pointed out that Holliday uses

the term 'learner-centredness' in a very different way from the present author.)

Learner training and involvement

8 Wenden, A. *Learner Strategies for Learner Autonomy.* 1991.
This is a very rich book which could belong in any of the three categories of recommended reading. Wenden provides a succinct review of many aspects of the literature on learning strategies and learner autonomy (in this sense, her book complements and updates *Learner Strategies in Language Learning*) together with practical guidelines for strategy-oriented classroom research by the teacher. It is recommended in particular, however, as a handbook to help the teacher plan and monitor learner training activities with her students. As Wenden herself points out, the book is most useful as a practical guide to action – to be dipped into and referred back to as and when the need arises. The methodology adopted by Wenden is task-based and reader-interactive, and the book thus embodies and supports a discovery-based approach to teaching.

9 Ellis, G. and B. Sinclair. *Learning to Learn English.* 1989.

10 Adult Migrant Education Program. *Teaching How to Learn.* 1989.
Both books are invaluable practical guides for any teacher or institution wishing to initiate a learner training programme. The teacher's edition should be consulted in both cases, as each contains a useful discussion of the approach in general and also of the rationale behind specific activities. Essential reading.

11 Clarke, D. F. Materials adaptation: why leave it all to the teacher? *ELT Journal.* 1989.

12 Clarke, D. F. The negotiated syllabus: what is it and how is it likely to work? *Applied Linguistics.* 1991.
In these articles, Clarke looks at two concrete aspects of learner involvement in a clear, realistic and undogmatic manner which teachers will find very helpful. Furthermore, the tone in which the articles are written is refreshingly down-to-earth: Clarke shows a committed but realistic attitude to the practicalities of learner involvement which is well worth thinking about.

Action research

13 Edge, J. and K. Richards. (Eds.) *Teachers Develop Teachers Research.* 1993.

This collection of papers provides a rich and varied perspective on the areas of classroom research and teacher development. The focus is on the type of localised, exploratory research which underpins the successful realisation of a learner-centred approach to teaching. The collection is of interest in terms both of the general approach to research it advocates and as a reference source for ideas on a range of specific issues.

14 Nunan, D. *Understanding Language Classrooms.* 1989.
Unlike the last reference, Nunan's book provides a systematic introduction to the small-scale, localised type of research which is generally referred to as 'action research', and which will play a role in the realisation of a collaborative approach to teaching and course development. The approach adopted is clear and practical, and explicitly seeks to demystify the concept of 'research'. Well worth reading in conjunction with the last reference.

8.6 Summary

a) The change in learner roles involved in a learner-centred approach to teaching has parallel implications for the role and responsibilities of the teacher. These need to be borne in mind both by the individual teacher and by educational authorities planning a move to a more learner-centred mode of teaching.
b) By making learners the central reference point for decision-making, learner-centredness places greater responsibilities on the individual teacher than traditional approaches; furthermore, it adds an explicitly educational dimension to teaching which is not necessarily present in content-based approaches.
c) This can represent a challenge to teachers with respect to their prior training, their habitual mode of teaching, and their individual interactional style (teachers, too, having subjective needs). Centring teaching on the learner therefore requires the teacher to be willing to examine critically her own assumptions and preferences in parallel with the reflective tasks she sets her students.
d) Specifically, the effective realisation of a learner-centred teaching also calls for:
    - needs analysis skills,
    - familiarity with a wide range of teaching methodologies, learning materials and study options,
    - course planning skills,
    - educational skills,
    - flexibility and adaptability.

e) The following advice is given to teachers wishing to develop a more learner-centred approach to their teaching:
  - share the process of discovery with your students,
  - do your homework,
  - take things gradually,
  - keep thorough notes and files,
  - share experiences with colleagues,
  - be realistic and pace yourself.

References

Allen, P. and M. Swain. (Eds.) 1984. Language Issues and Education Policies, *ELT Documents* 119. London: The British Council.

Allwright, R. 1982. Perceiving and pursuing learners' needs. In M. Geddes and G. Sturtridge: 24–31.

Allwright, R. 1991. The Death of the Method. Lancaster: Centre for Research in Language Education – Working Paper 10.

Altman, H. B. 1972. *Individualising the Foreign Language Classroom*. Rowley, Mass.: Newbury House.

Altman, H. B. 1977. Individualized instruction. In H. B. Altman: 76–83.

Altman, H. B. (Guest Editor) 1977. Special issue of *SYSTEM* (5, 2) devoted to Individualised Instruction.

Altman, H. B. and C. V. James. (Eds.) 1980. *Foreign Language Teaching: Meeting Individual Needs*. Oxford: Pergamon.

AMEP (Adult Migrant Education Program). 1989. *Teaching How to Learn* (Teachers' Guide). National Centre for English Language Teaching and Research, Macquarie University, Sydney.

Anderson, J. 1993. Is a communicative approach practical for teaching English in China? Pros and cons. *SYSTEM* 21: 471–80.

Assinder, W. 1991. Peer teaching, peer learning: one model. *ELT Journal* 45: 218–229.

Atkinson, D. 1989. 'Humanistic' approaches in the adult classroom: an affective reaction. *ELT Journal* 43: 268–273.

Au, S. Y. 1988. A critical appraisal of Gardener's social-psychological theory of second-language learning. *Language Learning* 38: 75–100.

Bachman, L. F. and A. S. Palmer, 1989. The construct validation of self-ratings of communicative abilities. *Language Testing* 6: 14–29.

Barber, C. L. 1962. Some measurable characteristics of modern scientific prose. In *Contributions to English Syntax and Phonology*. Gothenburg Studies in Linguistics 14. Stockholm: Almquist and Wiksell. Reprinted in J. Swales, 1985: 1–14.

Bassano, S. 1986. Helping learners adapt to unfamiliar methods. *ELT Journal* 40: 13–19.

Berry, J. W. 1981. Comparative studies of cognitive styles: implications for the education of immigrant students. Paper presented at the Conference on the Education of Ethnic Minorities and Immigrants, Miami, December 13–16, 1981.

References

Blanche, P. 1986. The relationship between self-assessment and other measures of proficiency in the case of adult foreign language learners. Unpublished Master's thesis: University of California.

Blanche, P. and B. J. Merino. 1989. Self-assessment of foreign language skills: implications for teachers and researchers. *Language Learning* 39: 313–340.

Blue, G. M. 1988. Self-assessment: the limits of learner independence. In A. Brookes and P. Grundy: 100–18.

Breen, M. 1985. Authenticity in the language classroom. *Applied Linguistics* 6: 60–70.

Breen, M. 1986. The social context for language learning – a neglected situation? *Studies in Second Language Acquisition* 7: 135–158.

Brindley, G. 1984. *Needs Analysis and Objective Setting in the Adult Migrant Education Program.* Sydney: New South Wales Adult Migrant Education Service.

Brindley, G. 1989. The role of needs analysis in adult ESL programme design. In R. K. Johnson: 63–78.

Brookes, A. and P. Grundy. (Eds.) 1988. *Individualisation and Autonomy in Language Learning.* London: Modern English Publications.

Brumfit, C. 1982. Some humanistic doubts about humanistic language teaching. In Humanistic Approaches: An Empirical View. *ELT Documents* 113: 11–19. London: British Council.

Brumfit, C. 1991. Problems in defining instructional methodologies. In K. De Bot, R. B. Ginsberg and C. Kramsch: 133–44.

Burkhalter, A. 1986. The expression of opinions: a preliminary needs analysis of discussion skills for academic purposes. MA qualifying paper, ESL Program: University of Minnesota.

Burnaby, B. and Y. Sun. 1989. Chinese teachers' views of western language teaching: context informs paradigms. *TESOL Quarterly* 23: 219–38.

Campbell, C. and H. Kryszewska. 1992. *Learner-based Teaching.* Oxford: Oxford University Press.

Clarke, D. F. 1989. Materials adaptation: why leave it all to the teacher? *ELT Journal* 43: 133–41.

Clarke, D. F. 1991. The negotiated syllabus: what is it and how is it likely to work? *Applied Linguistics* 12: 13–28.

Cornett, C. E. 1983. What you should know about teaching and learning styles. Bloomington: Phi Delta Kappa Educational Fountain.

Cortazzi, M. 1990. Cultural and educational expectations in the language classroom. In B. Harrison: 54–65.

Crabbe, D. 1993. Fostering autonomy from within the classroom: the teacher's responsibility. *SYSTEM* 21: 443–52.

Curran, C. 1972. *Counseling-Learning: A Whole-Person Model for Education.* New York: Grune and Stratton.

Curran, C. 1976. *Counseling-Learning in Second Languages.* Apple River, Ill: Apple River Press.

De Bot, K., R. B. Ginsberg and C. Kramsch (Eds.) 1991. *Foreign Language Research in Cross-cultural Perspective.* Amsterdam: John Benjamins.

Deller, S. 1990. *Lessons from the Learner*. Harlow: Longman.

Dickinson, L. 1978. Autonomy, self-directed learning and individualisation. In Individualisation in Language Learning. *ELT Documents* 103: 7–28. London: British Council.

Dickinson, L. 1987. *Self-instruction in Language Learning*. Cambridge: Cambridge University Press.

Dickinson, L. 1988. Learner training. In A. Brookes and P. Grundy: 43–53.

Dickinson, L. 1990. Self-evaluation of learning strategies. In R. Duda and P. Riley: 199–206.

Dickinson, L. 1993. Aspects of autonomous learning. *ELT Journal* 47: 330–36.

Dörnyei, Z. 1990. Conceptualising motivation in foreign language learning. *Language Learning* 40: 45–78.

Duda, R. and P. Riley. (Eds.) 1990. *Learning Styles*. Nancy: Presses Universitaires de Nancy.

Dudley-Evans, T. and W. Henderson. (Eds.) 1990. *The Language of Economics: The Analysis of Economics Discourse*. ELT Documents 134. London; Modern English Publications.

Edge, J. 1989. *Mistakes and Correction*. Harlow: Longman.

Edge, J. and K. Richards. (Eds.) 1993. *Teachers Develop Teachers Research*. Oxford: Heinemann.

Ellis, R. 1989. Classroom learning styles and their effect on second language acquisition: a study of two learners. *SYSTEM* 17: 249–262.

Ellis, G. and B. Sinclair. 1989a. *Learning to Learn English*. Teacher's Book. Cambridge: Cambridge University Press.

Ellis, G., and B. Sinclair. 1989b. *Learning to Learn English*. Cambridge: Cambridge University Press.

Ely, C. M. 1986. An analysis of discomfort, risktaking, sociability, and motivation in the L2 classroom. *Language Learning* 361: 1–25.

ETIC, 1978. *Individualisation in Language Learning*. ELT Documents 103. London: The British Council.

ETIC, 1982. *Humanistic Approaches: an Empirical View*. ELT Documents 113. London: The British Council.

Ewer, J. R., and G. Latorre. 1967. Preparing an English course for students of science. *ELT Journal* 21: 221–29.

Eysenck, H. J. 1965. *Fact and Fiction in Psychology*. Harmondsworth: Penguin.

Faerch, C. and G. Kasper. 1984. Pragmatic knowledge: rules and procedures. *Applied Linguistics* 5: 214–25.

Flowerdew, J. 1993. An educational, or process approach to the teaching of professional genres. *ELT Journal* 47: 305–16.

Flowerdew, L. 1995. Designing CALL courseware for an ESP situation: a report on a case study. *English for Specific Purposes* 14: 19–35.

Fok, A.C.Y.Y. 1981. *Reliability of Student Self-assessment*. Hong Kong University Language Centre.

Freeman, D. and J. C. Richards. (Eds.) 1996. *Teacher Learning in Language Teaching*. Cambridge: Cambridge University Press.

Freire, 1972. *Pedagógy of the Oppressed*. London: Penguin Books.

References

Fried-Booth, D. L. 1986. *Project Work*. Oxford: Oxford University Press.

Fröhlich, M. and T. Paribakht. 1984. Can we teach our students how to learn? In P. Allen and M. Swain: 65–81.

Gaies, S. and R. Bowers. 1990. Clinical supervision of language teaching: the supervisor as trainer and educator. In J. C. Richards and D. Nunan: 167–81.

Gardner, R. and W. Lambert. 1972. *Attitudes and Motivation in Second-Language Learning*. Rowley, Mass.: Newbury House.

Gattegno, C. 1972. *Teaching Foreign Languages in Schools: The Silent Way*. New York: Educational Solutions Inc.

Gattegno, C. 1976. *The Common Sense of Teaching Foreign Languages*. New York: Educational Solutions Inc.

Gattegno, C. 1988. *On Being Freer*. New York: Educational Solutions Inc.

Geddes, M. and G. Sturtridge. 1982. *Individualisation*. Oxford: Modern English Publications.

Gougher, R. 1972. *Individualisation of Instruction in Foreign Languages*. Philadelphia: The Center for Curriculum Development.

Gregoire, A. F. 1979. Learning/teaching styles: potent forces behind them. *Educational Leadership* 36: 234–36.

Gustafsson, M. 1975. *Some Syntactic Properties of English Law Language*. Finland: University of Turku.

Halliday, M. A. K. 1970. Language structure and language function. In J. Lyons. (Ed.): 140–65.

Handy, C. A. 1978. *Understanding Organisations*. Harmondsworth: Penguin Books.

Harrison, B. (Ed.) 1990. Culture and the Language Classroom. *ELT Documents* 132. London; The British Council.

Hofstede, G. 1983. The cultural relativity of organisational practices and theories. *Journal of International Business Studies* 83: 75–89.

Holden, H. J. 1990. Language as a facet in international business transactions: some research developments and conceptual challenges. Paper presented at the conference 'Business communication in multilingual Europe: supply and demand', University of Antwerp, February 22–4.

Holec, H. 1979. *Autonomy and Foreign Language Learning*. Strasbourg: Council of Europe.

Holec, H. 1980. Learner-centred communicative language teaching: needs analysis revisited. *Studies in Second Language Acquisition* 3: 26–33.

Holec, H. 1987. The learner as manager: managing learning or managing to learn? In A. Wenden and J. Rubin: 145–57.

Holliday, A. 1984. Research into classroom culture as necessary input into syllabus design. In J. Swales and H. Mustafa: 29–51.

Holliday, A. 1994a. *Appropriate Methodology and Social Context*. Cambridge: Cambridge University Press.

Holliday, A. 1994b. The house of TESEP and the communicative approach: the special needs of state English language education. *ELT Journal* 48: 3–11.

Holliday, A. 1994c. Student culture and English language education: an international perspective. *Language, Culture and Curriculum* 7: 125–43.

Holliday, A. and T. Cooke. 1982. An ecological approach to ESP. In A. Waters: 123–43.

Horwitz, 1990. Attending to the affective domain in the foreign language classroom. In S. S. Magnan: 15–33.

Huddleston, R. D., R. A. Hudson, E. O. Winter and A. Henrici. 1968. *Sentence and Clause in Scientific English*. London: Communication Research Centre, Department of General Linguistics: University College, London.

Hutchinson, T. and A. Waters. 1984. How communicative is ESP? *ELT Journal* 38: 108–13.

Hutchinson, T. and A. Waters. 1987. *English for Specific Purposes*. Cambridge: Cambridge University Press.

Huttenen, I. 1986. *Towards Learner Autonomy in Foreign Language Learning in Senior Secondary Schools*. Oulu: Acta Universitatis Ouluensis.

Hymes, D. 1972. On communicative competence. In J. B. Pride and J. Holmes: 269–93.

Janssen-van Dieten, A-M. 1989. The development of a test of Dutch as a second language: the validity of self-assessment by inexperienced subjects. *Language Testing* 6: 30–46.

Johnson, R. K. 1989. A decision-making framework for the coherent language curriculum. In R. K. Johnson: 1–23.

Johnson, R. K. (Ed.) 1989. *The Second Language Curriculum*. Cambridge: Cambridge University Press.

Kachru, Y. 1988. Cognitive and cultural styles in second language acquisition. *Annual Review of Applied Linguistics* 9: 149–63.

Kennedy, C. 1987. Innovating for a change: teacher development and innovation. *ELT Journal* 41: 163–70.

Kennedy, C. 1988. Evaluation of the management of change in ELT projects. *Applied Linguistics* 9: 329–42.

Kohonen, V. 1992. Experiential language learning: second language learning as cooperative learner education. In D. Nunan: 14–39.

Laing, R. D. 1970. *Knots*. The R. D. Laing Trust.

Larsen–Freeman, D. 1991. Research on language teaching methodologies: a review of the past and an agenda for the future. In K. De Bot, R. B. Ginsberg and C. Kramsch: 119–32.

LeBlanc, R. and G. Painchaud. 1985. Self-assessment as a second language placement instrument. *TESOL Quarterly* 19: 673–87.

Lee, Y. P. 1981. *Report on the Use of Student Self-assessment in the Testing Programme of the Language Centre of the University of Hong Kong*. Hong Kong University Language Centre.

Levin, L. 1972. *Comparative Studies in Foreign Language Teaching: The GUME Project*. Stockholm: Almquist and Wiksell.

Littlejohn, A. 1985. Learner choice in language study. *ELT Journal* 39: 253–61.

Lynch, T. 1988. Peer evaluation in practice. In A. Brookes and P. Grundy: 119–125.

Lyons, J. (Ed.) 1970. *New Horizons in Linguistics*. Harmondsworth: Penguin Books.

References

Magnan, S. S. (Ed.) 1990. *Shifting the Instructional Forces to the Learner.* Middlebury, VT.: Northeast Conference on the Teaching of Foreign Languages.

Makino, T-Y. 1993. Learner self-correction in EFL written compositions. *ELT Journal* 47: 337–41.

Mangelsdorf, K. 1992. Peer reviews in the ESL composition classroom: what do the students think? *ELT Journal* 46: 274–84.

Maslow, A. 1970. *Motivation and Personality.* New York: Harper and Row.

Moran, R. 1990. Watch my lips. *International Management* September: 77.

Moskowitz, G. 1978. *Caring and Sharing in the Foreign Language Class: A Sourcebook on Humanistic Techniques.* Rowley, Mass.: Newbury House.

Munby, J. 1978. *Communicative Syllabus Design.* Cambridge: Cambridge University Press.

Murphy, R. 1985. *English Grammar in Use.* Cambridge: Cambridge University Press.

Naiman, N., M. Frohlich, H. H. Stern and A. Todesco. 1978. *The Good Language Learner.* Toronto: Ontario Institute for Studies in Education.

Nunan, D. 1987. *The Teacher as Curriculum Developer.* Sydney: National Centre for Language Teaching and Research.

Nunan, D. 1988. *The Learner-centred Curriculum.* Cambridge: Cambridge University Press.

Nunan, D. 1989. *Understanding Language Classrooms.* Hemel Hempstead: Prentice Hall.

Nunan, D. (Ed.) 1992. *Collaborative Language Learning and Teaching.* Cambridge: Cambridge University Press.

Okoye, I. 1994. Teaching technical communication in large classes. *English for Specific Purposes* 13: 223–37.

O'Malley, J. M. and A. U. Chamot. 1990. *Learning Strategies in Second Language Acquisition.* Cambridge: Cambridge University Press.

O'Neill, R. 1991. The plausible myth of learner-centredness: or the importance of doing ordinary things well. *ELT Journal* 45: 293–304.

Oskarsson, M. 1980. *Approaches to Self-assessment in Foreign Language Learning.* Oxford: Pergamon, for the Council of Europe.

Oskarsson, M. 1981. Subjective and objective assessment of foreign language performance. In A. S. Read: 225–39.

Oskarsson, M. 1989. Self-assessment of language proficiency: rationale and applications. *Language Testing* 6: 1–13.

Oxford, R. 1990. *Language Learning Strategies: What Every Teacher Should Know.* Massachusetts: Heinle and Heinle.

Oxford, R. and M. Ehrman. 1993. Second language research on individual differences. *Annual Review of Applied Linguistics* 13: 188–205.

Oxford, R., M. E. Hollaway and D. Horton-Murillo. 1992. Language learning styles: research and practical considerations for teaching in the multi-cultural tertiary ESL/EFL classroom. *SYSTEM* 20: 439–546.

Prabhu, N. S. 1987. *Second Language Pedagogy.* Oxford: Oxford University Press.

Platt, P. 1989. The friction rubs both ways with the French and Germans. *International Management* May: 68.

Pride, J. B. and J. Holmes. (Eds.) 1972. *Sociolinguistics*. Harmondsworth: Penguin Books.

Read, A. S. (Ed.) 1981. *Directions in Language Testing*. Seameo Regional Language Centre: Singapore University Press.

Rees-Miller, J. 1993. A critical appraisal of learner training; theoretical bases and teaching implications. *TESOL Quarterly* 27: 679–89.

Richards, J. C. 1994. The sources of language teachers' instructional decisions. [Text of a] Plenary address given at the 1994 Georgetown University Round Table, Georgetown University, Washington, D.C.: March 13–16.

Richards, J. C. and D. Nunan. 1990. *Second Language Teacher Education*. Cambridge: Cambridge University Press.

Richards, J. C. and T. S. Rodgers. 1986. *Approaches and Methods in Language Teaching*. Cambridge: Cambridge University Press.

Richterich, R. 1973. *Systems Development in Adult Language Learning*. Strasbourg: Council of Europe.

Riley, P. 1988. The ethnography of autonomy. In A. Brookes and P. Grundy: 12–34.

Robinson, P. 1991. *ESP Today: a Practitioner's Guide*. Hemel Hempstead: Prentice Hall.

Rogers, C. R. 1961. *On Becoming a Person*. Boston: Houghton-Mifflin.

Rubin, J. 1975. What the 'good language learner' can teach us. *TESOL Quarterly* 9: 41–51.

Rubin, J. 1987. Learner Strategies: theoretical assumptions, research history and typology. In A. Wenden and J. Rubin: 15–30.

Sager, J. C., D. Dungworth, and P. F. McDonald. 1980. *English Special Languages: Principles and Practice in Science and Technology*. Wiesbaden: Oscar Brandtstetter Verlag.

Schank, R. C. and R. Abelson. 1977. *Scripts, Plans, Goals and Understanding*. Hillsdale, N. J.: Lawrence Erlbaum.

Scherer, G. and M. Wertheimer. 1964. *A Psycholinguistic Experiment in Foreign Language Teaching*. New York: McGraw-Hill.

Scovel, T. 1978. The effect of affect on foreign language learning: a review of the anxiety research. *Language Learning* 28: 129–42.

Selinker, L., E. Tarone and V. Hanzeli. (Eds.) 1981. *English for Academic and Technical Purposes: Studies in Honour of Louis Trimble*. Rowley, Mass.: Newbury House.

Sharwood Smith, M. 1981. Consciousness-raising and the second language learner. *Applied Linguistics* 2: 159–68.

Shavelson, R. J. and P. Stern. 1981. Research on teachers' pedagogical thoughts, judgements, decisions, and behaviour. *Review of Educational Research* 51: 455–98.

Skehan, P. 1989. *Individual Differences in Second-language Learning*. London: Edward Arnold.

References

Spolsky, B. 1989. *Conditions for Second Language Learning.* Oxford: Oxford University Press.

Stevick, E. W. 1976. *Memory, Meaning and Method: Some Psychological Perspectives on Language Learning.* Rowley, Mass.: Newbury House.

Stevick, E. W. 1980. *Teaching Languages: A Way and Ways.* Rowley, Mass.: Newbury House.

Stevick, E. W. 1990. *Humanism in Language Teaching.* Oxford: Oxford University Press.

Strevens, P. 1979.Differences in teaching for different circumstances or the teacher as chameleon. In C. A. K. Yorio and J. Schachter (Eds.) *On Tesol '79: The Learner in Focus.* Washington D.C.: TESOL: 2–11.

Swales, J. 1981. *Aspects of Article Introductions.* Language Studies Unit, University of Aston.

Swales, J. 1985. *Episodes in ESP.* Hemel Hempstead: Prentice Hall.

Swales, J. and H. Mustafa. 1984. *English for Specific Purposes in the Arab World.* Birmingham: Aston University Press.

Tarone E. and G. Yule. 1989. *Focus on the Language Learner.* Oxford: Oxford University Press.

Trim, J. L. M. 1980. The place of needs analysis in the Council of Europe Modern Languages Project. In H. B. Altman and C. V. James: 46–65.

Tudor, I. 1988. 'Yes, but ...?': interaction in learner-based video production. *Guidelines* 10: 24–32.

Tudor, I. 1991. Learner-centredness at two learner levels: a question of degree. Rapport d'Activités de L'Institut de Phonétique, Université Libre de Bruxelles, 27: 1–30.

Tudor, I. 1993. Teacher roles in the learner-centred classroom. *ELT Journal* 47: 22–31.

Tudor, I. and F. Nivelles, 1991. Assessing self-assessment: the case for an integrative profiling of L2 learners' strategic abilities. Rapport d'Activités de L'Institut de Phonétique, Université Libre de Bruxelles, 27: 67–90.

Underhill, A. 1989. Process in humanistic education. *ELT Journal* 43: 250–60.

Van Ek, J. 1975. *The Threshold Level in a European unit/credit system for modern language learning by adults.* Council for Cultural Cooperation, Council of Europe.

Von Elek, T. 1982. *Test of Swedish as a Second Language: An Experiment in Self-assessment.* Work Paper No. 31. University of Goteburg, Language Teaching Research Centre.

Wagner, J. 1988. Innovation in foreign language teaching. *AILA Review* 5: 99–117.

Wall, W. 1958. The wish to learn: research into motivation. *Educational Research* 1: 23–37.

Wangsotorn, A. 1981. Self-assessment of English skills by undergraduate and graduate students in Thai universities. In A. S. Read: 240–60.

Waters, A. (Ed.) 1982. Issues in ESP, *Lancaster Practical Papers in English Language Education* 5. Oxford: Pergamon Press.

Wenden, A. 1986a. Helping language learners think about learning. *ELT Journal* 40: 3–19.

Wenden, A. 1986b. What do second language learners know about their language learning? A second look at retrospective accounts. *Applied Linguistics* 7: 186–205.

Wenden, A. 1986c. Incorporating learner training in the classroom. *SYSTEM* 14: 315–25.

Wenden, A. 1987. How to be a successful language learner: insights and prescriptions from L2 learners. In A. Wenden and J. Rubin: 103–17.

Wenden, A. 1991. *Learner Strategies for Learner Autonomy*. Hemel Hempstead: Prentice Hall.

Wenden, A. and J. Rubin. (Eds.) 1987. *Learner Strategies in Language Learning*. Hemel Hempstead: Prentice Hall.

Wenden, A. and I. Dickinson. (Eds.) 1995. *Autonomy, Self Direction and Self Access in Language Teaching and Learning: The History of an Idea.* Special Issue of *SYSTEM* (23, 2).

West, R. 1994. Needs analysis in language teaching. *Language Teaching* 27: 1–19.

White, R. 1988. *The ELT Curriculum*. Oxford: Blackwell.

Widdowson, H. 1978. *Teaching Language as Communication*. Oxford: Oxford University Press.

Widdowson, H. 1981. English for specific purposes: criteria for course design. In L. Selinker, E. Tarone and V. Hanzeli. (Eds.): 1–11.

Williams, M. 1988. Language taught for meetings and language used in meetings: is there anything in common? *Applied Linguistics* 9: 45–58.

Willing, K. 1988. *Learning Styles in Adult Migrant Education*. Adelaide: National Curriculum Resource Centre.

Witkin, H. A. 1965. Psychological differentiation. *Journal of Abnormal Psychology* 70: 317–336.

Witkin, H. A., C. Moore, D. Goodenough and P. Cox. 1977. Field-dependent and field-independent cognitive styles and their educational implications. *Review of Educational Research* 47: 1–64.

Yeo, S. 1994. The ESP coursebook – effects on an in-service training programme in Slovakia. Paper presented at the conference 'LSP and Teacher Education', University of Edinburgh, November 16–18.

Index

References in italic indicate figures or tables.

Index

discovery process, sharing 253–4
diversity of learners *see* individual differences
domains of language use 78, 82–8
  cultural/affective 85–6
  occupational 82–4
  interactive 84–5
Dörnyei, Z. 45, 46, 47, 82

E-knots 234, 237
'ecological approach' 133
economic issues 19, 26
Edge, J. 214–15, 260–1
educational perspective 23, 27–8, 28
educational skills 250
Egyptian universities 146
Ehrman, M. 102, 104, 106, 113, 123
Ellis, G. 35, 36, 63, 68, 260
  learning preferences 53, 55, 56
ELT (English language teaching)
Ely, C. M. 105
'embedded figures' test 109–10
empowerment x–xi, xii, 25–8, 28, 29, 162
English language teaching (ELT)
  profession 130–2
error correction 207–8, 214–19
  peer correction 214–16, 216
  self-correction 216–17, 217–18
  written work 218, 218–19
ethnic differences 150–4
evaluation
  of learner training 59–61
  of learners *see* self-assessment
evaluative stage, self-assessment 171
evaluator, learner as 201
examination requirements 149–50
exercise preparation 210, 210–11
expectations *see* attitudes; motivation
experience sharing 255–6
experiential learning 9, 10
experimental laboratory, classroom as 142
expert-based needs analysis 30
expertise, use of learners' 15, –17, 82–4, 90–2
explicitness of purpose, and learner
  training 58
exploitable features of context 141
expressive intentions, exploring 180–1, 184
extroversion 101, 102–3, 104–5
Eysenck, H. J. 102

facilitating anxiety 107
factual knowledge 78–9

Faerch, C. 79–81
family socialisation 143
FD–FI (field dependence–field independence)
  109–10, 111–12, 114–17
femininity v. masculinity 153
field dependence–field independence (FD–FI)
  109–10, 111–12, 114–17
flexibility *see* adaptability
FLL (foreign language learning) contexts 45–6
Flowerdew, L. 254
foreign language learning (FLL) contexts 45–6
Fried-Booth, D. L. 219–20
Fröhlich, M. 40
functional goals 46–7
functional purpose grid 49
functional view of language 9

Gaies, S. 231
Gardner, R. 45
Gattegno, Caleb 4–5
general knowledge 78
'giving them what they want' approach
  246–7
global self-assessment 173, 174–6, 176, 177,
  178, 179
global self-esteem 106
goal formulation knowledge 80
goal-setting 70–3, 171–87, 231
  contextual factors 129
  global 174–7, 176, 177, 178, 179
  self-assessment 168
  task-based assessment 177–82, 184–7
goals, and motivation 44–8, 47, 49, 50
'good' language learners 38–9
'good learner' strategies 10–11
gradual innovation 255
grammar activities 208, 209–13
  exercise preparation 210, 210–11
  exploring textual material 211–12, 212
  story telling 212–13, 213–14
'group problems' project work 221, 221–2
group solidarity 15, 174
  collectivism 152–3, 154, 158
Grundy, P. 257–8

Halliday, M. A. K. 9
hands-on learners 113
Handy, C. 135–6
hemisphere processing 109
Hispanic students 144
historical survey 2, 3–12

274

Index